HARDPRESS.NET
HOME OF HARD-TO-FIND BOOKS

The Village Blacksmith, Or, Piety and Usefulness Exemplified, in the Life of Samuel Hick, Late of Micklefield, Yorkshire

by James Everett

Address:
HardPress
8345 NW 66TH ST #2561
MIAMI FL 33166-2626
USA
Email: info@hardpress.net

THE VILLAGE BLACKSMITH;

OR,

PIETY AND USEFULNESS EXEMPLIFIED,

IN A

MEMOIR

OF THE

LIFE OF SAMUEL HICK,

LATE OF MICKLEFIELD, YORKSHIRE.

BY JAMES EVERETT.

FROM THE SEVENTH LONDON EDITION.

NEW-YORK:
PUBLISHED BY T. MASON AND G. LANE,
For the Methodist Episcopal Church, at the Conference Office
200 Mulberry-street.

J. Collord, Printer.
1839.

"That not only the maxims, but the grounds of a pure morality, the mere fragments of which the 'lofty grave tragedians taught in chorus or iambic,' and that the sublime truths of the divine unity and attributes which a Plato found most hard to learn, and deemed it still more difficult to reveal; that these should have become the almost hereditary property of childhood and poverty, of the hovel and the workshop; that even to the unlettered they sound as *common-place*, is a phenomenon which must withhold all but minds of the most vulgar cast from undervaluing the services even of the pulpit and the reading-desk."

Coleridge's Biographia Literaria, vol. i, p. 226.

GLOSSARY.

Oftentimes, pronounced *offens.*

Our,	. .	*hower.*
Missionaries,	. .	*mishoners.*
Eaten,	. .	*hetten.*
Eat,	. .	*eight.*
Societies,	. .	*sieties.*
Would,	. .	*wod.*
Open,	. .	*hoppen.*
People,	. .	*pepell.*
Perfect,	. .	*parfit*, or *parfeat*, generally *purfit.*
Take,	. .	*tak.*
Make,	. .	*mak.*
Outpouring,	. .	*howtpowring*, exceedingly broad.
Gave,	. .	*gav.*
Sown,	. .	*sawn.*
Soon,	. .	*soen.*
Where,	. .	*whur, whor, wor.*
Ordered,	. .	*auder'd.*
Israel,	. .	*Hesrele.*
Should,	. .	*sud.*
Set,	. .	*setten.*
Who,	. .	*hoe.*
Mercy,	. .	*marcy.*
What,	. .	*wat.*
Enter,	. .	*henter.*
Awake,	. .	*wakken*
Methodists,	. .	*Metterdisses*, or *Metherdisses.*
Methodist,	. .	*Metherdis.*
Turned,	. .	*torned.*
Wet,	. .	*weet.*
A ladder,	. .	*a stile, a stee.*
Foot,	. .	*foet,* } divided nearly into two syllables.
Fool,	. .	*foel,* }
School,	. .	*skoel,* }
Noon,	. .	*noen,* }
Night,	. .	*neet,* }

Thus, agreeably to the above, Samuel, together with his less educated neighbours, would pray for the Lord to "*wakken*" the slumbering sinner.

PREFACE

TO

THE VILLAGE BLACKSMITH.

BIOGRAPHERS have occasionally, though perhaps unconsciously, glided into two opposite extremes: they have either depreciated the character of their subjects, or overrated their excellences. To the former extreme they have been led in various ways; and in none, among the less offensive, more than in writing far and near for *character;* and after securing their object, arranging the different materials in their works, like *witnesses* in a court of justice, to *speak* for the person in question. This, to say the least, is putting the subject on his *trial.* It is in this way that the Life of that excellent man, the late Rev. William Bramwell, has been doomed to suffer, and permitted to be swelled to a useless extent, by the publication of *opinions** which were never given with a view to appear in print; and which, if even given for that purpose, would have the same weight with the public that the "Names of Little Note, recorded in the Biographia Britannica," had with Cowper, especially in support of the character of *such* a MAN; a man who required no such adventitious aid, but who, after all the prunings

* This remark refers to a *second* volume published in England, but never republished in this country.—EDS.

and parings of those who least admired him, and, with only a tithe of his wisdom, looked upon him as a weak enthusiast, would have stood a lovely tree in the vineyard of the Lord, refreshing many with his verdure, protecting them with his shade, and enriching them with the weight and luxuriance of his fruit. When an author is reduced to the necessity of going *abroad* in quest of *character* for his subject, it is but too evident that the subject has not been sufficiently at *home* with himself to be *known*; or, that, in addition to a paucity of material, there is either incapacity for the work, or doubts of the propriety of its execution. In the present case, either the writer has not humility to spare for such condescension, or he wishes not to degrade his subject. Having no internal misgivings, no suspicion, he considers his hero *not* as on his trial, but one against whom no charge is preferred, and therefore deems the witness-box unnecessary. Let him not, however, be misunderstood; for though he has gone in quest of *materials*, he has not gone in search of *character*. He has procured materials, in order to form an *opinion* of his *own*; materials, which rose out of a *character already formed*—a character imbodied in a "living epistle" before the public, "seen and read of all;" and but for which character, such materials would not have existed.

The other extreme into which biographers have fallen has had its rise in an overweening anxiety and partiality, inducing them on the one hand to render the character as *perfect* as possible, in order to secure on the other an ample share of the good opinion of the reader. Here the writer has again to plead disinclination. He has taken up the character of Samuel Hick as it *was*, not as he *wished* it, nor as it *ought* to be; and has *left* the man as he *found* him—*in the rough*, and unadorned; somewhat resembling the block of marble upon which the first efforts of the artist have been employed, where the human form has been brought out of the unfinished mass, in whose *core* are to be found all those hidden qualities which give beauty to the surface, only waiting the masterly hand of a Phidias, for the purpose of imparting grace, and polish, and finish.

The circumstances under which the following pages commenced, were carried on, and completed, are these:—The good man, whose life and character they profess to portray, deposited with the writer, about three years prior to the period of his dissolution, some papers, with a solemn injunction to prepare them for publication. These papers were found to comprise broken materials of personal history, such as he himself alone was capable of throwing together, and such as it would fall to the lot of but few, without previous and personal acquaintance, to be able to separate and decipher. The pledge of preparation was given, without the specification of *time*, on either side, for its fulfilment. Such was the heterogeneal character of the papers, and such the complexion of many of the facts and incidents, that some of the former were totally useless, and some of the latter unfit to meet the public eye; the whole requiring another language, and bare allusion being sufficient in many instances where amplification had been indulged. Some time previous to the decease of the subject, a degree of impatience was expressed for the completion of the Memoir: but as no *time* had been originally specified, and as it was known that the good man was imprudently pushed on to request its publication during life, by injudicious friendship, the work, in mercy to himself, and for the still higher honour of the religion he professed, nor less richly enjoyed, was purposely delayed; from an impression that nothing short of the publication of the *whole* would give satisfaction. The writer's vow being still upon him, added to which, having been urged by others to furnish the public with a biographical account of the deceased, he has employed of the papers thus referred to, together with others which have since been put into his hands by different friends, whatever he has found convertible to the purpose of affording instruction to the Christian community, as illustrative of the grace and providence of God; the whole combining to furnish a living exposition of what has proceeded from the source of truth, where it is affirmed that "*God hath chosen the foolish things of the world to confound the wise; and God hath chosen the weak things of the world to confound the things which are mighty; and base things of the world, and things which are despised, hath God chosen, yea, and things which are not, to bring to naught the things that are: that no flesh should glory in his presence.*"

It may be proper to mention, that some time after the death of Samuel Hick, the writer learned, by an application being made to him for materials, that another person had it in contemplation to prepare a Memoir; but it was too late: he had gone too far to recede: and as he could not conceive what virtue his MS. could derive from the simple process of passing through a second person's hand to the press, or what advantage he could reap by placing the fruit of his labour at the disposal of one who had neither held the plough nor scattered the seed into the furrows, he preferred appearing before the public in his own name, without allowing the imperfections of his pages to be charged upon others, or their merit—should they possess any—to be claimed by any but their legitimate owner.

Among the persons to whom the writer has to acknowledge his obligations for information respecting the subject of the Memoir, he would not omit his friend, Mr. William Dawson, of Barnbow, near Leeds, to whom the work is inscribed,—the Rev. Messrs. H. Beech, A. Learoyd, J. Hanwell, T. Harris, and J. Roadhouse, together with Mr. Robert Watson, son-in-law of the deceased, and other branches of the family—the latter furnishing him with the use of his correspondence.

ADVERTISEMENT

TO THE

SECOND EDITION OF VILLAGE BLACKSMITH.

THE first impression of this Memoir having been sold in about the space of one month after its publication, and several orders remaining unfulfilled, the writer has been induced to send forth a second. Though any attempt to conceal his pleasure in the success of the volume would appear sheer affectation, he is far from attributing the favour with which it has been received to the *manner* in which he has performed his task; for, had it not been for the *subject*—which may be considered in some respects *new* in biography, and as holding the same relation to serious reading, as a *novel* bears to the graver character of historical details, the volume might have shared the same fate as many superior compositions—that of falling dead from the press. The literary world has heard a good deal lately respecting the romance of history; and they have here an approach to the romance of religious biography. Such forms of expression, the writer is aware, are liable to objections; but he is unable at present to find a more appropriate term to express his views and feelings in penning the Life of Samuel Hick—a character so singular, and yet so eminently devoted to God and to the best interests of man.

The reader will find some errors corrected in the present edition, which had found their way into the former,—several new incidents and anecdotes introduced,—and a public address appended, which the subject of the Memoir delivered in the East Riding of Yorkshire. It is not improbable that many of the facts stated in both editions may assume a new face to several readers—so much so, perhaps, as scarcely to be recognised by those who may be in possession of the hundredth *oral* edition; but to such persons as are aware how much the same tale will become metamorphosed, in its passage through a score of different lips and minds, it will not be surprising that the writer should differ in some important particulars from vague report. He might state that he has received communications from different persons, each professing to have received the intelligence from the lips of Samuel himself, yet widely different often, both in the principle and in the detail. This could be accounted for from the circumstance of Samuel having entered into particulars in one instance, and only named the naked fact in another; and also from the different impressions produced on the minds of the persons themselves, none of whom might have thought of a publicity beyond the domestic circle; and in each case the lapse of years seriously affected the memory. Yet, with these inconveniences, and others that will naturally suggest themselves to the reader, every individual is certain, in the integrity of his heart, that *his* is the *only* CORRECT VERSION. This, as so many extraordinary tales have been handed round respecting the subject of the Memoir, is admonitory of *caution;* and as the writer has had access to the *original documents*, as far as penned by the subject himself, and from only *part* of which a mutilated copy has been obtained, any other separately published Life—under whatever pretensions—should be received with suspicion, both as to its details and the motive for publication.

THE

VILLAGE BLACKSMITH.

CHAPTER I.

His birth—Parentage—Hears John Nelson—Disturbance during street-preaching—Is bound an apprentice to a blacksmith—His conduct—Attends a lovefeast—Becomes the subject of divine impressions—Hears Thomas Peace—Visits York—Scenes of riot—Hears Richard Burdsall—His conduct toward a persecuting clergyman—His heart increasingly softened—Conviction—Mr. Wesley—The good effects of that venerable man's ministry.

SAMUEL HICK, the subject of the present memoir, was in the moral world, what some of the precious stones are in the mineral kingdom, a portion of which lie scattered along the eastern coast of the island, and particularly of Yorkshire, his own county;—a man that might have escaped the notice of a multitude of watering-place visiters, like the pebbles immediately under their eye;—one who, to pursue the simile, was likely to be picked up only by the curious, in actual pursuit of such specimens, and thus, though slighted and trodden under foot, like the incrusted gem, by persons of opposite taste, to be preserved from being for ever buried in the dust, as a thing of naught in the sand, after the opportunities of knowing his real value—when above the surface, had been permitted to pass unobserved and unimproved;—one of those characters, in short, that could only be discovered when sought after, or forced upon the senses by his own personal appearance, in the peculiarities by which he was distinguished—who was ever secure of his price when found—but who would, nevertheless, be placed by a virtuoso rather among the more curious and singularly formed, than among the richer and rarer specimens in his collection.

He was born at Aberford, September 20th, 1758, and was one of thirteen children that had to be nursed and reared by the "*hand labour*," to employ an expression of his own, of poor, but industrious parents. Through the limited means of the family, his education was necessarily very circumscribed, being chiefly confined to his letters, in their knowledge and formation, without advaneing to figures:—and even these—such was the blank of being which he experienced for several years afterward—appear to have been either totally forgotten, or so imperfectly known, as to induce an inability to read and write when he reached the age of manhood. This led him, in after life, when Sunday-school instruction dawned upon the world, as the morning of a brighter day, to contemplate the times with peculiar interest, and to wish that he had been favoured with the privileges, in his younger years, which he lived to promote and to see enjoyed by others. The dream of childhood seemed to pass away, with all its dangers, its "insect cares," and its joys, without leaving a single trace of any interest upon his memory, till he reached the seventh year of his age; and one of the first of his reminiscences, when sitting down at a kind of halting-post, toward the close of his journey, to look back on *all the way which the Lord God* had *led* him *in the wilderness*, was just such an occurrence as a mind imbued with divine grace might be supposed to advert to,—anxious only to fix on favoured spots, where God is seen in his ministers, his providence, and his people.

Field and street-preaching had neither lost its novelty through age, nor was it rendered unnecessary by a multiplicity of commodious chapels: while the want of a suitable place, therefore, led a Wesleyan itinerant preacher to take his stand on the market cross, to proclaim, as the herald of the Saviour, the glad tidings of salvation, the inhabitants of Aberford were allured to the ground, in order to listen to his message. Little Samuel mingled with the crowd—gazed with a degree of vacancy on the scene—heard, but understood not. John Nelson was the preacher—a man whose life was full of incident and interest—who discovered no less prowess in the cause of God, than his namesake, Nelson, did upon the element for which he seemed called into existence—and who stood, for the fame he acquired, in a somewhat similar relation to Methodism, that the hero of the Nile did to the British nation. In the course of the service, a person prepared for the work by intoxication, having had three quarts of ale given to him by three Roman Catholics, who urged him to the onset, made considerable disturbance. The people were annoyed, and the preacher was thwarted in his purpose. The man exhibited in his hand a piece of paper, from which he either read or pretended to read; and being possessed of a powerful voice, he elevated it in true stentorian style, and by force of lungs rendered the feebler voice of the preacher inaudible. A chain of circumstances contributed to preserve the case alive in Samuel's recollection. The man was personally known to him—he continued to reside in the neighbourhood—afterward lost his sight—was supported by begging from door to door—solicited alms from Samuel himself, when the latter had become a householder—was reminded of the circumstance by him, and was either hypocritical or honest enough to confess his belief that it was a judgment from God—expressed his sorrow—and finished his course in a workhouse. The uses and improvements which Samuel made of circumstances and occasions even the most trivial, were invariably devotional, and often pertinent. From an occurrence like the present, he would, in stating it, exclaim, "Though hand join in hand, the wicked shall not be unpunished;" then, with his usual quickness, his eyes sparkling, and beaming with a fine flow of grateful feeling, he would advert to the difference between earlier and more modern times, exulting in the quiet which reigned around, "every man" being permitted, in patriarchal simplicity, to "sit" and to shelter himself "under his vine and under his fig-tree," the hand of persecution not being raised "to make him afraid."

His attention having been once drawn to the subject of religion, by the peculiarities of Methodism, it was soon reawakened by the return of the preachers, whose visits, from the comparatively small numbers of labourers employed, were more like the return of the seasons, setting in, earlier or later, and at wider distances, than the regular succession of week after week, or month after month. This irregularity, occasioned by calls to new fields of usefulness, rendered their visits, like the return of spring, the more welcome to religious persons, and preserved on the face of the whole an air of novelty among the profane, which frequent repetition, by producing familiarity, might have destroyed. Whoever might have been the ministers, whether in or out of the Established Church, that he heard—and whatever might have been the impressions received, not any thing of personal importance is recorded, till the lapse of a second seven years, when, at the age of fourteen, he was bound an apprentice to Edward Derby, of Healaugh, near Tadcaster, to learn the trade of a blacksmith. Here he appears to have been placed in a situation favourable, in some respects, for religious improvement; and in three sentences, the full power of which, when tried upon the mind of another person, he scarcely understood, he has struck off a sketch of his own conduct while filling that situation. He states, that he had a "comfortable time," that "the Lord gave" him "favour in the eyes of the people," and that he "never troubled" his "parents for any thing during" his "apprenticeship." We have in this, in the way of implication at least, his character as a *servant*, a *neighbour*, and a *child;* for had he not been *diligent* and *faithful* as a servant, *kind* and *obliging* as a neighbour, *tender* and *thoughtful* as a child, there is not any thing to induce us to believe that he could either have been *comfortable* in his service, participated in the *favour* of those around him, or that his parents would have been exempt from *trouble*, owing to demands made both upon their pockets and their patience.

He had not been long in his situation before curiosity led him to a lovefeast, which was held in a barn, at Healaugh. A good man of the same trade with himself was the door-keeper; and either through a kindly feeling on that account, or from his having perceived something in Samuel's general demeanour, which excited his hope, he permitted him to pass, and ordered him to mount the straw, which was piled up in a part of the building, in order to make room for the people. It was not long before the doorkeeper left his post, and advancing toward the body of the congregation, commenced the service. He remarked, in figurative language, when describing the influence of the Spirit of God upon his heart, that "the fire was burning," and that he "felt it begin at the door."

So gross were the conceptions of Samuel, so ignorant was he of the ordinary phraseology of Christians, that, like Nicodemus on another subject, he took the term *fire* in its literal acceptation, and in an instant his fears were roused, his imagination was at work, and his eye was directed to the door. He deemed his situation among the *straw* as one of the most hazardous, and in his imaginings saw himself enveloped in flame. He continued to fix an anxious eye upon the entrance, but on perceiving, as he expressed himself, neither "smoke nor fire," his fears were gradually allayed, and he again lent an attentive ear to the worthy man, who had borrowed his simile, in all probability, from the descent of the Holy Ghost, in "cloven tongues like as of fire," and whose feelings seemed to accord with those which stirred in the bosom of the psalmist, when he said, "My heart was hot within me: while I was musing the fire burned: then spake I with my tongue." There were two particulars which impressed the mind of Samuel, and which he afterward pondered in his heart; the one was the high value which the speaker stamped upon his office, and upon the place, dignifying the old barn with the title of a place of worship, and affirming that he "had rather be a door-keeper in the house of God, than to dwell in the tents of wickedness;" and the other was his declaration of a knowledge of the fact, that his sins were forgiven. Samuel could not conceive how the temporary appropriation of such a place to divine worship, &c., could constitute it "the house of God," or what honour or pleasure a man could derive from the apparently humiliating circumstance of keeping watch over a door that many would be ashamed to enter. But the knowledge of forgiveness puzzled him most, and in this he seemed to have a personal concern. His spirit clung to the fact, and he could not help wishing that the case were his own—that he knew it for himself; this plainly implying a knowledge of sin, though probably he was not painfully oppressed with his load. He took occasion the next day to ask his master how the man could know that his sins were pardoned, and to express what he himself felt on the subject,—a circumstance which would lead to the conclusion, that his master possessed something more than the mere semblance of Christianity, though not sufficient to lead him to establish the practice of family prayer.

Whatever was the knowledge which the master imparted, Samuel's feelings and inquiries are evident indications that he was visited with "drawings from above;" and these were fostered soon after by a local preacher from York, of the name of Thomas Peace, who, while preaching on the "remission of sins," and insisting on a knowledge of it, confirmed by Scripture all that had been heard from the lips of experience in the barn. While the preacher wept, and expostulated with the people, Samuel looked, and listened, and also wept: but with him they were tears of sympathy; for in his boyish simplicity he concluded that the man must have just come from the grave of his wife; and with equal simplicity, on his return home, he inquired of his master, who had become his oracle, whether it was not on account of the death of his wife that the preacher had been weeping. His master told him—and this is an additional proof of the light which he possessed—that the tenderness manifested was occasioned by the love of God which was shed abroad in his heart, inspiring him with love to his fellow-creatures. This was too high for Samuel's comprehension, but not beyond the feelings of his heart. He loved the man while hearing him preach, but loved him more now, ardently desired his return, and embraced every opportunity of attending his preaching. His heart was gradually softening—the great subject of religion was constantly revolving in his mind, like an orb of light, yet he was unable to fasten his thoughts down to the contemplation of its particular parts, with the exception of the doctrine of pardon—and withal, he had not power over moral evil.

In 1776, when he had attained his eighteenth year, it being customary for the young people of the neighbouring towns and villages to visit the city of York on Whit-Monday, in order to witness scenes of folly and dissipation, especially wrestling-matches and fights, the victors having prizes conferred upon them, he joined his companions, repaired to the spot, and became a spectator. But being naturally humane, and not having undergone any course of brutal discipline, to render callous the better and more tender feelings of his heart, he was not able to enter into the spirit of such gladiatorial scenes,—scenes more worthy of Greece and Rome in their pagan state, than of Christian Britain. This was not his element; it was to him a scene of "misery and cruelty," as he afterward stated; and averting his eyes from these objects, he was suddenly attracted by another crowd of people occupying another part of the same public ground, encircling a person who was elevated for the occasion, and seemed by his attitude to be haranguing his hearers. Samuel left his associates, and before the maddened yells and shouts of profanity had died upon his ear, and for which *that* ear had not been tuned, he was saluted with a hymn;—the two extremes furnishing an epitome of heaven and hell—the one seen from the other, as the rich man beheld Lazarus, only with this important difference among others, no impassable "gulf" was "fixed" between; "so that they which would pass from" one to the other might avail themselves of the privilege. This was a moment of deep interest; and on this single act, through the Divine Being putting special honour upon it, might hinge in a great measure the bearings of his future life. He was partial to *singing*, and as the hymn was sung in different parts he was the more delighted. The conspicuous figure in the centre was the late Richard Burdsall, of York, father of the Rev.

John Burdsall, who had, with his usual daring, entered the field against the enemy, and was mounted on what Samuel designated "a block," for the purpose of giving him a greater advantage over his auditory, while animadverting on the profligacy of the times.* Mr. Burdsall was remarkably popular in his day, and was just such a preacher as Samuel, from the peculiar construction of his own mind, was likely to fix upon,—one who would, on comparing the one with the other, have stood at the *head* of the *same class* at school, in which Samuel would have been placed at the *foot*; both being *fit* for the class, as well as *of* it,—only the one having attained to greater *proficiency* than the other, in a somewhat similar line.†

Samuel's attention was soon gained, and his affection won, which, to Mr. Burdsall, was of no small importance; for as he was proceeding with the service, a clergyman advanced toward him, declaring that "he should not preach there, not if he were the Lord Mayor himself," threatening to "pull him down from the

* The Wesleyan Methodists have always been distinguished for their zealous attempts to reclaim the *worst* part of human nature *first*: for this purpose they have resorted to markets, feasts, and fairs; and in looking at the situation of some of their oldest chapels, Whitby and other places, it will be found that they frequently pitched their tents in the most Sodomitish parts of a town, with a view to improve the more depraved as well as the lower grades of society.

† Quaintness, wit, and imagination, were rarely absent in Mr. B. Speaking to the writer once, in the city of York, on his early call to the ministry, he said, "I seem to have been something like a partridge: I ran away with the shell on my head."

block." Just as he was preparing to carry his designs into execution, Samuel, whose love to the preacher was such, that he felt, as he observed, as if he "could lose the last drop of" his "blood" in his defence, stepped up to the clergyman, clenched his hands, and holding them in a menacing form to his face, accosted him in the abrupt and measured terms of the ring upon which he had but a few minutes before been gazing,—"Sir, if you disturb that man of God, I will drop you as sure as ever you were born." There was too much emphasis in the expression, and too much fire in the eye, to admit a doubt that he was in earnest. The reverend gentleman felt the force of it—his countenance changed—the storm which was up in Samuel had allayed the tempest in him—and he looked with no small concern for an opening in the crowd, by which he might make his escape. Samuel, though unchanged by divine grace, had too much nobleness of soul in him to trample upon an opponent who was thus in a state of humiliation before him; and therefore generously took him under his protection, made a passage for him through the audience, and conducted him to the outskirts without molestation, when he quickly disappeared. The manner in which this was done, the despatch employed, and the sudden calm after the commotion, must have produced a kind of dramatic effect on the minds of religious persons, who, nevertheless, in the midst of their surprise, gratitude and even harmless mirth at the precipitate flight of their disturber, who was converted in an instant by a mere stripling from the lion to the timid hare, would be no more disposed to justify the clenched fist,—*the earth helping the woman* in this way,—than they could be brought to approve of the zeal of Peter, when, by a single stroke, he cut off the right ear of the high priest's servant. Samuel instantly resumed the attitude of an attentive hearer, without any apparent emotions from what had just transpired. In the launching forth of his hand, he gave as little warning as the thunderbolt of heaven; the flash of his eye was like the lightning's glare—a sudden burst of passion, withering for a moment—seen—and gone.

The following good effects resulted from this sermon—a high respect for the preacher, and a stronger attachment to the Methodists as a people; both having a tendency to lead him to the *use* of the *means* by which the Divine Being conveys *grace* to the hearts of his creatures. He remarked, that after this period, in following Mr. Burdsall from place to place, he travelled "many scores of miles," and that he "never heard" him without being "blessed" under his preaching. His feelings were in unison with those which dictated Ruth's address to Naomi, "Whither thou goest, I will go; thy people shall be my people, and thy God my God;" and as far as circumstances would admit, and he had light to discover the truth, he laboured to give vent to the overflowings of his heart.

His case was one which would lead to the conclusion, that his religion commenced in *heat* rather than *light;* that he continued for some time, even beyond this period, more the subject of *impression* than of *instruction;* felt, in short, what he was unable to express to others, and for which he could not account to himself. He had been touched by the wand of Moses at Horeb, which had unlocked some of the secret springs of his heart, and put them in motion, rather than been in the tabernacle with Aaron the priest, illuminated and perfected by the Urim and the Thummin. His heart was much more assailable than his head, and, as will afterward appear, was much more at work through life, and had a more commanding influence over his conduct. Divine light was admitted but slowly, not so much through any violent opposition to it, or any process of reasoning carried on in his mind against any of the particular doctrines of the gospel, as through a want of power to arrange and classify his thoughts, to connect one subject with another, to trace effects to their causes; a want of the means of information, as well as a relish for reading, had the means been at hand; a certain quickness in catching particular points, which led him to think as some Hibernians are led to speak; and a peculiarly animated temperament, which disposed him to warm himself at the fire of the Christian altar, rather than silently gaze upon a cloudless sky, the splendid canopy of the great temple of the universe.

He seemed, in fact, to carry the more fiery part of his trade into his religion, as he subsequently carried every part of his religion into his trade. Full of the best and warmest feeling *for* the religion of Christ and its professors, and using the means in order to *attain* it, he was now in a hopeful way, not only of verging *toward* it, but of entering *into* its genuine spirit.

To these kindlings, yieldings, and advances, was at length added *conviction*, though not the most poignant. The clouds which overhung his mind began to break away. This was effected by the ministry of the Rev. John Wesley. The chronology of this event is placed by Samuel's widow in the fifteenth year of his age; but by himself, after the period of his having heard Mr. Burdsall: and although the memory of the former is generally more to be depended upon than that of the latter, yet in this case Samuel was probably the more correct of the two. It was in the old chapel at Leeds where he heard the founder of Methodism; and he scarcely appears to have been sufficiently impressed with the importance of personal salvation, during the first year of his apprenticeship, to lead him so many miles from home to hear a sermon; nor does he refer to any thing that seems to amount to *conviction* prior to his York excursion. Still, the date is of minor importance, provided the fact be secured; and the principal point to be attended to is that of tracing the progressive steps by which he was led to the knowledge of himself and of God, and to the enjoyment of "pure and undefiled religion." On entering the chapel, he was awed and delighted at Mr. Wesley's appearance, who, according to his conceptions of angelic beings, seemed at first sight to be "something more than man," even "an angel" of God. This prepossession in favour of the preacher, naturally prepared the way for a speedy reception of the truths delivered. There was one subject, however, and all in favour of the preacher which Samuel was at a loss to comprehend. Mr. Wesley's prophetic soul was led out, in some part of the discourse, to connect with the revival of religion which was going on, more glorious times; intimating that when his dust should mingle with the clods of the valley, ministers more eminently successful than either himself or others by whom he was surrounded, would be raised to perpetuate and extend the work. Not distinguishing between ministerial *talent* and ministerial *usefulness*, Samuel thought Mr. Wesley intimated that *greater* preachers than himself would supply his place; thus giving Mr. Wesley the credit of indirectly associating himself with the *great*, though *greater* were to tread in his steps. Samuel, according to his own exposition of Mr. Wesley's words, could not conceive it within the range of possibility for any one to equal, much more to surpass him; for, to use his own language, "he preached like an angel." The text was, "Show me thy faith without thy works, and I will show you my faith by my works," James ii, 18. In addition to Mr. Wesley's appearance, and his exalted character as a preacher, we discover part of the secret of Samuel's estimate of him in himself. It might now be said of him, as of Saul of Tarsus, "And there fell from his eyes as it had been scales;" immediately his mental vision was rendered more acute, as well as enlarged. On hearing Mr. Wesley, he emphatically "received his sight," and that too in the most important sense; he had listened to one, of whom he might have said, not indeed as the woman of Samaria, "*Come, see a man* that has *told me all things that ever I* DID," but "*Come, see a man that has told me all things of which I am* DESTITUTE." Though he could not give any correct account of the manner in which the subject was treated, there was one conclusion which he was enabled to draw from the whole, and which penetrated too deeply for him ever to *forget*, that he possessed neither *faith* nor *works* which God could either approve or accept.

In no previous instance had the hand of God been so visible as in this; and the state of the subject of the memoir may be illustrated by that of one of two persons shut up in a dark room, where the other, having seen it by daylight, expatiates to his fellow an hour or two on its height, length, width, and form, the nakedness and colour of the walls, with all its other peculiarities. From the description given, aided by his blind attempts to feel his way into every corner, and lay his hand upon every thing within his reach, the hearer may be able to form some conception of the apartment and situation in which he stands. But it is easy to conceive that a third person opening the door, and entering the room with a lighted taper in his hand, would throw more light upon the subject in one single moment, than a person of the highest descriptive powers, through description alone, could do in twelve hours. This, though not a perfect illustration, is sufficient for the present purpose: Samuel had heard preaching repeatedly; a *description* of the moral condition of man, of the new creature in Christ Jesus, of the awful and glorious realities of an invisible world, of every thing, in short, connected with man as the subject of the moral government of God, had been given in the discourses which he had heard; but through his own supineness, his not asking for divine aid, or, if he asked, his asking amiss, he remained in the "darkness" of ignorance, error, and unbelief, without "light" to guide him either in his conceptions, his decisions, or his walk. HE, however, who commanded light to shine *out* of darkness, commanded it here to shine *into* darkness; a pure ray was shot from the Sun of righteousness, illuminating all within. Samuel found the "house" *empty* of all good, not *swept* of evil, nor *garnished* with holiness. It was light which produced a *conviction*, not so much of the *presence* of evil, as of the *absence* of good. He saw that he was "*poor*" and "*naked*," and had till now been "*blind*;" but the negative character of his conviction did not constitute him "*wretched*" because of *sin*, or "*miserable*" because of the *enormity* of *that* sin. The flaming sword was permitted to turn only in one direction; other operations were apparently restrained, when the present had its full effect, and the subject was more fully prepared for their exercise. The Holy Spirit had been already in operation, softening and gently impressing the heart, all preparatory to a farther work of grace. There was fire, as has been previously stated; but it was fire without flame, fire smouldering under ashes, and consequently incapable of emitting the beneficial light. It was now that the shades of night, in which he had been so long enveloped, seemed to say, as the angel said to Jacob, "Let *us* go, for the day breaketh."

CHAPTER II.

He leaves his master before the expiration of his apprenticeship—Is providentially directed to a suitable situation, and commences business for himself—His marriage—His benevolence—Death of his wife's mother—Is alarmed by a dream—Obtains mercy—Suddenness of his conversion—Its fruits—His zeal—Answer to prayer, and effects of his expostulation with a landlady—Summary of the evidence of his conversion.

IT has been quaintly, but significantly observed, in reference to the providential lot of human beings, that "every peg has its hole."

Whatever may have been the primary design of the remark, it is certainly applicable to the notions of personal *comfort* and probable *usefulness;* the former effected by the *adaptation* of the *pin* to the place and of the *place* to the pin, and the latter by its *projection,* going beyond itself, so to speak, affording an opportunity, both to friends and strangers, of suspending upon its form whatever they may desire, whether from inclination or necessity. And the man who permits his Maker to "*choose*" his "*inheritance*" for him, will rarely be placed in a *situation* in which it will be impossible for some of his fellow-creatures to hang upon him their hopes, their weaknesses, and their wants. This will apply with equal propriety to persons in humble life, as to persons in the more elevated ranks of society. We are taught the doctrine of a wise and bountiful Providence in the fall of a "sparrow," and in the adornings of "the lilies," of a Providence which is both *permissive* and *active* in its operations, directing in the *outset,* and entering into the minutest circumstances of human life. General observation would almost warrant the belief, that there is a starting point for every man, later or earlier in life, subject to his own choice: and in proportion as he proceeds along the line, or deviates from it, will be the amount of his success or adversity, connecting with the situation, in the person that holds it, industry, economy, and integrity. The principal difficulty is in the *choice.* Religiously to determine this, we ought never to lose sight of the circumstances of the case, personal competency, and general usefulness. Several of these remarks will apply to the subject of this memoir.

Though Samuel had acted in the capacity of a faithful servant to his master for some years, a circumstance took place which led to a separation before the expiration of his apprenticeship. His master's daughter had conceived an attachment to him, which was returned, though not to the same extent, by Samuel. This naturally led to certain domestic attentions, in which the young woman contributed to his comforts; and having a little money at command, she occasionally assisted him, with a view to give strength to the bond which subsisted. His master coming down stairs one morning, a little earlier than usual, found him seated with Miss Derby on his knee. He instantly returned, and told his wife, whom he had left in bed; and after opening the circumstance, said, "I believe she is as fond of the lad as ever a cow was of a calf." On again descending the stairs, he chided them both, and signified his disapprobation of all attachment. The day passed on, with evident indications that the master was brooding on the subject; and at length he ordered Samuel, with a good deal of angry feeling, to leave his house and his service. The dismissal having been given at an evening hour, Samuel requested permission to remain till the next day, which was granted. To prevent any matrimonial connection from taking place between them, the father, on Samuel's removal, contrived to form a union between his daughter and a person of some property, but much her senior, offering as an inducement a handsome dowry. Miss D. wrote to Samuel the day previous to her marriage, requesting him to meet her at a specified time and place, pledging herself to him for ever, as the sole object of her first affection. Poor Samuel was placed in circumstances at the time from which it was impossible to escape; and the fitful moment glided away from both without improvement, to their inexpressible grief. As this was a compulsory measure, the bride gave her hand without her heart; her spirits shortly afterward became depressed, and confirmed insanity ensued. Samuel was sent for by her friends—he obeyed the summons—the sight of him increased her malady, and added to the poignancy of his own feelings—he hastily withdrew—and she died soon after. As an affair of *honour*, it may be said, "In all this" Samuel "sinned not."* Abandoned, however, as he was, by his master, the Lord directed him by his providence.

Without giving the West Yorkshire dialect, which he *wrote* as well as *spoke*, and which it would be as difficult for persons in the southern

* Old Mrs. Derby, who survived Samuel, and was living at Healaugh, in 1831, in the 90th year of her age, was very partial to him, always styling him, "*Our Sam*;" and Mr. D., on seeing his daughter's distress, was heard to say, "O that I had let Sammy have my lass!" Samuel paid occasional visits to his old mistress to the end of his days.

counties of England to read and to understand, without a glossary, as the "Lancashire dialect," the substance of his relation, when "entering upon the world," to employ a familiar phrase, is clear, simple, and touching. "When I was one and twenty years of age," he states, "there was a shop at liberty, at Micklefield, and my father took it for me. I here began business for myself; and when I had paid for my tools, I was left without a penny in my pocket, or a bit of bread to eat. But I was strong, in good health, and laboured hard; and that God who sent the ravens to feed his servant, fed me. One day, while at work, a man came into my shop, who told me that his wife had fed the pig so fat as to render it useless to the family, and that he would sell me the one half of it very cheap. I told him that I wished it were in my power to make the purchase—that I was much in need, but that I was without money. He replied, he would trust me: and I agreed to take it. I mentioned the circumstance to a neighbour, who offered to lend me five pounds, which I accepted: and out of this I paid the man for what I had bought. I continued to labour hard, and the Lord, in his abundant goodness, supplied all my wants." From this it would seem that he had not been anxiously looking in every direction for a situation, and that, on finding every providential door shut had sat down to quarrel with the dispensations of God, or made some hazardous attempts to force an opening: nor was the situation at first either perceived by himself, or the door—to proceed with the allusion—but slightly turned upon its hinges, leaving the possibility or propriety of entrance still problematical. It was thrown open by the hand that regulates all human affairs—circumstances invited the father to the spot—he took his survey—Samuel, having been released from his connection with his master, found the occurrence seasonable—poverty was his portion, but no capital was requisite for the purchase of stock—previous industry and economy prepared him to meet the expense of tools—his father led him up to the door which his Maker had opened—labour was instantly furnished, and the "daily bread," for which he was commanded to pray, was supplied—the confidence and kindness of friends encouraged him to proceed—and *there* he continued, succeeded, and was afterward useful. Providence appeared to meet him at every turn, and, as in a piece of wedge-work, adapted its movements to all the peculiarities of his case.

After having been established in business for the space of eighteen months, without apparently elevating his mind above the drudgery of the day, he meditated a change in his domestic circumstances. "The Lord," he observes, "saw that I wanted a helpmeet"—he knew the character that "would suit me best" —and was so "kind" as to furnish me with "one of his own choosing." From the form of expression employed, it would seem that there was an allusion to his first attachment, which he might be led to consider as not of God, from the circumstance of his having been thwarted in his purpose. His courtship, in its commencement and termination, preserves the singularity which distinguished most of the leading transactions of his life. His partiality to singing led him to unite himself to the choir that attended Aberford church, which union continued for the space of ten years. Here he became acquainted with her who was destined to be his bride, and to survive him as his widow. The first time he saw her, which was during divine service, it was powerfully impressed upon his mind that she would one day become his wife. Under such impression, and in great simplicity, he walked up to her immediately on leaving the church, and unbosomed his feelings and thoughts on the subject. She heard his first lispings with surprise, and felt their force; for from that period they delighted in each other's society, and were finally united in holy matrimony in Spofford church. She was six years older than himself. On leaving the hymeneal altar, and reaching the church door, a number of poor widows pressed around him to solicit alms. His heart was touched; the tear was in his eye; "I began the world," said he to himself, "without money, and I will again begin it *straight*." The thought was no sooner conceived, and the generous impulse felt, than the hand, which emptied the pocket, scattered the last pence of which he was possessed among the craving applicants. The bride being entitled to some property, and work pouring in upon him, his exhausted stores were soon recruited: and believing that a blessing followed the donation, he appended to a narrative of the event, in a tone of triumph, "The Lord gave me a good wife, and I have never wanted money since that day."

The fine glow of devotional feeling occasionally experienced in his youth, had for some time become extinct; and he had not in his present situation been brought into contact with any decidedly religious character to revive it, except the mother of his wife, who was a member of the Wesleyan connection. He complained that at this period his wife and himself were "both strangers to saving grace"—that "the parish" could not boast of a single Methodist, and that there was not "one" of his "own family that knew the Lord." His mother-in-law, who, it would seem, did not reside in the same parish with himself, often spoke to him on the subject of religion, and interceded with God both for him and his partner. Example, exhortation, and prayer were ineffectual. The appeal was to be made to the passions; and through these was the entrance to be made, which would effect his deliverance from the thraldom of Satan. His mother-in-law sickened and died. The happiness she experienced in her last hours softened the heart and reawakened the attention of Samuel to the concerns of his soul. This however, but for what he denominated a "vision," had been "as the early dew that passeth away."

Three days after her dissolution, he dreamed that she appeared to him arrayed in white, took him by the hand, and affectionately warned him to flee from the wrath to come; stating, that if he did not repent he would never meet her in the paradise of God. At the close of the address, the visionary form vanished; conviction, while he slumbered, seized his spirit; he awoke in terror, and, to use his own language, "jumped out of bed," thus furnishing another exposition of the language of the "man in the land of Uz,"—"When I say, My bed shall comfort me, my couch shall ease my complaint; then thou scarest me with dreams, and terrifiest me through visions." This sudden spring from the bed roused his wife: his groans and distress alarmed her; and supposing him to have been suddenly seized with some complaint that threatened his life, she was proceeding to awaken the neighbours, and to call them to her assistance, when she was arrested in her course, in the midst of the darkness with which she was surrounded, with a sentence wrung from the depths of his agonized spirit, and uttered in sobs: "I want Jesus—Jesus, to pardon all my sins." It was sufficient for her to know that he was not in immediate danger from affliction; her fears were therefore quickly dissipated, but she could afford him no consolation. This he seemed to feel, and observed, "I had no Paul to say to me, 'Believe on the

Lord Jesus Christ, and thou shalt be saved;' nor any praying wife to pray for me." It was the midnight of desolation; and the only light by which the way of mercy could be discovered, was from within. The flood of day which was poured upon his mind was as strong as it was sudden; and differing in degree from that with which he was visited under the ministry of Mr. Wesley, he now beheld both sides of his case, not only the *absence* of all *good*, but the *presence* of real evil. "My eyes," said he, "were opened—I saw all the sins I had committed through the whole course of my life—I was like the psalmist—I cried out like the jailer." He added with considerable emphasis, "I *did* say my prayers," continuing, "as I never did before;" meaning that he had *only* SAID them previously to this period. He further observed that it might have been said of him, as of Saul, "Behold he *prayeth*."

The ministerial instruction which he had at different periods received, led him, in the midst of much ignorance on other subjects, to adopt the proper means, and to look to the true source of happiness, in order to its attainment. He had *heard* of one Jesus of Nazareth, like Saul; and though that Jesus had not before been experimentally revealed to him, yet such was the nature of the *light* which he received, that it enabled him to recognise in HIM from whom it proceeded the face of a Saviour, and a Friend. The Sun of righteousness, like the orb of day, discovers himself by his own shining. It is in his light that we see light. Samuel was in the light, in the midst of natural darkness; and though he could not hear the prayers of a wife, he had confidence in the intercession of a Saviour. "Jesus," said he, "was my advocate; I put in my case, and he pleaded for me before the throne of God. I believed that the blood of Christ was shed for me; and the moment I believed, I found peace. I could adopt the language of the poet:—

'My God is reconciled,
His pard'ning voice I hear;
He owns me for his child,
I can no longer fear;
With confidence I now draw nigh,
And, Father, Abba, Father, cry.'"

His state, as an inhabitant of the natural world, afforded a fair exemplification of the change through which he passed. He reposed himself in darkness—lay in that darkness, like the dead in the tomb—and was passing through this insensible state to the light of another day. On the same evening, as a sinner before his God, he lay down in the darkness of a deeper night than that which veils the face of nature—was the subject of a more terrible death than that of which sleep is but the image—awoke in spiritual light—and was, ere the natural light broke upon his eye, enabled to exult in the dawn of a fairer morning than ever beamed upon our earth—a morning which can only be surpassed by the morning of the resurrection, when the just shall kindle into life at the sight of the Sun of righteousness, to which this, through the vivifying rays of the same Sun, formed the happy prelude. Spiritual *life* succeeded spiritual light. To object to the *genuineness* of the work, because of its *suddenness*, would be to plead a "*needs be*" for our continuance in a state of comparative darkness, danger, misery, and death, in opposition to the end proposed by the scheme of human redemption through Jesus Christ, which was to complete our deliverance from such a state—would be to prescribe limits to the power, goodness, and purity of "the HOLY ONE of Israel," as though he were unable to effect such a change but by degrees, unwilling at once to soothe our sorrows, and approving of our continuance in a state of moral defilement—would be to doubt the veracity of the Holy Ghost, in his statements of the sudden illumination of Saul, the sudden conviction of the multitude under the preaching of Peter, and the instantaneous pardon of the penitent thief—and would, finally, be to obstruct the course of our obedience, in compliance with all the exhortations which urge us, and all the injunctions which bind us to an immediate preparation for another state of being, as well as needlessly expose us, through sudden death, to the "bitter pains" of death eternal.

But the doctrine of *sudden conversion* is becoming every day less objectionable; and the "holy ground" on which *that* conversion takes place, is not barely visited by the hymning seraphs of the Christian Church, who chant their songs *within* the sacred enclosure, but is respected and honoured by some of our first epic poets from *without*, through whose pen the ground has at length become poetically classical.* Thus, in "THE POET'S PILGRIMAGE TO WATERLOO," the author, in his moments of vision, after tasting the tree of knowledge, sings :—

"In awe I heard, and trembled, and obey'd;
The bitterness was even as of death;
I felt a cold and piercing thrill pervade
My loosen'd limbs, and losing sight and breath,
To earth I should have fallen in despair,
Had I not clasp'd the cross, and been supported there.

'My heart, I thought, was bursting with the force
Of that most fatal fruit; soul-sick I felt,
And tears ran down in such continuous course
As if the very eyes themselves should melt;
But then I heard my heavenly Teacher say,
'Drink, and this mortal stound shall pass away.'

"I stoop'd and drank of that divinest well,
Fresh from the Rock of ages where it ran.
It had a heavenly quality to quell
My pain:—I rose a renovated man,
And would not now, when that relief was known,
For worlds the needful suffering have foregone."

These sentiments, though highly poetical, take their root in fact, and owe their beauty and their excellence to truth, of which they are the fictitious representatives. The deep distress, the *heart-sickness* referred to, would, by a simple-hearted Christian, be styled *deep conviction* for *sin*, or the pains of *repentance* antecedent to

* See the writer's Letter to Dr. Southey, Poet Laureate, on the Life of Mr. Wesley.

pardon; by a philosopher, a species of religious madness. The passing away of the "*mortal stound*" would be contemplated under the notion of *peace of mind*, after the penitent had by faith "*clasped the cross*," or rather the Crucified. The brief space of time allotted for the whole would at once entitle the work to the general appellation of *sudden conversion:* for the poet had only to *stoop*—to *drink*—to *rise*, and to rise too a *renovated man*. This bears such a striking analogy to the case of the sin-sick village blacksmith, whose personal history is passing in review—who knelt in distress before his God—implored mercy—and rose renewed and happy—that the poet, had he known the fact, could scarcely have been more felicitous in its illustration.

So fully satisfied was Samuel himself of the genuineness of the work, that he frequently, in after life, when dwelling upon his religious views and feelings, recurred to the very "flag" on which he knelt, and where he remained as he had risen from his couch, unannoyed by the cold, till he experienced peace with God. No sooner was he put in possession of the "pearl of great price," than he waited with the anxiety of the watchman for the morning, to be delivered from a situation which had become burdensome through overwrought joy,—a joy which could only find relief in the hearts of others—hearts ready, as the recipients of its overflowings, to share in its fulness. But where were *hearts* to be found to become the receptacles of such joy?

It was not for him to say, with the psalmist, "Come and hear, all ye that fear God, and I will declare what he hath done for my soul;" or, "I will declare thy name unto my brethren: in the midst of the congregation I will praise thee." Though *congregations* were not remote, yet there were no *brethren* with whom he could claim religious affinity, none that *feared* God, with whom he was acquainted. He resolved, therefore, to proclaim the goodness of God to his "neighbours;" and like Melancthon, to whom truth appeared at first so simple, and yet so forcible, that he instantly calculated on the conquest of others, but had soon to complain that old Adam was too strong for young Melancthon, Samuel—and the thought has haunted many beside these, both learned and illiterate—contemplated nothing short of the sudden conversion of every person in the neighbourhood. "I thought," he remarked, "I could make all the world believe, when day-light appeared. I went to my neighbours, for I loved my neighbour as myself. I wished them all to experience what I felt. The first that I went to was a landlady. I told her what the Lord had done for *me*; and that what he had done for me he could do for *her*, exhorting her to pray and believe." This was no new language to the ear into which it was poured, for the woman seemed to know to what source it was traceable. "What," she retorted, "have you become a *Methodist?* You were a good neighbour, and a good man before; and why change? The

Methodists are a set of rogues, and you will soon be like them." Samuel, who was at least guiltless of Methodism, had too important a subject in hand to spend his time in disclaiming his brotherhood, and therefore continued to press upon her attention the necessity of personal religion, telling her, if her "sins" were "not pardoned," it would be impossible for her to go "to heaven." Unprepared for such service, partly from the early hour, partly from the personal nature of the discourse, but more especially from the character of the preacher, who, only the day before, had given so little promise of any thing of the kind, she became indignant, and in her ire turned him out of the house, in which he might have remained till evening, reducing himself, by intoxication, beneath a level with the brute creation. Fiery as was his zeal for her salvation, he received the requital of his good intentions with meekness; and instead of repining at the rebuff, retired to a field, and poured out his soul in prayer to God on her behalf. He had just been favoured with a proof of the efficacy of prayer in his own case; and the simple thought that "what God had done for himself he could do for others," so fully occupied his mind, that, in its strength and simplicity, he was led on from one part of prayer to another—from *confession*, *supplication*, and *thanksgiving*, in reference to himself, to that of *intercession* for those around. The fire of divine love burned upon the altar of his heart, faith was in exercise, hope was on the wing, every feeling, though infantile, was strong—he again returned to the contest, but what a change! "To my surprise," he observed, "when I went back she was crying in the doorstead. She asked me to forgive her. 'O yes, that I will,' I said; and if you will let me go in, and pray with you, the Lord will forgive you too." His words and his manner, when the woman was left to herself, had been the subject of reflection; and, from the impression made, she readily acceded to the proposal. "She took me," continued he, "into a room; and there I prayed for her. It was not long before the Lord blessed her; and he thus gave me the first soul I asked for. He can do a great work in a little time. She lived and died happy. This encouraged me to go on in the duty of prayer."

If an inward renewal is known by its effects, the *tree* by its *fruit*, the evidence of Samuel Hick's conversion to God is not less certain than if it had been less sudden. He had employed the *means*, prayer and faith, instituted by God himself for the attainment of his favour—he experienced *joy* in the Holy Ghost through believing, having been made a partaker of "*salvation*;" and being "upheld with" God's "free Spirit," he immediately began, in primitive style, to "teach transgressors" the "ways" of righteousness, and a "sinner" was "converted" to the truth. The *temper* of mind which he manifested under opposition, his readiness to *forgive*, the *constraining* influence of the love which he felt, the *persevering* quality of the principle by which he was actuated, his *joy* over a sinner repenting, only to be compared with that possessed by angelic beings, all, all are indications of one of whom it might be said, "Old things are passed away: behold all things are become new." Add to this, every part of his personal history, from this time to the hour of his death, is confirmatory of Christian character. While a career of between forty and fifty years of Christian usefulness, connected with a strictly moral conduct, renders it improbable that he should, for such a length of time, impose upon others; his views of his state and of his services, and his abhorrence of sin, authorize the belief that there was no deception practised upon himself. It was not a state of mere improved feeling, not the whitewash of pharisaism; the change entered the *grain* of the man, turning him inside out to others, to whom any thing in the shape of *guile* was invisible, and *outside in* upon himself, while he declared, from the internal and external evidence which a depraved nature and a previously sinful life had furnished, that he had been "as big a *heathen* as any of the natives of Ceylon," having "had gods many, and lords many;" but that "the Lord, when he awakened" his "soul, enabled" him "to cut them off at a stroke." He reasoned not with flesh and blood; he spared no Agag, he reserved no sin.

CHAPTER III.

He seeks church fellowship—Advises with a pious clergyman, with whom he meets in band—Unites himself, on the clergyman's leaving the neighbourhood, to the Wesleyan Methodists—The kind of preaching under which he profited—Society at Sturton Grange—A revival of religion—Two colliers rendered extensively useful—A solitary barn the resort of the devout—Samuel's distress on account of indwelling sin, and his deliverance from it—Singular occurrence—Deep distress compatible with a state of justification.

MAN, who was originally formed for society, and furnished with its felicities in paradise, carries with him into every climate, and into all circumstances, those elements which, when properly improved and directed, not only fit him for social life, but render him restless without it, as well as inspire him with a solicitude for its blessings. A few solitary hermitical and misanthropic exceptions, or an occasional wish for "wings like a dove," to "fly away" from its bustle, in order to "be at rest," are not to be adduced as arguments against the general principle; for even among those who are most partial to retirement, who are least in love with the world of beings around them, and who, in opposition to the designs of God in helping man by man, convert themselves into *misers'* treasure, a kind of moral and intellectual *cash*, hoarded up in the *safe* of a monastery or a nunnery, *useless* to such as are most in need of their aid, and whose wants might be essentially relieved by an expenditure of their time and of their talents; even among these the love of society is inherent, and is manifested by their institutions, where groups are permitted to dwell and mingle with each other, if not as the *coin* itself, as the *misers* of Christianity. This love of society is not destroyed, but regulated and strengthened by religion; and by no one is it more needed, or more ardently desired, than by a person newly "found in" Christ. The notion of "going to heaven alone," of preserving our religion a "secret"—which, by the way, belongs only to those who have no religion to exhibit—is instantly annihilated on the reception of pardon. The charm of secrecy is broken, and why? There is now "*something to say*"—subject matter for conversation. "A new song" is put into the "mouth," and it must be *sung*; a "morsel" has been received, and it cannot be eaten "alone." Nor is the wish to communicate confined barely to a person's entrance on the divine life; "it grows with his growth." "They that feared the Lord spake often one to another."

Samuel, who was in danger of *casting his "pearls before swine*," and who had confounded attempts at usefulness with "the communion of saints," was instinctively led to seek the latter from the nature of his own wants. "I was at a sad loss," says he, "for church fellowship, there being no society near." This "*loss*" could not allude to any privation of privilege, with the enjoyment of which he had been previously favoured; for no such enjoyment had been known. The want was created with the character which he now sustained. It was the want of a child—himself being only a *babe in Christ*—looking for some one to guide and support his steps; the want of another regimen than that to which he had been accustomed—of other food for the support of a new life. His connection with the Methodists, as a *hearer*, whether occasional or constant, seems to have broken off with his servitude at Healaugh; and no persons of that persuasion being near, a closer connection could not be immediately and conveniently renewed. Having been accustomed to attend the service of the Established Church, after his residence at Micklefield, he naturally looked to its members for communion. The light, however, which he had received, was sufficiently discriminative in its character to guide him to the right spot. Instead of "wending his way" to Aberford, where he had distinguished himself as a chorister, he proceeded with the infallibility of instinct to Ledsham, and with great simplicity solicited an interview with the resident clergyman. "I asked him," he remarks, "what I should do; and he told me to call on him the next Lord's day morning, when he would advise with me." He accordingly repaired to the house at the time appointed, and was cordially received, as well as religiously instructed. Samuel's testimony of him—because the testimony of *experience*—is of more value, in an evangelical point of view, than the highest panegyric from the pen of a literary nominal professor of Christianity. It is the lisping of childhood, as yet unaccustomed to artifice. "He was a very good man, and preached the gospel. I went to Ledsham some time; but he was at length obliged to leave, for his salary would not keep him. Then I was at a loss for my band-mate." The last expression, the full import of which can only be known and felt by persons enjoying the sweets of Christian fellowship, shows the tenderness, the condescension, the solicitude, the sympathies of this ecclesiastic—the VILLAGE PATRIARCH stooping from his dignity, and taking, as a *band-mate*, "sweet counsel with the VILLAGE BLACKSMITH!*

* Ledsham is the village, [in which stands the church] in which the late Rev. Walter Sellon, who was vicar of the parish, lived and died; and Ledstone Hall, at no great distance from it, is the place where the renowned Lady Betty Hastings also resided, and finally resigned her soul into the hands of her God. •The clergyman, of whom Samuel speaks, is supposed to have been Mr. Wightman, who was curate to Mr. Sellon; the former a Calvinist, and the latter an Arminian in creed; and though *salary* might have its share of influence in the question of removal, it is strongly suspected that *doctrinal sentiments* aided in turning the scale. Mr. Sellon was a sturdy supporter of the doctrine of general redemption, and fought some hard battles in early life against the Calvinistic view of the subject, under the auspices of Mr. Wesley; but toward the close of Mr. Wesley's pilgrimage, Mr. Sellon manifested a degree of coldness toward his old friend. In a manuscript correspondence of Mr. Wesley with Mr. Sellon, in the possession of the writer, it appears that the warmth of friendship began to subside when Mr. Sellon resided at Ashby-de-la-Zouch. From 1772 to 1784, there is a chasm in the correspondence. Up to the former period, Mr. Wesley's address was, "Dear Walter," with all the familiarity of close friendship: but on Mr. Sellon's residence at Ledsham, at which place he lived during the latter period, the address was altered to "Dear Sir," one of the letters concluding with, "You used to meet me when I came near

This was a gracious providence to Samuel, through which he was enabled, in the childhood of his Christianity, to acquire strength; and but for which he might have found it difficult to walk alone. He had not long, however, to bemoan his bereavement. The Lord, on removing one stay, speedily supplied its place with another. It was with Samuel, therefore, as with the child, a *change* of *nurses*, rather than a privation, or even a serious suspension of the kindly offices requisite for the support and guidance of his weakness and inexperience. "The Lord," he observed, "sent Mr. Wade to Sturton Grange, where they took in the preachers, and had a society. As I felt my want of church fellowship, I went to ask them to take me into society. They offered to take me on trial; and I continued a member till we got a society in our own place, which was not long, for I never let them alone." He had an ardent desire for the salvation of sinners; and his *not letting them alone* refers as much to his conver-

you; but you seem of late years to have forgotten your old friend and brother, John Wesley." Among the manuscript letters referred to, are some curious epistolary specimens written by Mr. Charles Wesley to Mr. Sellon; also some rare ones, addressed to the same person, from the Rev. Messrs. J. Fletcher, Vin. Perronet, E. Perronet, Sir Richard Hill, and the Countess of Huntingdon—all tending to throw light on the controversies and passing events of the times—which another occasion may render it proper to present to the public. How long Mr. Sellon remained at Ledsham, the writer is unable at present to ascertain; but it is probable, from the Wesleyan Meth. Mag. for 1818, p. 53, that he was either in the village or its immediate vicinity, in a state of great affliction, in 1790 and 1791.

sational efforts to reclaim his neighbours, as to any request that a portion of the privileges of the society to which he had united himself, which was little more than a mile distant, should be transferred to Micklefield. Thus, adverting to his situation to promote the religious welfare of others, he remarks, "I had a good opportunity, as nearly the whole town came to my shop; and I was always at them. I found my share of persecution; but this did not daunt me, nor prevent me from calling on sinners to repent, believe, and be converted."

It was not barely by reproof and exhortation that he sought to multiply the number of travellers to Zion, but also by earnest and affectionate *invitation*. The first fruit of this description of labour—labour which has been extremely productive in a variety of instances—was a wealthy agriculturist. "Mr. Thomas Taylor," said he, "came to preach at Sturton Grange, and I invited all I could to go and hear him. One of these was Mr. Rhodes,* a large farmer, who lived in the parish; and who said if I would call upon him he would go with me. Blessed be the Lord! on the same night the gospel proved the power of God to his salvation. I remember the text; it referred to the *tares* and the *wheat*. The tares were gathered and tied

* In a letter from Mr. Dawson, dated April 3d, 1830, referring to Mr. Rhodes, he observes, "He is still living at Micklefield. I saw him yesterday. He is nearly blind, and his constitution is fast breaking up. He will not survive Samuel long. The Methodists always preached, and still preach at his house."

into bundles. There was a bundle of sabbath-breakers, a bundle of swearers, &c. These bundles were to be burned; and before the sermon was finished, the preacher got Mr. Rhodes bound up in one of them. From that time the Lord added to our number; we got preaching to our place, and soon had a class-meeting." This, it should seem, from a reference to the Minutes of Conference, was either in the year 1785, or 1786, when Mr. Taylor was stationed in the Leeds circuit. Such preaching was as much calculated to instruct the uneducated mind of Samuel, as it was to arrest the attention of the farmer. Keach would have been a superior preacher in his estimation to Saurin, and he would have profited more by the *metaphors* of the one, than by the *sermons* of the other. He could fasten upon some of the more prominent parts of a highly figurative discourse, and turn them to good personal and practical account; but would have been in danger of running wild with the remainder. He knew much better when to commence, than how to proceed, or where to close.

But it was not in criticism that he was skilled; nor was it into the niceties of Christian doctrine that he could enter. He knew the truth much better in its operation on the heart, than in its shinings on the understanding; and could tell much better how it felt, than in what position and connection it stood. He seemed to possess the faculty in religion, which some blind people are said to possess, in a rare degree, in reference to colours; a faculty of describing it by the *touch;* for scarcely any thing advanced amounted with him to truth, unless it fell with power upon his heart. He had received the doctrine of justification as an *experimental* truth, though utterly unable, in puritanic style, to enter into a detail of its *moving, meritorious, remote, immediate,* and *instrumental* causes; and this led to another doctrine equally momentous; a doctrine of experience, no less than of theory; the *sanctification* of the heart to God. "After he had enjoyed the blessing of conscious pardon," says Mr. Dawson, "he discovered that there was a higher state of grace to be attained; that such state was purchased for him by the blood of Jesus Christ; and was to be applied to his soul by the Holy Ghost, through faith. This he sought in the way which God appointed, and found the promise realized. 'Every one that asketh receiveth; and he that seeketh findeth; and to him that knocketh it shall be opened.' He was enabled to believe for a higher enjoyment of divine love, and from the hour he believed, obtained a richer measure of it, through which he was empowered to 'rejoice evermore; pray without ceasing; in every thing give thanks.'"

This farther change was wrought in his soul in the year 1794, and the following are some of the circumstances connected with its attainment. "About this time, (1794,)" he observes, "there was a great revival of the work of God at Sturton Grange, near Micklefield. The meetings were held in Rig *Lair*.* Some hundreds of souls were converted to God, and many were sanctified. I was one of the happy number, not only convinced of the necessity of Christian holiness, but who, blessed be the Lord! proved for myself, that the blood of Christ cleanseth from sin." Mr. Dawson, in adverting to this extraordinary work of God, in connection with Samuel's progress in religion, states that "there was an extraordinary outpouring of the Spirit upon nearly the whole of Yorkshire, and that it was most remarkably felt in the neighbourhood of Micklefield. At a solitary barn," continues he, "which stands on a farm belonging to Mr. Wade, at Sturton, near the Roman road leading from Castleford to Aberford, a prayer meeting was held every Sunday morning and Monday evening. These meetings were especially owned of God. The glory of the Lord filled the place, and the power of God was present to wound and to heal, to kill and to make alive. Two colliers,† men who gave themselves to prayer, were very successful instruments in the hand of the Lord in the conversion of scores, if not hundreds of persons, in the course of the summer. Our late brother Hick took his full share in the work, and experienced a full share

* *Lair*—a BARN, in the west of Yorkshire.

† One of these men was supported by the bounty of the late Mr. Broadhurst, of Swinton, for the sole purpose of enabling him to devote his time to the visitation of the sick, &c., and died lately at Manchester, where he had resided several years. His brother William, the other person alluded to, married a person belonging to Pollington, a village about three miles from Snaith, Yorkshire, where he continued

of the glory. Sabbath after sabbath the barn was filled with people; the cries of penitence were heard in different places, and were frequently succeeded by songs of praise. The colliers were invited to the neighbouring villages, whither friend Hick accompanied them in their work of faith and labour of love. Often has he been heard to relate the conquests of redeeming love, as witnessed in these journeys, from which he frequently returned home rejoicing—rejoicing more than earthly conquerors when they find great spoil."

Under the general influence referred to, Samuel was led, as stated above, to seek a farther work of grace. At the midnight hour he retired to this "*barn*," whose solitude was deepened by the season, for private devotion. He bowed the knee in one of its unfrequented nooks; but before he had proceeded to offer a petition to God whom alone he supposed to be present, he heard the voice of prayer in an opposite corner. He paused; he listened; the shadows of night had fallen too thickly around to permit him to see any one. Unexpected as it was, it was the voice of melody to his ear: still he listened, and at length he recognised the voice of PRAYING GEORGE, one of the colliers, who was

useful as an exhorter and class-leader for a considerable length of time—ended his days in peace, about five years ago—and left a widow and two or three children. They received the appellation of the "*Praying Colliers.*" The one who resided in Manchester, and who was personally known to the writer, was generally designated by the title of "Praying George." Their proper name—the one by which they were least known—was Mosely.

wrestling, like Jacob, repeating again and again, "Lord, wash my heart; Lord, wash my heart;" adding emphasis to each repetition—elevating his voice as he rose in fervour—but as little suspecting that he was heard by a fellow creature, as Samuel did that he should find any one in the place at such an hour. He soon gave the response to George's prayer, who, in his turn, was surprised to find that Samuel had stolen into the place for the same purpose. They mingled their petitions and spirits together, and increased each other's ardour. "I thought," said Samuel, "if the Lord could wash George's heart, he could also wash mine; and I was fully convinced that if George's heart wanted washing, mine required it much more; for I considered him far before me in divine grace." He proceeded from the very first on the principle, that "*God is no respecter of persons*," and that, from the immutability of his nature, the same power and goodness exercised in one case could, and really *would*, be exercised in another, where a compliance with the means proposed to attain the end was observed.

He experienced much of the presence of God in prayer, but no satisfactory evidence of the blessing which he sought. Having in all probability remained in the same position for a great length of time, and having been earnest in his pleadings, he was so affected and enfeebled when he rose, that he was unable to stand erect, and was obliged, as he expressed himself, to "walk home almost double." On passing along one of the fields, he heard a sudden and "mighty rush" over his head, as he termed it, the sound of which he compared to a large covey of "pigeons," sweeping the air with their wings. Being partially bent toward the ground, and the morning light not having dawned upon the earth, he was unable to perceive any thing, had any appearance been visible. He started—but all was gone in an instant. Having just come from the spot where he had been holding converse with God, and linked as he was in spirit to the invisible world, it was natural for him—whatever becomes of either the rationality or the Christianity of the act—to direct his thoughts thither; and the sound had but just passed, when it occurred to him, "This is the prince of the power of the air." On reaching home, he named the circumstance to his wife, who was still more struck with it, when, on having occasion to go into the fields some hours afterward to milk the cows, she heard the same noise as described by Samuel, but saw nothing from whence it could proceed.*

Instead of retiring to rest, he spent the whole of the morning in private prayer: and such was

* Though no anxiety is felt by the writer for his credit as an author, in giving publicity to this circumstance; and though he has no particular wish to give a supernatural character to it, he would, nevertheless, lend an attentive ear to the solution of a few difficulties with which the subject is involved. The *sound* was heard by *two persons* at *distinct periods*; no *appearance* was *visible* in either case; the sound was like that of *birds* upon the *wing*:—the *hour was unseasonable*, in the first instance, for any *birds* to be *abroad*, except

his distress—being, as he forcibly expressed himself, "under deep conviction for holiness," —that he could "neither eat, sleep, nor work." He continues, "I went mourning and pleading the whole of that day and of that night, but could find no rest to my soul. The next morning, about eight o'clock, I knelt me down upon the same flag on which God had pardoned my sins: and while I was pleading his promises, faith sprung up in my heart; I found that the blood of Christ did indeed cleanse me from all sin. I immediately leaped up from my knees. I seemed to have gotten both a new body and a new soul. The former appeared like cork wood, it was so light. I was clear in my sanctification. It was received by faith in Christ. All was joy, peace, and love. My soul was constantly mounting in a chariot of fire; the world and the devil were under my feet."

The martyrdom of spirit which Samuel experienced on the death of the depravity of his nature, can only be understood by those who have suffered on the same rack; and there are not a few who have suffered more because of indwelling sin, than under conviction of its enormity and punishment, as was evidently the case with

the *owl*;—in the second instance the *night-bird* must have disappeared;—and what might have been invisible to Samuel, through the *darkness* of the hour, ought to have been seen by his wife in the *morning light*;—and on the supposition that the imagination of the former might have been a little affected, still the case of the latter—a person of a much cooler temperament, and one who had not been passing through the same nocturnal process—preserves the whole in its native force.

the subject of this memoir. It is not difficult to explain this, except to the "natural man," to whom every experimental subject is mysterious. But to the purely enlightened it is well known that the discipline experienced in the school of repentance, in which the "*heavy-laden*" sinner "*labours*" under an oppressive burden prior to his entering into "*rest*"—into that *first* or *preparatory* state of repose consequent on his justification or discharge from guilt—is occasionally less severe than the discipline which is afterwards exercised in the school of Christ—into which school the penitent enters immediately on the reception of pardon, and in which, prior to his reception of what the poet styles "that *second* rest," he is taught to "*learn*" of Him who was "meek and lowly in heart," and while under his tuition, has, even in that state, to bend the neck of his spirit to the "*yoke*" which his divine Teacher imposes. Human nature is not made of sufficiently tractable materials—has been too long accustomed to an improper bias, to sit composed under the restraints of such a *yoke*, or instantly to yield to its forms. The workman called "the old man," is hostile to all the works of "the new man:" and will not supinely give up his possessions. On the justification of a sinner, peace, sweet peace, falls upon the soul with the softness of flakes of snow; and to persons in an imaginative mood, it is as easy—barring the coldness of the metaphor—to perceive the soul beautifully covered with it, and shining in its external whiteness:

but in the sanctification of the spirit, the work goes deeper than the soul's surface. And, to change the metaphor, it is not till after a person's justification, that God takes the lid from off the top of the sepulchre of the human heart, and unfolds to view its hidden filth—the beholder, like an unamiable being looking at himself in a mirror, being startled at his own appearance. The *pain* experienced in both states, though severe, differs in its character, because produced by widely different *causes*. *Actual transgression* is the immediate cause of *penitential distress*, and *innate depravity* that of a *believer's grief*—the one finding relief in an act of *pardoning mercy*, and the other in a work of *purifying grace*; or in other words, both in the death of Jesus Christ, through the *merit* of whose blood the *guilt* of *sin* is *cancelled*, and by the *virtue* of whose blood the *pollution* of the *soul* is *cleansed*; and the *taint*, if such an expression may be allowed, is as painful and odious to the enlightened mind as is its guilt to the awakened conscience. To the woodman who wishes to eradicate, to have the ground perfectly clear, it is as mortifying to have the *roots* left in the earth, as to see the *tree* standing; and having cleft the one, he is the more solicitous to have the other plucked up, not only that he may not lose what he has already wrought, but that he may prevent its again shooting upward, and by farther growth producing still more pernicious fruit. While the misery of a penitent is to be found in the accusations of a guilty conscience, followed up by awful forebodings of "wrath to come," the believer's distress arises from a fear of falling—an inward abhorrence of every thing rising in the soul incompatible with unsullied purity—an anxious desire after a full conformity to the divine image—an exquisitely constituted conscience, which is as tender to the touch as the apple of the eye—the consciousness of still possessing a heart prone to wander from the living God, and of a nature upon which temptation, without great watchfulness, may still operate to the ruin of the soul—a keener insight into the spirituality of the sacred law—a quick-sightedness and frequent anticipations of danger—the whole working the mind into a state of earnestness and of agony to be "freed from the yoke of inbred sin." In the latter state there is no sense of guilt, nor consequently of the divine displeasure, and therefore no fear of punishment; yet there is a continual loathing of self—"war in the members"—dying to live. All this appears to have been known and felt by Samuel Hick, whose own statement leads to the conclusion, that he suffered much more as a believer than as a penitent, through the union of which two characters the man of God is made perfect.

After he had risen from his favourite "flag," for which he entertained a kind of superstitious respect, and which was now rendered "doubly dear," he walked forth some time in brightness. The *blessing* of purity, which he had received, was never lost through actual transgression; and although he was twice in a state of deep distress respecting its *evidence*, it was soon regained by the exercise of the same means, and an application to the same source through which it was first obtained. "He experienced it," says Mr. Dawson, "upwards of thirty years—lived and died in the full possession of its excellences. O, with what warmth, affection, and pathos, he used to speak of his enjoying the perfect love of God in his heart!—that love which casts out tormenting fear, and strongly and sweetly constrains the whole soul to engage in the whole will of God, as revealed in his word." This love expanded his naturally affectionate heart, and his bowels yearned for the salvation of his friends, his neighbours, and the world."

CHAPTER IV.

Samuel's public character—His call to speak in public—A dream—Reproves a clergyman—Assists in prayer meetings—Visits Howden and other places—A remarkable outpouring of the Spirit of God—His power in prayer—Labours to be useful—Suits his language and thoughts to the employment of persons addressed—A general plan laid down for the spread of religion in the villages of Garforth, Barwick, &c.—Samuel received as a regular local preacher—His person—Intellect—Influence—Peculiarities—Tenderness—Language—Style of preaching—An apology for his ministry.

Two things have contributed essentially to the spread of Wesleyan Methodism; first, the *adaptation* of its *rules* and *regulations* to *every condition* of *man;* and secondly, the *provision* which its rules have made for the *encouragement* and *exercise* of *every description* of *talent.* Having risen out of *circumstances*, it accommodates itself to *that* nature which is the same in every climate to which those circumstances belong; and it can furnish employment for *all*, from the youth that lisps in prayer to the eloquence of the pulpit—from the Village Blacksmith to the man crowned with academical honours. The system, under God, brought into exercise the powers possessed by Samuel Hick, who has been heard to say, "I know that the Lord has given me *one* talent, and I am resolved to use it. He has given friend D. *ten*, but I am determined that he shall never run away with my *one*." And to his honour it may be recorded, that he made his *one* go much further in real *interest* to the cause of God, than many with ten times the intellect and influence.

He appears to have exercised occasionally in public, prior to the revival of the work of God at Sturton Grange. Mr. Dawson remarks, "that he first engaged in the prayer-meetings, and next spoke a word by way of exhortation. The last was done *like himself*, and always gained the attention of his hearers." Exclusive of a distinct impression upon his mind that it was his duty to call sinners to repentance, he was not a little influenced by a dream which he had, and to which he might be excused for paying the greater attention, as God employed a dream for the purpose of rousing him from spiritual slumber; and more especially might he be excused, when revelation warrants the belief, that "IN A DREAM, in a VISION of the night, when deep sleep falleth upon men, in slumbers upon the bed; then" God "openeth the ears of men and SEALETH their INSTRUCTION." The substance of it was this:—He dreamed one night that he set sail to the West Indies in the character of a missionary, to preach the gospel to the poor negroes—that, on his landing, he saw a pulpit, the stairs of which he ascended—and, on unfolding the leaves of the Bible, which was laid before him, a perfect blank was presented to his eye. "A pretty thing this," said he to himself; "a Bible, and not a text in it!" He turned over the leaves again and again, and suddenly on one of the white pages several beautiful gold letters sprang into form, and dazzled his sight. The words were, "Prepare ye the way of the Lord," &c. These he announced as his text, and began to preach. In the course of the sermon a poor woman was so affected while intently listening to him, and gazing upon him, that she cried aloud for mercy. He instantly quitted the pulpit, descended its steps, directed his way to the penitent, prayed with her, and soon had the unspeakable pleasure of hearing her proclaim the mercy of God in the forgiveness of her sins. From this pleasing dream he awoke; and under its warmest impression, exclaimed to his wife, accosting her by name, "Matty, I believe I am called to preach the gospel." Martha, less awake to the subject than himself, requested him to go to sleep again, not a little infidel in her principles respecting it.

This relation was given in *his own way*, on a platform, at the first Wesleyan missionary meeting held at Selby, November 16th, 1814, before a crowded audience, when the writer of this memoir was present, together with Mr. Dawson and others, and for the first time was favoured with the sight of Samuel. The description of the vessel in which he made his voyage, which is too ludicrous to appear among graver associations—his suddenly turning to the pulpit, and pointing to it as a model of the one in which he supposed himself to have preached—the familiarity of some of his comparisons, his views rising no higher, in reference to the gold characters, from his days having been spent mostly in the country, than some of the more costly sign-boards of the tradesman—his grotesque figure, and still more characteristic action, for the latter of which he was not a little indebted to his trade, his arms being stretched out, with his hands locked in each other, while he elevated and lowered them as though he had been engaged at the anvil; varying in his movements as he rose in zeal and quickened in delivery, becoming more and more emphatic—his tears—his smiles—his tenderness—his simplicity—the adroitness with which he turned upon the text, the effects of the sermon, &c. to strengthen his call to the work—the manner in which he brought the subject to bear upon the object of the meeting—and his offering himself in the fulness of his spirit at the close as a missionary, telling the people that his "heart was good," his "health was good," and his "appetite was good;" that he wanted not their money, but would bear his own expenses; and that, sustaining his own burden, he should consider it, provided family connections would admit, the highest honour that could be conferred upon him;—the whole, in short, producing, both upon the platform and among the people, an effect rarely witnessed, and a scene calculated to move on with the memory, and live as a distinct picture in the imagination.

That he had other and more substantial proofs of his call to exercise in public, there is no question; but the above shows the peculiar cast of his mind, and his attention to what was passing *within*, whether asleep or awake, together with his readiness to convert every thing to pious purposes—manifesting, in innumerable instances, stronger evidences of *piety* than of *judgment*.

He regularly attended Micklefield chapel-of-ease, in which service was performed about this time, once a fortnight on the Lord's day, by the Rev. —— T., of Monkfryson, a village about five miles distant. Mr. T. had ten shillings and sixpence per day allowed him for his labour; but neither exhibiting the morality of the gospel in his life, nor preaching its doctrines in the pulpit,—denying the inspiration of the Spirit in his sermon, after the people had been praying for it in the liturgy, Samuel took the liberty of addressing him on the subject one day, as he was passing his door on his way to Fryson. "Sir," said he, "I must tell you that you do not preach the gospel. You say that there has been no such thing as inspiration since the apostles' days. Your sermon contradicts your prayers; and I know by experience that there is such a thing as inspiration." He added, "I have been praying to my Lord either to convert you, that you may preach the truth, or that he would send some one else to preach it; and I fully believe that he will not let you come here much longer." Mr. T. said little in reply: and though Samuel's rebuke might be deemed a compound of ignorance and of impudence, by those who knew him least, yet such was the event, that Mr. T. only preached in Micklefield church chapel two or three times afterward, and an evangelical clergyman supplied for some time his place. The fact is simply stated; every reader may select and enjoy his own inference; but place Samuel's prayer out of the question, his fidelity—and this is the chief design of the relation—is of more real value in the illustration of character, than any conjecture as to the cause of the change.

In the earlier part of his public history, to which it is proper to return, an extensive field of usefulness was laid before him, in the line which Providence apparently marked out for the "Praying Colliers," with whose labours his own were soon identified. Wherever he went he was popular and useful; but his popularity was rather the result of *singularity*, than drawn upon him by any peculiar display of pulpit talent; while his usefulness was chiefly among those of his own order—though he was highly respected by his superiors in talent and in property. Not being as yet, however, a regularly accredited local preacher, remarks on his mental powers, and the character and style of his public addresses, must be reserved for the period when he was fairly brought upon the local preachers' plan.

One of his earliest public excursions was into the Hull circuit, whither he was invited in company with the "Colliers," and from the outskirts of which no less than seven horses were sent to carry them and their colleagues to the first scene of labour—Spaldington Outside, where they were met by the Rev. James Wood, the superintendent:—a pilgrimage this, which, while it might have furnished Chaucer with an episode for his "Canterbury Tales," would have greatly enhanced their devotional character. Samuel was in the full enjoyment of the heaven which the witness of his sanctification had imparted, and was ready to conclude, as he observed, that "the enemy of souls was dead, because" he himself "was dead to sin;" but he found that he was only entering the field of battle; rejoicing meanwhile that he "was provided with the whole armour of God."

Mr. Wood, whose judgment, gravity, and experience, would operate as a suitable check to the ebulliency of spirit of these revivalists, accompanied them to several places. Howden was the first place at which an extraordinary influence of the Holy Spirit was manifested; and was especially felt in a prayer-meeting, in the awakening of sinners, many of whom, Samuel observed, "cried out like the slain in battle." Several of the old members, offended with the noise, left the chapel. "They could not stand this," said Samuel; adding in his peculiar turn of thought, "It was a mercy they went out; for it rid the place of a deal of unbelief, which they took away with them." Previously to leaving the chapel himself, he had a rencounter with one of his own trade, a genuine son of Vulcan, who might have been drawn to the spot from what he had heard of the Village Blacksmith. Samuel was pressing home, by personal appeal, the subject of experimental religion upon an old man, when the person referred to came up to him, and requested him to let the old man alone, declaring him to be exceeded by no one in the town for honesty, and affirming his belief that he would go to heaven when he died. Samuel brought him to the test of "sin forgiven;" stating, if he knew not this, he doubted of his safety. His opponent immediately fired, telling him, if he said so again, he would "fell" him. This was language which Samuel would not have brooked on the day he heard Mr. Burdsall, at York, without the metal of his own temper being heated to the same temperature with that of the person who stood before him; but he was now another man, and fought with other weapons. He replied with undaunted brow, "I have no fear of *that*: if you lift your hand up, I believe you will not get it down again." So saying, he dropped upon his knees, and began to pray for the man, who, apparently afraid lest the prayer should turn upon *judgment* rather than *mercy*, made a precipitate flight.

After the service was closed, he went to the house of Mr. Ward, a local preacher, where he was invited to spend the night. The good lady of the house, being of the Baptist persuasion, was less prepared than her husband for the feverish agitation attendant on some of the prayer-meetings, and, agreeably to her own views, lectured Samuel on the subject, declaring that he and his associates were destroying the work of God, and that they had made the house of God a house of confusion; warmly recommending decency and order. "Confusion!" he exclaimed; "I believe there was such confusion, and great confusion, too, on the day of pentecost." But it was not for him to stand and reason the case with his hostess, however competent to the task; he therefore adopted his "short and easy method" of settling disputes, by going to prayer; "for I thought," said he, "she and I should agree best upon our knees." He there poured forth his petitions with great simplicity and fervour for her and for the family. When he arose, she affectionately took him by the hand, which to him was the right hand of fellowship. On finding another spirit in her, he told her, that in most revivals of religion "three sorts of work" might be recognised—"the work of God, the work of man, and the work of the devil;" stating, that when the latter two were destroyed, the first would stand; and that we should be careful not to injure the one in suppressing the other. The good lady was so completely overcome by the sincerity and simplicity of his intentions, his spirit, and his manners, that she made it her study to render his stay as agreeable as possible, by heaping upon him every social comfort. His mode of conducting a discussion, or more properly of terminating one, was the best adapted to his own case, and might be safely recommended in nine instances out of every ten, where the best side of a question is entertained with the worst arguments for its support; for certainly a question is not to be decided by the merits of the person who takes it up; and the best of causes may have the feeblest advocates.

The next day the party went to Spaldington Outside, at which place a gentleman of the name of Bell at present resides; and such was the concourse of people collected together from neighbouring and distant parts, that no building could be found sufficiently large to accommodate them. The horses of those that rode were tied to the gates and hedges,—giving the distant appearance of a troop of cavalry, and the company divided themselves into two distinct bands, and occupied two large barns. In the barn originally intended for the meeting, a temporary platform was erected for the accommodation of the prayer-leaders, exhorters, and more respectable portion of the female part of the auditory. The latter, in the estimation of Samuel, were mere *spectators* of the work of God upon others. The influence, however, becoming more general, one of these, under deep awakenings of soul, cried aloud for mercy; and as though determined to be avenged of her besetting sin, her love of finery, she made a sacrifice of part of her adornings upon the spot, by throwing them among the poorer people below. With the exception of two or three extravagances—the absence of which had been more remarkable than their manifestation, and which are subjects of *forbearance* rather than *approval* under all such circumstances—the meeting was attended with great good.

From this place they proceeded to Newport, where several persons were convinced of sin, and others found peace with God; the service continued till midnight: Mr. James Wood conducted the meeting, which was distinguished by great decorum. Instead of going to Hull the succeeding day, as previously arranged, Samuel was obliged to return home. But it was of no importance where he was: on the road, in his shop, in the field, he was ceaseless in his attempts to benefit those who came in his way.

Journeying homeward, he saw a young man sowing seed in a field, whom he accosted in his usually abrupt, yet affectionate manner;—

"You seem in earnest. Have you had time to water your seed?" "No," returned the sower; "we never water this kind of seed: it is wheat, not rye, that we steep, and sprinkle with lime." Samuel had another object in view, and said, "That is not what I want to be at: have you been on your knees this morning, praying to God to give his blessing to the seed?" This instantly brought the charge of Methodism upon him. "O, you are a Methodist! If you had been at our church yesterday, you would have heard our parson give them their character." "You had a poor errand there," was the reply: "if the Methodists are wrong, you ought to pray for them to be set right." It was in this way that he was constantly scattering seed—not always *skilfully*, yet often *seasonably*; for there were many instances of its falling into "good ground."

He did not always escape with the same triumphant feeling as that with which he withdrew from the sower just noticed, in his attempts at usefulness. Though his knowledge was limited within very narrow bounds, yet, as far as it extended, his sense of propriety always led him to delight in seeing any employment attended to in a workmanlike manner. On another occasion he perceived a youth turning up a piece of land with the plough. His patience, which was occasionally one of his most vulnerable parts, being a little touched with the carelessness and awkwardness of the lad, he shouted out, as he paused a moment to look at him, "How dare you attempt to plough *my* Lord's land in that way?" proceeding to give some directions, when he was stopped short by him,—thus showing not only his quickness in comprehending Samuel's allusion to the Divine Proprietor, but his smartness in so promptly meeting him in his own character,—"I am turning up a *bowling-green* for the *devil*:" intimating as much as though any thing done, and in any way, was good enough for the purpose to which the ground was to be devoted. This was so much relished by Samuel, that the notions of agricultural propriety which were fluttering in his imagination, and to which he was about to give utterance, broke up like a congregation of swallows in autumn—took instant flight, only to return with the appearance of the plough in the course of the ensuing spring; as also did all the moral lessons which he intended to found on the employment in which the lad was engaged.

Another field of labour opened to him after this period, more regular and permanent in its character, and much more accommodating to his circumstances. "About the year, 1797," says Mr. Dawson, "a plan was laid down to engage the talents of all the prayer-leaders and exhorters in the villages of Garforth, Barwick, Kippax, and Micklefield, together with other places in the vicinity; all of whom were to be united, and to itinerate through the whole neighbourhood. Brother Hick very readily agreed to have his name entered upon the plan, and having a horse at command, he could go to the most distant places without difficulty. He attended promptly and conscientiously to his appointments, so long as the union existed; and it was this plan that brought him to the notice of many persons who otherwise would not have been acquainted with him, and laid the foundation of his future and more widely extended usefulness. After this, his name was placed upon the regular local preachers' plan, of the Pontefract circuit, the places of which he supplied with pleasure to himself and profit to the people, to whom he recommended the person and salvation of Jesus Christ. When Micklefield was taken into the Selby circuit, his name was inserted in the plan of the local preachers belonging to that circuit; but residing on the borders of the Selby and Pontefract circuits, his name stood on both plans."* In reference to the last particular, Mr. Dawson proceeds, "I remember calling upon him one day, when he observed that his time was pretty well filled up, saying, 'You see I have my name upon both Pontefract and Selby plans;' emphatically adding, '*there is no living with half work.*'" It was his "*meat* and his *drink*,"

* This was considerably subsequent to the period of 1797, when the general plan was made, which associated the prayer-leaders with the exhorters. One of Samuel's contemporaries thinks it was not till 1803 that he was regularly admitted on the plan, though he had addressed public assemblies from the time stated as above. Prior to the year 1807, the plans of the Pontefract circuit were written; after that, they were printed. Selby became the head of a circuit in 1812.

like Him "who went about doing good," to do the will of his Father; and in the execution of that will he alone could LIVE.

The first time he ventured to take a text was in a school-room in Aberford, his native place; and it was the one with which he was dazzled in his dream. The room was crowded; and it is probable that the success of this, and a few similar attempts, might have led the way for the insertion of his name on the plan among "exhorters." That the attempt was prior to such insertion, is likely from the fact of the person belonging to the school-room having joined Mr. Kilham's adherents soon after the division, on the event of which there would be but little disposition to grant the loan of the place, owing to the state of party feeling which was then at the highest point of elevation. He had large congregations in those days; and when he had no regular appointment, he very often, in company with his friend William Brandfoot, travelled from ten to fifteen miles to a love-feast;—an example, by the way, which is not much to be commended, and which becomes criminal—though far from the case with Samuel—when persons give the preference to a love-feast in the country to the sacrament of the Lord's supper in the town, and nearly at their own door. Being now fairly before the public, it is desirable that a distinct image of the man should be put into the possession of the reader, that he may have a more correct conception of the personage with whom he passes along, instead of being in the presence of a kind of invisible agent, with whom he is permitted to converse in the dark, till the writer, in the usual biographical mode, and as though his pen had been previously employed on some other person, is pleased to unveil his subject at the close of his work in the exhibition of a summary sketch of his character. The subject of this memoir may be considered at this period as possessing *that* which, in the general acceptation of the term, properly constitutes *character*, and that too perfectly distinct in itself. Instead, therefore, of throwing the mind of the reader *back*, at the close of the book, upon that which has *grown out* of character, and not character from it, he must carry forward with him a distinct recollection of *the* MAN, through which he will be the better prepared for all that may follow, as well as judge of the likeness given—the one proceeding from the other like the tree from the root, the bough from the stem, and the fruit from the minor branches; just as character gives rise to circumstances, and circumstances become the medium through which the tempers of the mind and dispositions of the heart are manifested, unfolding themselves to others, either as wholesome or pernicious *fruit*.

There was but little that might be deemed prepossessing in his *person*. He was tall and bony, rising to the height of about six feet. Hard labour, and the nature of his employment —lowering one arm with the iron, and raising the other with the hammer, while he stooped at the anvil—gave a roundness to the upper part of his back, and a slight elevation to his right shoulder. His hair was naturally light—his complexion fair—his face full, but more inclined to the oval than the round—and his general features small, with a soft, quick, blue-gray, twinkling eye, partaking of the character of his mind, twinkling in thought, and sending out occasional and inexpressible natural beauties, like streaks of sunshine between otherwise darkly rolling clouds.

His *mind* was peculiarly constructed, and had all the effect in preaching and in conversation of an intellect broken into fragments—not shining forth as a whole, like the sun diffusing light and day; but the scattered portions shining separately, like stars in the heavens; and these too not silently and slowly stealing out, one by one, but suddenly breaking upon the eye in numbers, and from unexpected quarters, some of them but indistinctly visible, and others as lovely as Venus in all her glory. He appeared utterly incapable of classifying his thoughts;*

* In the more lengthened extracts given from his papers, the writer has occasionally taken the liberty of transposing some of the thoughts, for the sake of preserving something like unity and order; attending at the same time, with the strictest scrupulosity, to the *sense* intended to be conveyed to the reader. Samuel was not altogether ignorant of the character and extent of his intellectual powers, any more than of his moral condition. Speaking of him to Dr. A. Clarke once, the writer found that Samuel had visited him at his residence, Haydon Hall, near Pinner, Middlesex, in the neighbourhood of which the doctor sent him to conduct a religious meeting, with a view to communicate, under God,

and it is doubted by the writer, whether any mode of mental discipline which could have been adopted, even in youth, would have reduced his then comparatively chaotic mind to order; and equally doubtful, whether any society, with such a peculiarly constructed mind, would have given ease, and grace, and polish to his manners. Yet rude, or, perhaps, more properly unwieldly, as were the latter, there was nothing to offend; for while persons in the middle ranks of life were not at a sufficient remove from him to form a contrast, those in the higher walks of society were instantly arrested by an undefinable something about him which taught them, that *that* which might not comport with good taste, was, nevertheless, that which ought to be borne, and by an impression in his favour, which would instantly compel every high-wrought feeling, and all etiquette, to bow

a quickening influence to the people, for which, as an instrument, he was tolerably calculated. The doctor had met with him at Bristol, in Yorkshire, prior to this period; and related with a degree of pleasantry—for it was impossible for the most grave to relate some of his conversations without a slight contortion of the facial nerve—his first interview with him. Samuel, with his usual openness and simplicity, covered with smiles, stepped quickly up to the doctor, shook hands with him, and after a few words, artlessly proceeded thus:—"You can get through with preaching better than me: I cannot bear to be disturbed: I have but one *idea*, you see: and if I lose that, why, I have then no more to go to: but you, sir, you have a many *ideas*; so that if you were to lose one, you could pick up another by the way, and go on with it." By "one *idea*," he meant the leading thought on which he intended to dwell. While the relation assists in the illustration of intellectual character, it shows also the desolation which sometimes appeared to himself, occasioned by a want of reading, when he turned his eye inward.

before the untutored blacksmith—entering, before he was long in their presence, into the real enjoyment of his society and conversation, and delightfully embracing opportunities for again holding converse with him. To persons in the polished circles it was a relief to the mind to be with him—one of those novel scenes but occasionally met with in the landscape of life. Instead of the dull, monotonous plain, whose richest garb becomes common-place by constantly gazing upon it, in Samuel it was like broken rocks, wood and water; a piece of moor land, with patches of rich soil beneath the heath, with here and there a flower of surprising beauty springing up in the midst of the wilderness scene; the whole contributing to show the effect of *grace* upon *nature*—and a nature too which, without that grace, could never have been subdued into any thing like decorum or sobriety. This might appear to some, and may not improbably be subjected to the charge, as partaking a little too much of the pencil and colouring of the artist; as permitting, in the real character of romance, the imagination to be let loose upon a subject which ought to command the graver exercise of reason. The fact is—for not any thing shall be permitted to operate to the suppression of truth, and the Christianity of the case has nothing to fear in the way of consequence—the fact is, that such a man, and such a life might—and it is penned with reverence—might, without the aid of imagination, without any art or exaggeration, form the groundwork of a lighter exhibition, say—a *farce*, to the awfully solemn, and splendid representation of the Christian religion. But then, religion had nothing to do in the construction of the man's mind—a mind more nearly allied to the comic than the tragic, in its operations, and whose effects, though perfectly *undesigned* on the part of the actor, laid a more powerful hold upon the lighter than the graver feelings. Chistianity took the man as it found him, and performed upon him its grand work, which is not to change the *construction* of the mind so much as its *nature*; to effect, in other words, its *illumination* and *renovation*: nor is it requisite, to compare temporal things with spiritual, in cleansing a building, to change the position of either a door or a window. The grace of God was observed to lay a strong hand upon an otherwise untractable nature—making light shine into darkness, as well as out of it—straightening the crookedness of fallen humanity—planting flowers where nothing but the rankest weeds would have grown—forcing by an irresistible power, an untaught, and, in some respects, though not in the strongest sense, an uncouth being—upon society, and compelling the wisdom, the wealth, the dignity of this world to bow before that being—one, who, without the grace of God, would have been in danger of being despised, and yet the despisers, through that grace, acknowledging the power of the Supreme in a thing of naught.

This is not a subject slightly to be dismissed.

Samuel Hick was untaught in the *school* of this world; *art* would have been lost upon him; he was one upon whom education and polished society, as already hinted, could never have had their full effect; he seemed formed by nature, as well as designed by Providence, for the forge; and not any thing short of the grace of God appears to have been capable of constructing more than a blacksmith out of the materials of which he was composed. It was never intended that the hand of a Phidias should work upon him. Such was the peculiar *vein*, though excellent in itself, that it would never have paid for the labour. No man with greater self-appropriation—not even the apostle himself—could exclaim, "By the grace of God I am what I am;" or with the poet, "O, to grace how great a debtor!"

Not any thing, however, that has been advanced on his mental endowments and capabilities, and as applicable to him as a fallen being, in common with others of the same species, is intended in the least to deny him the credit of possessing *great openness* of disposition, and unbounded *generosity*. The latter was expressed, not always *gracefully* but *honestly* and *warmly;* and like the sea-anemone, which feels the first returning wave upon the rock, and throws out all its tendrils, his tender nature would give forth all its sympathies on the slightest intimation of human wo. United to uncommon tenderness of heart, there was a sincerity and a simplicity which no one could resist, which linked him to every spirit he came near, and which, while his own yearnings led him to weep over distress, to seek it out in all its haunts, and to relieve it to the leaving of himself pennyless, ever secured to him fellow-helpers in any projected work of benevolence. And yet, with his own bowels of compassion thus yearning over human misery—misery both of body and of mind—his eyes suffused with tears, and his face beaming with patriarchal benevolence, melting the hearts of those that stood before him, who mingled their tears with his—it was impossible—such were the outbreakings of intellect, such the sudden transitions of thought, such his similes for illustration, such his peculiar mode of expression, his half-solemn, half-comic, or undesignedly ludicrous representations—it was impossible to suppress the smile; and smiles would have been actually flickering, like patches of light, over the same face down which the big gushing tears were seen chasing each other in rapid succession. Before a few seconds had elapsed, all smiles had subsided, and the listener was left almost angry with himself for indulging in them, when he was aware that the speaker never intended them to appear in company with tears on such occasion and on such a subject; and still larger tears would start—the auditor employed in wiping them away with his pocket-handkerchief.

In preaching, as in conversation, he was never at "one stay," in reference to subject; but ever and anon there were fine strokes of wit, touches of keen repartee in his addresses to sinners, and occasional beautiful illustrations of Scripture, turning often upon a single thought capable of furnishing *hints* for superior minds and better thinking, not only by being themselves improved in the laboratory of the brain, but by leading to another and still nobler train of thought, which might ultimately enrich the individual, and which—except for having thus been struck out by Samuel, like a spark from his own anvil—would never have been elicited by long and previous study. In this way inferior minds often become steps by which superior intellects attain a higher character of thought. To the uninstructed and depressed, his preaching was especially adapted; and by bringing a great deal of what was familiar to the lower orders of society into his addresses, he was extensively useful in encouraging and raising the minds of the humble poor, who could indulge with a relish in such food as he had to give, without satiety; when more costly and highly decorated dishes would have been much less savoury. Not a few of his strokes in the pulpit were as sudden as those which were manifested in his regular calling, when sparks as profusely seemed to fly all around, warming and enlightening, and bidding the profanely heedless stand out of the way.

His *language* in the pulpit was the same as in social life—the *broadest*, and yet, as has been already intimated, most closely *abbreviated*

West Yorkshire dialect; the former giving a fulness and quaintness to many of his intellectual clothings; and the latter operating, to employ a homely simile, like a pair of scissors in the organs of speech, clipping a piece from off each word, and not unfrequently from the same word at both ends.* This to a Yorkshireman,

* The writer had it once in contemplation to give the whole of Samuel's remarks in the dialect in which he spoke. But though this would have given greater prominence to his character, it might have diminished the effect which it was otherwise desirable to produce. Nor is it necessary for purposes of accuracy to give a man's *pronunciation* in the *words* he employs. Fidelity in such a case would be as absurd as unnecessary, since it would require every piece of biography to vary according to its subject, from the peer to the peasant. An ingenious apology therefore might be framed for honest Samuel, from either Walker's or any other Pronouncing Dictionary, in which the *eye* and the *ear* are almost perpetually at variance with each other, in the difference which subsists between the *spelling* and the *pronunciation* of the same word; and also in the fluctuations in the same language among the same people, at different periods of time. A few words from the vocabulary of the deceased, which the reader will find in a Glossary at the close of the volume, as exemplified in his papers, drawn from his conversations, &c., will furnish a correct conception of his language, and will support a remark made in a preceding page. As the language cannot operate as a reflection against Samuel in any other way than that in which the whole of the lower grades in society in the west of Yorkshire are participators; and as the inhabitants of different portions of the island are not exempt from conversational peculiarities and provincialisms, one county or district is as much entitled to the laugh as the other, and also forbearance. The following specimen of the English language, in a letter of Robert Waterton, to King Henry V., 1420, dated from Methley, where the king had his lodge, and where Samuel, some centuries afterward, moved, conversed, and, in a *few* instances, entrenched on the very same pronunciation with the worthy letter-writer, will be a curiosity to some readers :—

"Os [as] I have conceyvid by zour right honourable lettres

and particularly one of the least educated, gave Samuel an advantage over many of his brethren—he always appearing to such a one like an instrument in tune: but to another than a Yorkshire ear, the instrument often gave an "uncertain sound," the sense being to be gathered, not from detached parts, but from the whole; and as his speech was rather rapid, his preaching, to persons unacquainted with his provincialisms and pronunciation, had the effect of a broken English from the lips of a foreigner, where attention is constantly kept up, in order to come at the sense of the speaker, and where the interest continues to heighten in proportion as we are let into the meaning of what is heard. To keep perfectly grave through one of his pulpit addresses was extremely difficult: yet the most grave found it impossible to be angry,

wrytin at zour Cytee, the which I have receyvid right late syth Pask [Easter] wyth othir zour lettres undir zour Pryve Seale, charging me to assaye by all the menese [means] that I kan to exytc and stirre sych as bene able gentilmen wythin the shyre and the contree, that I dwell in, to kome [come] ovyr to zowe at zour Wage, armyd and wrayde as langys [belongs] to thaire astate, to do zowe servyce, and for to certifie als well to zowc os to zour Counsell of thaire answere and thaire will, the whych zour hegh comaundement I have bygune to labour apon and sall trewely forthe [further] dayly wyth all my myght till I have perfourmd zour forsayd comaundement. And upon Wedynsdaye next sall zour Justice sitte at Zork [York] apon the deliverance of the Gaole there and a Cession of the Pees [Peace] also, at which tyme I suppose to speke with many of the gentyls there, and als sone aftyr as I maye be answered I sall certifie os zowe hase lykid to comaunde me, wyth all the haste, &c. Writin at zour awne logge at Metheleye the xii daye of Aprill zour trewe leige man and subgitte, &c.' See Ellis's Original Letters, vol. i, p. 6.

because they saw at once there was no design to produce a smile on the part of the speaker, and that he seemed unconscious of its presence while there. It resolved itself into a *peculiarity* rather than a *fault*—an *imperfection* in the *medium* of *communication*, rather than a *sin*, in the first instance, in the man; and hence the line of forbearance—forgiveness being uncalled for—ran parallel with the failing or infirmity.

To advocate, in unqualified terms of approbation, the establishment of such a style of preaching, would argue as little taste, judgment, skill in Christianity, and knowledge of human nature, as it would, in another view of the subject, have been criminal to deny such a man opportunities of usefulness, since numbers might have remained unbenefited to the same extent by more highly polished instruments. The Divine Being, who found a place in the Old Testament church for the employment of one of the *herdmen* of TEKOA, and in the New, for a *fisherman* of GALILEE, and a *tentmaker* of TARSUS,* has

* The writer is aware that it was customary for the higher ranks in society among the Jews, as well as the poor, to teach their children a trade; it being a maxim among them, that "he who teaches not his son a trade teaches him to be a thief," and that one of the Jewish rabbies was surnamed the *Shoemaker*, another the *Baker*, *&c.*: nor is he less aware that it constituted a part of the education of others of the easterns, and was practised down to the time of Sir Paul Ricaut; the grand seignior, to whom he was ambassador, having been taught to make *wooden spoons*—taught not only as an amusement, but as necessary to support life under adverse circumstances, on any unexpected change of fortune: and may be told from hence, that the mechanical arts thus connecting themselves, not only with rank, but with the literature of the times, ought not to be ad-

certainly not altered the constitution of his church so seriously as to deny the *mechanic* an official situation in it now? He who divided public teachers of old into different classes, giving "some *apostles*; and some *prophets*; and some *evangelists*; and some *pastors* and *teachers*;" not despising the humbler office of an *exhorter*; does not now surely find human nature in such a delightfully improved state as to render *exhortation* useless? He who required the use of from *one* to *ten* talents in the days of his flesh, does not find the highest number multiplying so fast, certainly, that he cannot, in the order of his providence, and in the government of his church, furnish employment to persons

duced as a precedent to support the modern custom of granting mechanics a license to preach the gospel. There are two classes of objectors; and those who are not met by one example receive a check from another. Some persons contend for a systematic, classical education, and condemn the smallest interference with the arts, as though they either lowered the dignity or contaminated the purity of the priesthood. Such are referred to the case of St. Paul, who, after his consecration to the priest's office, was not ashamed to labour with his own hands. The second class of objectors include such as would tolerate a *literary* character, but persist in maintaining that the *illiterate* mechanic has no right to assume the office of a Christian teacher. These are directed to the case of Peter—Peter, who could never boast of a classical education, and yet under the tuition of the Holy Ghost, could speak of "*unlearned*" men *wresting* the *Scriptures* to their own destruction, establishing by that a claim to another kind of *learning* from that which is taught in our public schools—without which a man may be a novice in the things of God, and with which, the unlettered plebeian rises, in church affairs, superior to the most erudite who is otherwise unschooled in the experimental verities of Christianity. It is not a little singular, that among some of the persons who object to receive instruction from the lips of a poor mechanic, there are those who can see no impropriety in a possessed of only *one* or *two?* Such a ministry, owned of God; and he has deigned to own it; ought to be *borne* by the more highly gifted and cultivated, for the *sake of* the *poor*, to thousands of whom the preaching of the Village Blacksmith, and others as unlettered as himself, has been of essential service. It may occasionally produce the blush of *learning;* but, in doing this, *piety* at the same moment is compelled to blush at the very *life* which some of the literati lead; and thus blushes are blushed at in their turn; for what in the one is criminal, in the other is an infirmity; and to see such as in the eye of learning appear halt, and maimed, and infirm, rise in arms against the common

clergyman attending to his glebe through the week. In "A Charge delivered to the Clergy of the Deaneries of Richmond and Catterick, within the Diocess of Chester, on Thursday, July 4th, 1816, by John Headlam, A. M., Rector of Wycliffe, and Deputy Commissary of the Archdeaconry of Richmond," *agricultural pursuits* are highly *recommended* to the clergy. Since then, Mr. Headlam has been elevated to the dignity of an archdeacon, and one of the clerical agriculturists in the neighbourhood died in a state of insolvency. This case—should a second edition of the Sermon be demanded, should lead Mr. Headlam to reconsider the paragraph in which the advice is given. Though such failure might be urged as a caution against ministers already set apart for the sacred office entering into the business of the world, who possess a competency of personal property, or are otherwise respectubly supported by their separate charges, or as by law established; it could not be so successfully urged against men already engaged in commercial pursuits, who received their call in the midst of such pursuits—who, from various causes, may be prevented from devoting themselves exclusively to the work—who toil like Samuel Hick, without salary—and who have no other way of supporting themselves and their families, but by manual or other labour.

enemy of man, argues, at least, as in civil affairs, a nobler public spirit; a higher degree of patriotism; than is possessed by persons of superior *ability*, who remain inactive, and who ought to be led on by a sense of duty to labour for the public good. The moment it is established as a truth, that "God hath" NOT "chosen the foolish things of the world to confound the wise, and weak things of the world to confound the things which are mighty;" that very moment a substantial plea is instituted against the preaching of Samuel Hick.

CHAPTER V.

His diligence—The light in which he beheld mankind—The substance of a conversation held with Earl Mexborough—Samuel's circumscribed knowledge in natural history—His views of the Bible—Proofs in favour of the doctrine of future rewards and punishments—His visit to the seat of Earl Mexborough—A point of conscience—A painting—Fidelity in reproving sin, at the hazard of being injured in his trade—The millennium dexterously hitched in, as a check to pleasure-takers—Three hunting ecclesiastics rendered the subject of merriment among the titled laity—Ministerial fruit a proof of the power of truth, not of a call to preach it—Duty on saddled horses viewed as a hardship—Samuel's more extended labours—Privations—Persecutions—A poor widow—A conquest over bigotry at Ledsham.

BEING now recognised as a regular local preacher, Samuel conscientiously attended to his various appointments, though he was far from parsimoniously confining himself to them. as if duty proceeded no further than the limits prescribed to him by his brethren. His zeal was not to be bounded by the appointments of a plan. He observed his appointments as he did his *regular seasons* for *private prayer*—as duties to be performed—not to be neglected but with peril—and attended to with delight; but extra work was like a special season for retirement—something out of the regular track—and was enjoyed by him as children revel in the enjoyment of a holyday. In the Church of Rome he would have had the credit of being wealthy in works of supererogation. He imitated, on a miniature scale, the great apostle of the Gentiles, and was "in labours more abundant:" and why? He was *in* his Master's *work*, as St. John was *in* his Lord's *sabbath*, "in the Spirit;" and in the spirit of the thing itself, too, he was always found.

His zeal, however, as has already appeared, was not a mere crackling blaze in the pulpit. His workshop was his chapel, and many were the homilies which he delivered over the anvil and over the vice, to both rich and poor. In this he was no respecter of persons. He looked upon every human being as possessed of an immortal spirit; depraved by nature; redeemed by Christ; within the reach of mercy; and himself as accountable to God for the improvement or non-improvement of opportunities of usefulness to them; and hence, to repeat his own language, he "was always at them," because always yearning over them in melting compassion. Adverting to the more early part of his history, he observes, "At this time I feared no man, but loved all; for I wanted all to enjoy what I felt. I remember Lord Mexborough calling at my shop one day to get his horse shod. The horse was a fine animal. I had to back him into the smithy. I told his lordship that he was more highly favoured than our Saviour, for he had only an ass to ride on, when he was upon earth." The earl suspecting that Samuel was not very well instructed in natural history, replied, "In the country where our Saviour was born, the people had rarely any thing but asses to ride upon; and many of them were among the finest animals under heaven, standing from sixteen to seventeen hands high." This information was new; and as grateful apparently for the improved condition of his divine Master, as for an increase of knowledge, Samuel exclaimed, "Bless the Lord! I am glad to hear that; I thought they were like the asses in our own country." Samuel's simplicity might excite a smile; but there were other biblical subjects, which gave him a superiority over many of his more learned fellow creatures. The Bible was better known by him as a *revelation* of God, on subjects of a *spiritual* and *experimental* nature, than as an *historical* record.*

* It is stated that Dr. Doddridge, while engaged with his Expositor, was in the habit of consulting one of the old members of his church on those texts of Scripture, which contain in them the heights and depths of Christian experience—conduct equally complimentary to the doctor's condescension and the venerable man's piety. The doctor, though a pious man himself, knew that experimental religion

While Samuel was engaged with the horse, the earl, says he, "sat down on the steady clog," and with great condescension and familiarity, entered into conversation with him. "I am inclined to think, my good man," said the noble visitant, "that you know something of futurity. Pray, what becomes of the soul when it leaves the body?" As Samuel had no doubt of the divine authority of the Scriptures himself, he took it for granted—more from the strength of his own faith, than presuming upon it out of courtesy, as St. Paul might have done in the case of Agrippa, when there was no evidence to the contrary—that the earl was also a believer in their truth, and proceeded to state, that, in the times of old, "there was a certain rich man, which was clothed in purple and fine linen, and fared sumptuously every day—that this man died and was buried—that, though the body was committed to the dust, the soul was sent to hell—that both would remain till the morning of the resurrection—and that, at that period, the body and soul, which had shared in each other's wickedness, should also share in the

was *progressive* in its character and operations, and beheld his hoary auditor as having many years the advance of him—beheld him like mellow fruit ready to drop off, or to be plucked for heaven. He was aware that he himself wanted age and sunning for several passages; and although he brought all the experience he possessed to bear upon them, he suspected there was still something beyond. To his own *head*, he required the advantage of the old man's *heart*; and united *knowledge* and *experience* tell upon the understandings and affections of others.

miseries of the damned, and the smoke of their torments would ascend for ever and ever:—that there was likewise a poor man named Lazarus, which was laid at the rich man's gate, full of sores—that he died too—that angels carried his soul to Abraham's bosom—that the soul would remain there till the great archangel's trumpet should sound, when rich and poor, small and great, should stand before God—and that the soul and body which shared in each other's sufferings upon earth, would share in each other's joys in heaven." It never entered into Samuel's mind to inquire whether the narrative came in the shape of a *history*, or of a *parable*; and neither was it indeed necessary to his purpose, as parable is the representation of truth—truth in the *spirit*, though not in the *letter*: nor had he any thing else in view—unless it were that of making the subject speak through the "rich man" to his noble auditor—than to establish, in the best way he was able, the existence of the soul, and the doctrine of future rewards and punishments. If the character before him had been such as to have admitted an approach to the probationary character of the "rich man," a thorough knowledge of Samuel's intellectual powers would at once have destroyed the supposition of any thing like design to institute a parallelism; and yet, there were few subjects—considering his own piety and station in society, and the exalted rank of the interrogator—more calculated to fix attention, or that could better afford ground for reflection and inference. The earl remarked that he was of the same opinion with Samuel himself on the subject of a future state, and wished the whole world possessed the same faith.

Having thus received a little encouragement, Samuel proceeded to show that something more was implied in faith than a bare assent to the doctrines of the Bible; and to guard the earl against any error, gave him an account of his experience, which was as *artless* in its design and detail as that of St. Paul's was *seasonable* in the presence of Agrippa. In evidence that it was taken in good feeling, "he stopped," says Samuel, "till I related it, and gave me half-a-crown for preaching this short sermon to him."

Not long after this, he was planned to preach at Methley, and had some of the servants of the same nobleman for his hearers, to one of whom—a female—he was uncle. Partly out of respect to Samuel, and partly to his niece, the servants united in inviting him to spend the evening with them at the Hall. But before he could comply with the request, he had a piece of casuistry to settle with his own conscience. The Earl and the family were in the metropolis, and he could not conceive how he could live at the noble proprietor's expense, without his consent, and remain guiltless. This point was soon disposed of, by the servants informing him, that, during the absence of the family, they were "living at board wages." "When I knew that they could keep me at their own expense," he observes, "I went with them, and stopped all night." This was one of those punctilious movements in social life, which would have escaped the notice of multitudes, but upon which the eye of an enlightened conscience—the guardian of property—instantly flashed, and through which the Christian was commanded to pause and inquire before he advanced. In the course of the next morning Samuel was shown through the rooms; but of all that he saw, not any thing attracted his attention or made an impression equal to a painting of Joseph and Mary, the latter of whom was placed upon an *ass*, with the infant Jesus. He instantly recollected his conversation with the noble owner of the mansion, and knowing little of books, very innocently, and not unnaturally for a person of his cultivation, considered this painting as the source from whence the earl derived his knowledge. "It was one of the finest creatures," says he, "I ever saw; and I thought my lord got his information from it." Then, instead of indulging in what was passing before the eye, he breaks away in a tangent, and shows where his heart is, by adding in the next sentence, "I am informed that his lordship has family prayer, morning and evening;*

* This nobleman died in the course of last winter, (1830,) and was succeeded in his titles and in his estates by his son, Lord Pollington. It was to Earl Mexborough that the village of Thorner, in which the late Rev. John Pawson was born and is buried, belonged; and his kindness and benevolence as a master and a landlord were not the only excellences for which he was beloved, and for which he is still had in remembrance.

and I fully believe, that if Christians of all denominations were faithful to the grace given, both rich and poor would be saved. I am privileged with getting into the company of gentlemen, and I never let these opportunities slip. I consider it a privilege to speak a word for my Master, whom I so dearly love."

It will be easy to perceive, that his association with persons of distinguished rank only extended to transactions in business, and that not any thing more than this is intended by himself; a circumstance which tends not a little to elevate his piety above all earthly considerations, as many in a similar situation to himself would have shrunk from the discharge of what appeared to him to be a Christian duty, from a dread of suffering in business by giving offence to their employers. An instance of his fidelity in this respect—and by no means a solitary one—was exemplified in his conduct toward Mr. Wh—t—n,* whose horse had lost a shoe in the heat of the chase. Having had the horse in the hands of another blacksmith only the day before, and being interrupted in his enjoyments, he swore at the man for having, as he supposed, put on the shoe so carelessly. Samuel turned to the squire, and without further ceremony, told him, that he paid the

* The widow and family of this gentleman resided at Aberford. Speaking of the lady, "Samuel," says Mr. Dawson, "stood very high in her estimation. He had full liberty to inform her of any case of distress which came under his observation; and on information being given, he was frequently made her almoner."

rent of the shop—that while it was in his hand he would not suffer any man to take the name of God in vain within its walls—and that if he persisted in swearing, he would not set the shoe on. He availed himself of the gentleman's anxiety to return to the field, and the gentleman knowing that his enjoyment depended solely on his attention to the prohibition which had just been issued, very prudently desisted. The compassion of Samuel was excited both for the horse and for the rider. "The poor animal," says he, "could scarcely stand till I set the shoe on; and while I was shoeing him, I began to preach, and said, 'It is a pity, sir, that these good creatures should ever be abused.'" Mr. W., passing over the rebuke he had received for swearing, and finding, as he believed, the ground on which he stood as a hunter, somewhat more tenable than that on which he stood as a swearer, replied, "The dogs were made on purpose to hunt the fox, and the horse to follow the dogs." "God," said Samuel, who felt that the honour of his Maker was interested, "God was never the author of sin. He sent these creatures for the use of man, not to be abused by him. But the time will come, sir, when the hounds will not run after the foxes." Mr. W., either not apprehending his meaning, or disposed to amuse himself with the reply, asked, "Do you really think that such a time will ever arrive?" "Yes, sir," returned Samuel: "it will come, as sure as God made the world; for he has prophesied that the lion shall lie down with the lamb, and that all flesh shall know him, from the least to the greatest." The shoe having been replaced, a period was put to the conversation, when Mr. W. very pleasantly tendered him some silver, which he refused to accept, saying, "I only charge a poor man twopence, and I shall charge you, sir, no more." The difference which Samuel observed between Earl Mexborough and Mr. W.—having accepted silver from the former for a similar office, and declined receiving it from the latter—shows the acuteness and discrimination occasionally manifested by him. "Did he," said Samuel to the biographer, some years after, when relating the circumstance in reference to Mr. W., "Did he think that I was going to give up my chance at him for half-a-crown?"—thus renouncing every thing which in his estimation was calculated to deprive him of the privilege of freedom of remark, and rebuke—though undoubtedly erroneous in the supposition, that Mr. W. had any need to have recourse to the gift as a bribe. Mr. W. soon remounted, and set off to pursue the chase. On his return, he pointed Samuel out to the party that accompanied him, as he passed the shop, and entertained them with his notions of the Millennium. A few days after Mr. W. on again passing the shop on his way to the field, endeavoured to divert himself at Samuel's expense, by asking with some degree of pleasantry, "Well, do you think the dogs will run the foxes to-day?"

"O yes, sir," replied Samuel, with unexpected smartness, "the Jews are not brought in yet." Mr. W. seemed to have possessed as much millennial knowledge as enabled him to comprehend Samuel's meaning, and rode off like a person who had been shot at by the archers.

He was pretty generally known by the sportsmen of the neighbourhood, and few of them, though partly dependant upon them for employment, remained unreproved by him. earl C—th—t was one, among others, who had felt the force of some of his sayings, and who enjoyed their effects upon others. The earl had an opportunity of this kind furnished, when several gentlemen were waiting one morning for the hounds. "They met *anent* (opposite) my shop," says Samuel, "and stopped till the hounds came." Among the party were the Hon. C. C—, vicar of K—, the earl's brother; the Rev. W—, rector of G—; the late Rev. C—, vicar of A—; and Dr. E—, who followed the medical profession at K—. "It came into my mind," continues Samuel, "that the three clergymen had no business there." His movements generally corresponding with the rapidity of his thoughts, he instantly "threw down the hammer and the tongs," darted out of the shop door, like an animal from a thicket of underwood, and appeared in the midst of them with his shirt sleeves turned up, his apron on, his face and hands partaking of the hue of his employment—as fine game, in the estimation of some of them, to occupy the lingering moments, till other game should be started, as any that could present itself in human shape. "Most of them," says he, "knew me. I said to them, Gentlemen, this is one of the finest hunts in the district. You are favoured with two particular privileges; and they are privileges which other districts have not." This excited curiosity, which was as quickly gratified; for the inquiry relative to "*privileges*" was no sooner proposed, than the answer was given—"If any of you should happen to slip the saddle, and get a fall, you have a *doctor* to *bleed* you, and three *parsons* to *pray* for you: and what are these but privileges? THREE PARSONS! O yes, there they are."* The odd association produced in the minds of some of

* The three reverend gentlemen were not equally implicated in an adherence to the chase. With one—the first—it had become a *passion*; and though possessed of other good qualities, especially benevolence to the poor, yet so much did the turf engross his attention that he thought very little of setting off for Doncaster and Pontefract races after service was over on a Sunday. The second was not remarkable for following the fox-hounds, and is supposed to have proceeded little further than that of attending to see them "throw off." Greyhound coursing was less objectionable, as being less hazardous. The third, the late Mr. C., like the first, was a genuine lover of the sports of the field. He received, however, what would have been sufficient as a rebuke for others, before he left the world to give an account of his apostleship. On a shooting excursion, his dogs, as usual—having been well trained—set some partridges; the birds started, and flew over a hedge, behind which his servant was standing; he fired:—whether or not he winged a bird, is not for the writer to state, but it is well known that he killed his servant.

the gentlemen, between *hunting* and *devotion*—the huntsman's *shout* and the clergyman's *prayer*, the inconsistency of which not a few had light sufficient to perceive, and of which, by the way, we are furnished with a somewhat similar ridiculous appearance in some of our cathedrals and churches, where some of the ancient knights—not very remarkable for prayer during life—are represented as praying in marble, booted and spurred, clad in armour, with uplifted hands, about to rise to the victor's heaven, of which—abstractedly considered—the Bible knows as much as that of the hunter's—this odd association operated powerfully upon the risible faculties, and turned the laugh upon the clergymen, who, in the language of Samuel, "lowered their heads, and never spoke a word in their own defence," though forward enough at other times, and with open front too, to condemn him for occupying any share of the priest's office. But *right* and *truth* give one man an amazing advantage over another; guilt stands abashed in the presence of innocence; a child, under peculiar circumstances, becomes a Hercules, and wields truth—though in irony—like Elijah, with all the power of the imaginary deity's club. Towards one of the divines Samuel experienced an unusual leaning of spirit; for he states, that it was "under Mr. C—, of A—, that" his "dear mother was converted to God in A—b—d church. The word preached," he proceeds, "proved the power of God to her soul's salvation. She died happy in God. I do not know that she ever heard a Methodist sermon in her life."*

A nobleman who occasionally courted remark from Samuel, and who was more disposed to tease than to injure him, having told him that he ought to be surcharged for placing a saddle on his cart-horse on the Lord's day; he immediately threw back upon his noble implicator the mischiefs of the chase; stating, that there would be a greater propriety in *surcharging* his lordship himself for breaking down the hedges

* To argue from hence, that a Christian minister is at liberty to pursue what line of conduct he pleases, because the Divine Being may vouchsafe to honour his ministry with success, as though he thereby sanctioned the proceedings of the man, would be absurd. *Truth*, and the *medium* of its conveyance, are two distinct things—as much so as the *water* and the *conduit* through which it passes; nor are any of the cleansing effects or refreshing qualities of the water to be attributed to the instrument of communication, as any other medium of conveyance, whether of wood, lead, or silver, would have equally served the purpose, and the effects had been produced as easily without as with the one employed. This may be carried even a little further; for it would be no difficult matter to prove, that ministerial *fruit* is not an exclusive proof of a *call* to the ministry. Open this door, and the greatest latitude is given to female preaching. *Fruit*—independent of other evidence—is only a proof of the *power of truth*—not a *call* to *preach* it. Truth belongs to God, and he will honour his own truth whoever may be the instrument employed to deliver it. Should the instrument himself be unconverted, he will receive the honour which the *scaffolding* receives from the *builder*, when it has served his purpose, in contributing its share to the completion of the erection—be thrown aside as constituting no part of the goodly edifice. This is not intended to apply to the clergyman in question, however much out of place in the field, but to protect the simple-hearted from deducing false inferences from apparently legitimate, but, in point of fact, otherwise false premises.

of the farmer, than that he should be surcharged for saddling his horse, riding peaceably along the king's highway, and going about doing good by preaching the gospel. The *law* of the case was not what occurred to Samuel: he looked at it with the eyes of a *Christian*, without connecting with it for the moment, the relation in which he stood to the British Constitution as a *subject*; and although he would have yielded to no man in point of loyalty, and no man was more ready to pay the taxes imposed upon by government than himself; yet this was a case, like many others, of which he could only see one bearing; and that was a bearing of *hardship*. The naked principles of *good* and *evil* arranged themselves on opposite sides, and so completely was his mind absorbed with these, that all the reasoning that could have been employed, would never have made the subject appear otherwise than as unreasonable to him—that one man should be permitted to do *evil*, and that another, from the purest motives, at his own cost, and with his own horse, should not be permitted to proceed in his own way to do *good*, without an extra charge. To have suggested that his lordship had to pay for his pleasure, by a tax upon both his dogs* and horses, would not have re-

* It would have been a little amusing to have witnessed Samuel's feelings, and heard his remarks on the following items occasioned by *British devotion* to DOGS. In a parliamentary paper, ordered to be printed, it appears that the total number of dogs of different descriptions (exclusive of packs of hounds) upon which duty was paid in the United Kingdom, during the year ending 5th April, 1829, was

moved the impression of hardship from the mind of Samuel. His logic was simple and untrammelled by legal subtleties. His reply would have been, that his lordship had no right to do evil, though he paid for it—that creation belonged to his divine Master—that man was in misery—that he himself, as a servant of the Most High, was commanded to do good unto all men—and that, to the performance of acts of mercy, not only should "every let or hinderance" be removed out of the way, but every person should contribute to the furtherance of such work—forgetting that if all were contributors, there would be an end to receivers—and that in forming laws for the multitude, it was impossible so to construct them as not, in certain cases and under certain circumstances, to bear hard upon a few individuals. If any class of men had a right to institute a claim to exemption from such a tax, it was such men as Samuel Hick; and had our legislators deemed exemption prudent, there is no doubt that to such men it would have been extended.

Many of the circuits continued very extensive long after Samuel was admitted on the local preachers' plan, and such were his "outgo-

353,058. The amount of duty paid upon them was 187,581*l.* The packs of hounds upon which duty was paid amounted to 69; the duty on each being 36*l*, the sum total amounted to 2,484*l*. The duty paid upon dogs within the bills of mortality was 15,307*l.*—To have given a rough calculation of not only the tax upon hounds and horses, but the expenses of purchase, keep, keepers, &c., Samuel would have pitied the man who could spend so much upon so little.

ings," occasioned by the ardour of his zeal, that a horse became absolutely necessary, in order to enable him to accomplish his "labours of love." As an exemplification of part of his toil and of his treatment, he observes, "In those days there were not many noble, not many rich called. For my own part, I have travelled many scores of miles, and neither tasted meat nor drink till I got home [in the evening.] I have very often had snowballs thrown at me, and been abused by the enemies of the cross of Christ: I have been turned out of places where I have been preaching, by the clergy and the magistrates: but, bless the Lord, I have lived to see better days." After noticing the cessation of persecution, he again, by a sudden transition of thought, turns to his favourite subject—the grand Millennium, which appears like a vision breaking upon his "gifted sight," and "more golden bright than the rich morn on Carmel"—in a vision often repeated, in which there was to him, in the language of the poet, "a mingling of all glorious forms"—of "angels riding upon cloudy thrones, and saints marching all abroad like crowned conquerors:" nor had the fair poetical Jewess, so finely portrayed by Milman, in his "Fall of Jerusalem," more delightful visions, when "nightly visitations" poured over her mind, "like the restless waters of some pure cataract in the noontide sun," than had Samuel Hick of "the latter-day glory," toward which he was constantly turning, like the sun-flower, toward the orb of day, and in the splendours of which he was constantly basking and brightening.

Whatever might have been the length of the journey, and whatever the fare with which he was treated, the spirit of Samuel remained unbroken, his gratitude unabated. He had bread to eat of which the world had no knowledge; the religion of the soul appeared to bear up the animal frame, and to render it frequently insensible to pain, and want, and toil. The hut afforded him higher entertainment than the dwellings of the wealthy. The following relation furnishes an insight into his spirit. "I remember," says he, "I was planned to preach at Hemsworth* once, and being a stranger in the town, I inquired where the Methodist preachers put up their horses. I was informed that there was not any body in the place that would take them in; but that a poor man received them at the common side. I went to my INN, and found a place to put up my horse, which they had built on purpose for the preachers' horses. When I got into the house, I soon found that the poor people had Jesus Christ with them. They were glad to see me, and to receive both me and my horse. These dear friends had a great many enemies, because of their taking in the preachers. The people

* In 1811 and 1812, when the writer was in the habit of visiting the village, in which there was then a neat Wesleyan chapel, it was in the Barnsley circuit. At the period referred to by Samuel, it was probably connected with Leeds, Wakefield, or Pontefract. It is about six miles from Pontefract, and fifteen from Micklefield.

who had supplied them with milk refused to let them have any more; and the publicans would not let them have yeast for their bread. They were also in a strait for food for the preachers' horses. The poor woman begged a few *land ends* of grass, got it dried, and preserved it; and she gleaned a little corn in the fields. She made us very comfortable. Some time after this, I was again planned for the same place. The Lord had opened the hearts of some of the farmers, and they opened their houses; but I went to my old *inn* at the common side. The woman cried for joy to see me. She said she was sorely troubled, because the preachers had left her house: but I told her not to be troubled about it—that she would get her reward for her labour of love. I went to the same place about thirty years after this, and found the same widow. She was very happy in her soul. We see that the Lord is as good as his promise, 'Them that honour me I will honour'—'With long life will I satisfy' them, 'and show' them 'my salvation.' She was very glad to see me; and I told her that I would put her into my life for a memorial of her love to the preachers and their beasts. It was like the widow's mite."

The simplicity of the man is at once seen, in telling the aged matron that she should occupy a place in the memoir of his life; and that he intended nothing more in what he termed his "Life," than to show forth the goodness of God to himself and others, will readily be credited:

nor shall his innocent intentions, though bordering upon the childishness of simplicity, in reference to the poor widow, cease to be fulfilled to the very letter. "Ruth the Moabitess" did not cleave closer to "God" and his "*people*" than did this poor woman; nor did the young widow appear more interesting to Boaz among the "reapers," than did this *gleaner* in the corn-fields to Samuel Hick. He, however, in consoling her for the loss of the preachers, seemed to be unaware that he was furnishing a substantial reason, in his notice of some of the farmers having "opened their houses," why they should take up their abode elsewhere; a point upon which many would have fastened, and would from thence have argued the propriety of relieving her of a burden—though deemed by her a privation—which she had so long and so nobly borne, and which others, now made willing in the day of gospel power, were equally ready, and much more able to bear than herself. For complimentary as it had been for a poor widow, like her of Zarephath, whose "cake" and "cruse" never failed, to supply the wants of the prophets of the Lord, it would have reflected little honour on the more wealthy to have looked on with a stupid indifference, and to have permitted its continuance. Some of the very first expressions uttered by the *new-born* soul are, "What shall we do?" These are the mere nursery expressions of the babe, in reference to the cause of God. Some persons, it is true—not very remarkable for self-denial, or turning the good things of this life aside when within their reach—would have availed themselves of the opportunity of exuding a little bad feeling, by insinuating that the preachers were always on the alert to better their condition. But the very fact of their having stooped so long to lodge in the hovel, of their readiness to accommodate themselves to any fare, however scanty, and to any situation, however humble, while labouring to promote the happiness of their fellow-creatures, shows that they carried about with them the spirit of self-denial, and have it yet at hand whenever Providence opens the door and bids them enter: and the wailings of the widow for their loss are evidence of their worth; for, having been cheered by their presence, their advice, and their prayers, on the social hearth-stone, she sighed and wept at their removal; and sighed the more, as she valued their society.

Samuel took his own way of consoling her, and directed her attention to the "recompense of reward" for what she had done. And it was here, both as to subject and place, that he was in his element. To behold him thus, in one of his happiest moods, the reader has only to sketch a thatched cottage, tottering, like its inmate, with age; its whitewashed walls and mud floor; a few homely pieces of furniture, impaired by long-continued use; Samuel himself seated upon the remains of an old oaken chair, on the opposite side of the fire to the good old woman;

there talking of the joys of the heaven to which they were both hastening, throwing a beam of sunshine into the heart of her with whom he conversed, and which seemed dead within her, till he stirred it into life. Now he crouched forward, with the crown of his head toward the fire—his eyes fixed upon the ground—his elbows occasionally supported by his knees—the palms of his hands turned upward—his thumbs and fore-fingers in constant motion, as though he were in the act of rubbing some fine powder between them, in order to ascertain the quality; or like some of our elderly matrons at the distaff, twisting the fibres of the flax into a thread—dropping for a moment the conversation—next chiming in with a few notes of praise—again taking up the theme of Christ and future glory—his face meanwhile glistening through the rising emotions of his soul—his hands now gliding into quicker action—the fountains of the beating heart breaking up—till at length, elevating his frame, and with his eyes brimming with tears, he seems to throw, by a single glance, all the tenderness of his soul into the bosom of the object of his solicitude, which at once softens, animates, and transfixes the eye of the beholder in grateful return upon himself for the conversational benefits thus conferred.

One of the cases to which Samuel refers, when he states he had been "turned out of places by the clergy," occurred in his own neighbourhood. On the death of Lady Betty

Hastings, and the termination of the Rev. W. Sellon's labours at Ledsham, the living was given to a young clergyman, in a delicate state of health, who came from London to take possession, and who, in his first sermon, made a warm attack upon enthusiasm, and denied the influences of the Holy Ghost, stating, that there had been no such thing as inspiration in the world since the apostolic age. To this he might have been led, from a persuasion that the people had been deluded into the belief of such things through the mistaken piety, as he supposed, of her ladyship, and the preaching of his predecessors. But while thus proclaiming his own nakedness of soul, of every hallowed influence, the poor people, "clothed with the Spirit of holiness," were better instructed, and instead of being satisfied with this collegian, sent for the "Village Blacksmith," to build them up in the faith of Christ.*

* The people's choice, in this case, must remind those who are acquainted with the facts of Mr. Baxter's account, in the Preface to his Disputations, pp. 186–7, of the election of Alexander. When Gregory conferred with the church respecting the choice of a pastor, several of the people were for having a man of rank and splendid abilities; but recollecting that the prophet anointed David, a shepherd, to be king over Israel, he requested them to look among the lower orders of society, and to see whether a person could not be found, possessed of piety and ministerial qualifications. This was received with indignation by several of the inhabitants of Comana; and one lofty-spirited gentleman, whose views as little accorded with those of Gregory as they would have done with those of the little Christian flock at Ledsham, in after ages, told the worthy bishop, by way of derision, that if he wished them to take a person from the scum of the people, they might as well select Alexander the

Samue yielded to their entreaties; but found it difficult to obtain a house to preach in, as nearly every house was under clerical influence, and those who sent for him were afraid of incurring the clergyman's displeasure. A good woman at length obtained the consent of her husband to lend their house for the occasion, indifferent to consequences. A congregation was soon assembled, and Samuel commenced with singing and prayer. During the second hymn, a noise was heard at the door, when Samuel left his stand, and went to inquire into the cause. He was met at the entrance by the clergyman, accompanied by another gentleman, to whom he announced himself as the preacher.

Clergyman. "We want none of your preaching here, and are resolved not to have it."

Samuel. "Sir, I preached the gospel here

collier from their ranks. Gregory took the hint, and sent for Alexander, who appeared before them, ragged in his apparel, and besmeared, like Samuel, with the filth of his employment, exciting the laughter of the less sedate among the assembly. The bishop soon perceived him to be a man of both talent and piety; and after withdrawing with him, and instructing him how to act, returned to the assembly, and delivered a discourse on the nature of the pastoral office. It was not long before Alexander, who was a comely-looking man, was again presented to the brethren, washed, and attired in the canonicals of the episcopal order, and was chosen—collier as he had been—bishop of Comana, with only one dissenting voice! Though there is no doubt, that Alexander was by far Samuel's superior in point of intellect, yet the coal, the smoke, and the soot had an amazing influence on the more elegant in both cases; and the Wesleyan body was as great a help to the latter as Gregory was to the former.

before you were born, and I will live to preach it when you are gone."

Cler. "I tell you, I will not suffer you to preach here. This house is my property."

Sam. "Why, sir, you do not preach the gospel to the people, for you deny inspiration; and no man can preach it but by inspiration of the Spirit of God."

Cler. "I discharge you from preaching in this house."

To this authority Samuel reluctantly submitted, as it would have been imprudent to encourage the occupants to persist in resisting their landlord: the people were therefore dismissed. The clergyman, however, mistook his opponent, if he concluded that the field was his own; for though the preacher was driven from the house, he was not driven from his purpose. On returning home, he wrote a long, faithful letter to the reverend gentleman; informing him, in connection with the admonitions sent, that on the following sabbath he should again visit Ledsham—occupy a piece of waste land in the village, to which he could lay no claim, as it belonged to the lord of the manor—and should there, in his own cart, preach to the people; giving him an invitation at the same time to attend, and to correct him in any thing he might advance contrary to the Scriptures or the Book of Common Prayer. As he made no secret of either his letter or his intentions, the report of his visit to Ledsham, in defiance of the newly inducted minister, soon spread among the neighbouring villagers. The day arrived—the people flocked to the place from a circle of some miles. Samuel, after unyoking his horse, appeared in his cart, occupying it as a pulpit for the occasion, accompanied by four local preachers—the air rang with the song of praise—and a gracious influence attended the word. The clergyman and his lady stood at a distance hearkening to what was said. Samuel, toward the close, told them that he loved the Church, and hoped that, "as soon as the bells" gave "over *tinkling*," they would accompany him, and join in its service. "We all went," he observed, "and I never saw a church so full in my life. The aisles, the communion-place, and bell-house, were all crammed full. What was best of all, the clerk was on our side, and gave out a hymn tune. Such glorious music I never heard in a church before. The parson, poor young man! was overfaced with us, and could not preach; so that he had to employ another person." As a substitute is not so easily obtained, in an emergency of this kind, in the Establishment as among the Dissenters, it is probable that the person was prepared for the duties of the day, independent of this circumstance, and that Samuel attributed to the congregation that which originated in indisposition. This is the more likely, from what Samuel adds:—"The poor young man went off to London next morning, where he died, and was brought back to be buried about six months after." This fact, taken in connection with

Samuel's declaration, "I preached the gospel here before you were born, and will live to preach it when you are gone," falls upon the heart with peculiar solemnity. It ought not be omitted, that the clergyman beckoned the churchwarden to him after the service, and stated that he had inquired into the character of the old blacksmith—found that he was a very good man—and wished him to be informed from himself, that he might preach in the village whenever he judged proper.

CHAPTER VI.

His qualifications for soliciting pecuniary aid—An unsuccessful application to a clergyman—Relieves his circuit from a debt of seventy pounds—His anxiety to obtain a chapel at Aberford—A miser, and his manner of addressing him—A chapel erected—Contests with different avaricious characters—A visit to Rochdale—Administers seasonable relief to a preacher's family—His Scriptural views of charity—Supplies a poor family with coals—Regales part of a company of soldiers on a forced march—An amusing domestic scene—Visitation of the sick—Gives up the use of tobacco from principle—His indisposition, and inattention to the advice of his medical attendant—The good effects of his state of mind upon others—Raises a subscription for a poor man—Relieves a poor female—His love to the missionary cause—Origin of missionary meetings among the Wesleyans.

SUCH was the native restlessness of Samuel's character, that, like quicksilver, the slightest impulse propelled and continued him in motion. With the exception of sleep, or the utter exhaustion of his physical powers he scarcely knew a pause in the work of God. This promptitude to be serviceable to others, the general esteem in which he was held, together with a peculiar fitness for benevolent enterprise—the latter of which was founded on his own generosity—his simplicity of manners, a certain straightforwardness, which knew no fear, and saw no difficulties, rendered him a desirable person to engage in any purpose of soliciting pecuniary aid. Accordingly, he was selected by a committee formed for the occasion, and was commissioned to go through the circuit in which he resided, to collect subscriptions in order to relieve it from its financial embarrassments. Clothed with proper authority, and furnished with a book in which to enter the names of his subscribers, he went forth with the freshness and spirit of the husbandman entering for the first time in the season into the harvest-field. He saw the fields white, and in his view had nothing to do but put in the sickle. He found few obstructions; and among those few—created, by the way, by his own imprudence—he records one which may be considered more amusing than vexatious.

"I went to Ricall," says he; "and as I purposed going to all the houses in the town, I thought there would be no harm in calling upon the Church clergyman. I did so; and found him in his garden. I presented my book, which he gave me again, and looked at me." The look would have had a withering effect upon many of Samuel's superiors; but the same spirit and views which emboldened him to make the application, supported him in the rebuff with which he met. "I am surprised," said the clergyman, "that you should make such a request; that you should ask me to support dissenters from the Church of England!" Samuel instantly interposed with, "No, sir, we are not dissenters; the church has *dissented* from us. The Methodists are good churchmen, where the gospel is preached. And as for myself, I never turned my back on a *brief* when I went to church." Though wiser heads than his own would have found it difficult to charge dissenterism upon the Church, except from Popery, he was correct in his denial of the application of the epithet to the Methodist body. The retort was more equitably supported when he defended himself, by adding, to his reverence, "I think there is no more harm in you helping to support us, than there is in us helping to support you." The clergyman here very properly took shelter under the wing of the state—his only ground of defence—by replying, "You are obliged to support us; the law binds you to do it." Samuel, in return, resorted to the only code of laws with which he had any acquaintance, and which he consulted daily—the *Christian code*—saying, "Ours is a law of love; and if we cannot all think alike, we must all love alike." He concludes, on retiring with his Wesleyan "*brief*," which met with a better reception elsewhere, "We parted after a long contest; and although I did not get any money from him, I would not have taken five shillings for my cause;" or, as in all probability he meant, the opportunity he had just had of pleading and supporting it.

His summary of his labours, treatment, and success, during the remainder of his tour, is worthy of notice: "I had a very good time in going around the circuit—had very kind friends—preached and prayed—and got seventy pounds toward the debt. While employed in this noble work, I got my own soul blessed; and I grew like a willow by the waterside. I got many a wet shirt, and many a warm heart; and while I was begging for money, I did not forget to pray for the souls of my fellow-creatures."

Some money which had been lent upon a chapel in the neighbourhood some time after this, being about to be called in, Samuel felt very uncomfortable lest the sum should not be forthcoming when required. Relief seemed to present itself in a moment, while musing in his shop. He laid aside his tools—went into the house—washed—and attired himself in his best apparel. His friend, Mr. R., surprised to see him thus habited, inquired, "Where are you going, Samuel?" "I am *bown* (going) to Frystone, to get some money for the chapel," he replied. "Of whom?" it was asked. "Of Mr. ——," was rejoined. Mr. R., knowing the gentleman, and considering him from his prejudices and habits, to be a very unlikely person for such an application, endeavoured to dissuade him from his journey. His entreaties were fruitless: Samuel set off—obtained an interview with the gentleman—was courteously received—and after naming the object of his mission, the circumstances in which the trustees would be placed, and the nature of the security, was told that the money was at his service at any hour. Samuel returned delighted, and it is doubtful, whether any man besides himself would have obtained relief from the same source. Mr. R. had given all up in despair.

Samuel Hick was a man who would not solicit charities from others, in order to save himself, or even a loan, which he would not have cheerfully advanced, provided he had the amount in his possession. He gave to the extent of his ability, and might even be associated with those of the Corinthians who, "beyond their power, were willing of themselves" to impart gifts to others. Many interesting instances of liberality might be selected from different periods of his personal history, and here concentrated. As specimens of others which must henceforth remain curtained from earthly gaze, the following charities, without attending to any chronological arrangement, will tend to illustrate one of the more important traits in his character.

He had long looked upon Aberford, his birthplace, as his Redeemer had beheld Jerusalem—with the compassionate emotions of a soul alive to the spiritual dangers and necessities of the inhabitants. His wish to see a Wesleyan chapel erected in it amounted even to anxiety, if not pain. In the year 1804, his wife had £200 left her by a relation. This was placed by the side of the fruits of his own industry, and the union gave the appearance of wealth in humble life. As his property increased, so did his anxiety for a place of worship at Aberford; and he at length declared, that if not a farthing should be contributed by others, rather than the village should be without a chapel, he would give the £200 which he had lately received. He stated his views and feelings to Mr. Rhodes,* and remarked, that he thought he could procure a piece of ground from a gentleman, who, though a Methodist, had not come so far under the influence of its spirit as to subdue the covetousness of his nature.† Mr. Rhodes intimated to him, that he doubted his success in the direction toward which he was looking, unless the old gentleman was either about to die, or some extraordinary change had taken place in the disposition of his heart. Samuel was not to be diverted from his purpose: he could have rendered nugatory, by a

* This venerable man, who was living when the 44th page of the first edition of this memoir was in the press, has since joined the world of spirits. "He died May 18th," says Mr. Dawson, "and entered the same heaven with Samuel."

† Samuel had some odd notions and expressions relative to such characters. Looking abroad at the fine feeling of benevolence which had gone forth, and not often associating with persons of a parsimonious disposition, he exclaimed to a friend one day, "The breed of misers is nearly run out, and not one of the few that are living dare get married, so that in a little time we shall see no more of them."

single sentence—"The Lord has the hearts of all men in his own keeping"—all the reasoning of the most skilful logician—could have dissipated every doubt like mist before the sun. Away he proceeded to the late Sir Thomas Gascoigne, Bart., the lord of the manor, in order, in the first instance, to obtain permission to procure stone upon Hook Moor, since without building materials the land would not have answered his purpose. This was readily granted. He next proceeded to the gentleman loaded with "thick clay," who was instinctively led to raise objections against the proposal. Samuel, in perfect *keeping* with the other portions of his thinkings and remarks, combated every objection, not in the detail, but with one of his *wholesale* sweeps—"The *land* is the *Lord's; you* are only the *occupier ;* and the Lord wants some of his own land to build his own house upon." Mr. T., who already had the "nine points" in law on his side, was not to be subdued by a single blow in the onset; nor was Samuel to abandon himself to despair by the notion of possession, as he could have instantly conjured up the argument of death to dispossess the occupant. Such, however, were the irresistible appeals of one untutored mind upon another, such Samuel's importunity, that the miser in the man actually gave way before him, and the old gentleman told him, that he thought he should not live much longer, and would therefore let him have the piece of ground which he had selected for the purpose. Samuel went home rejoicing; but his joy, alas! was of short duration; it was like the fold of a cloud, which, by suddenly opening and reclosing, only veils the heavens with additional darkness: the miser started into life again during his absence, the proprietor altered his resolution, and every hope was frosted. All, however, was not lost. "It is but justice to state," Mr. Dawson observes, "that though Mr. T. died before a chapel was erected at Aberford, yet he expressed a wish to his executors that they should give *five* pounds toward such erection, should one at any future period be built. With this request, though only orally delivered, they cheerfully complied."

About eight years after this, there was a favourable opening for a chapel, which Samuel promptly embraced. He was desirous, however, of associating Martha with him in this charity; and having more confidence in his God than in himself, he retired to pray, that her heart might be prepared for its exercise. On withdrawing from his privacy, and appearing before her, he scarcely felt satisfied respecting his success, and again retired without opening his mind on the subject. He prayed—he believed—and rising from his knees, descended from the chamber in confidence. Martha knew that a chapel was on the eve of being built; and the moment now arrived for ascertaining the temperature of her charity. Samuel opened the business: "You know, we are *bown* to have a chapel at Aberford, Matty, and we must give something to it; what do you think it should be?" "Well," returned Martha, whose proper character only required a fitting occasion for disclosure, "We mun gee summut haunsom." Never did music sound sweeter to the human ear than did this sentence to Samuel, who was instantly in tears. But there was still a degree of uncertainty remaining, in reference to the standard which each had separately, and privately, fixed upon, as reaching the point, which, in their circumstances, was deemed *something handsome*. Samuel, therefore, solicitous to come to a conclusion, asked, "And what shall it be?" "Twenty pounds," replied Martha. This was almost too much for his feelings, not only on account of the generosity displayed, but because it was the very sum upon which he himself had previously determined; and the opportunity for noticing it is the more readily embraced, in order to place Martha's character in a correct light. It was intended as the dwelling-place of her God—it was a charity in which immortal spirits were concerned—and was also to be erected in the birth-place of her husband. A gentleman farmer undertook the work of soliciting subscriptions for its erection, and Samuel had the unspeakable pleasure of seeing it rise in the face of the sun, vying with all around it for neatness and accommodation. Samuel had the honour of laying the first stone, upon which he devoutly knelt, and most fervently prayed for the blessing of God upon the house which was to overshadow it: "And as he offered the *first prayer* upon the *first stone* that was laid;" so, says Mr. Dawson, "in the *pulpit* of the *same chapel*, he *preached* his *last sermon*, and poured forth his *last public prayer* for the prosperity of Zion." The chapel was crowded on the occasion, and a collection made by him in the evening, for the purpose of defraying the expense of cleaning, lighting, &c., which far exceeded any sum that had been obtained for the same object before; the auditory thus, both by their attendance and liberality, rendering that homage which they would have paid him, had they been certain he was about to make his exit, and expected to hear him announce for his farewell address, "Ye shall see my face no more."

A conquest no less complete, but much more rapid than the preceding, was one which he obtained over another son of the earth, in one of his Yorkshire tours. Having met on former occasions, they were known to each other, and as great an intimacy subsisted between them as was possible in the admixture of fine gold and the coarsest clay. Samuel addressed him on the behalf of Christian missions, but found every part of the fortress provided with arms against any regular and deliberate attack. Poverty was pleaded—objections to the object urged—and reasons given why help should be sought in other quarters. On finding all "special pleading" ineffectual, and as though aware that a city, which would be proof against a regular siege, might nevertheless be taken by surprise, he dropped in his accustomed manner upon his knees, and turning from the miser, directed his addresses to God. Every sentence was like inspiration, and penetrated the soul of the miser like the fire of heaven—withering him with fear. Impressed apparently with a dread of the Being before whom he was immediately brought in prayer, in whose hearing he had pleaded poverty, though possessed of thousands of gold and silver, and who could in an instant as easily take away life as annihilate property, he exclaimed with hurried vehemence,—"Sam, I'll give thee a guinea, if thou wilt give over." Samuel, unruffled in his pleadings by the oddity of the circumstance, and who, in fact, had too many of his own to be moved by those of others, and encouraged withal by the symptoms which appeared, proceeded with earnestness in his addresses, and changing the subject with the quickness of thought, told his Maker how inadequate a guinea was to effect the conversion of the world, and how trifling a sum it was in return for the thousands which the recipient had received in the dispensations of Providence. The miser was again met in an unexpected way, and in the genuine "love of money," which seemed to excite a fear lest he should be further wrought upon by the prayer of the petitioner, or God should extort from him, in the moment of excited feeling, more than the selfishness of his nature would allow, he again roared out,—"Sam, I tell thee to give over,—I'll give thee two guineas, if thou wilt only give it up."

Anxious to maintain his ground, Samuel started up with the same abruptness with which he had knelt—held the miser to his word—secured two notes—and bore them away in triumph to a missionary meeting about to be held in the neighbourhood, where he exhibited them on the platform, with the high-wrought feelings of a man who had snatched a living child from the clutch of an eagle. To be grave in the rehearsal or hearing of such facts, is as difficult as it is to believe in the sincerity of the giver; and were it not for the general artlessness of conduct and disposition manifested by Samuel, it would have been impossible to view it otherwise than as a species of dexterous acting, practised with a view to impose. But a preconcerted plan would have spoiled it; he had not a mind to carry him forward in such a thing beyond the length of his own shadow, beneath a meridian sun; he was the mere creature of impulse—knew no mere of plot than a child.

He was less successful in another case, when called upon to visit a professor of religion possessed of from six to eight thousand pounds, and yet, as a proof of the hollowness of his professions, would not allow himself the common necessaries of life. Samuel, having heard he was dying, and being well acquainted with him, entered his habitation of wretchedness. The furniture was poor, and appeared to have served two or three generations in a regular ancestral line; the room was filthy, and the air fœtid; and yet the general survey was less repulsive than the scene in one of the corners of the room, where the wretched man was lying on a still more wretchedly dirty bedstead, covered with an old horse-cloth, and scarcely an article of linen visible. Samuel was shocked at the sight, and accosted him, "Man, what art thou about? Thou hast plenty,—why dost thou not make thyself comfortable? Thou wilt leave thy money to those, *happen*, that will make none of the best use of it."* Turning his dim eye and squalid face toward Samuel, and thrusting his withered arm from underneath the filthy coverlet, like the skeleton arm of death stretching into sight, he pointed his finger downward and said, "Look there—I do endeavour to comfort myself." Samuel inclined his head, till he was enabled to look beneath the bed, where he beheld a small phial-bottle, within one of his shoes, the heel of which was high enough to support it. "That," added he, "is a sup gin." After dealing faithfully with him, Samuel knelt by his side, and supplicated Heaven for mercy. "But," said he to a friend

* As a specimen of what he had to expect, and of the profusion of avarice, the man saw his nephew and heir, some time prior to this, coming out of a public-house opposite to his own, staggering, and throwing off the contents of a sickened stomach as he crossed the street. "See thee," said he to his brother, who was sitting beside him, "how our money will go when we are gone;—come, there is a *penny*—go thee, and get some ale, and let us make ourselves comfortable while we live." This *ale*, by the way, was sold at a penny per quart, which nothing short of sheer want and feverish thirst could induce a human being to drink. But it was the *comfort* of a MISER.

afteward, "bless you, *barn*,* I could not pray; the heavens were like brass; there was no getting to the other side of them; and how was it possible to get over all yon old crooks, rusty iron, and hob-nails, heaped up in the corner, which had been collecting for years, and which, if every body had their own, were *happen* none of his!"

During part of the life of two of Martha's sisters, who resided in Rochdale, he paid an annual visit to them in that town. On one of these occasions, in 1801 or 1802, while Mr. Percival was stationed on the circuit, he went as usual to tender him his respects. Mr. P. engaged him to preach in the country the next day, which was the sabbath, and a person was appointed to conduct him. Samuel ascended the pulpit, preached in his accustomed way, but failed to secure the attention of his rustic hearers. He gave up preaching, and commenced a prayer-meeting. It was not long before a person manifested deep distress of soul, on account of personal guilt. Samuel's companion was alarmed lest some of the irreligious part of the congregation should become unruly: but the service passed off much better than was anticipated. Samuel called upon Mr. Percival the next morning, to inform him of his sabbath's excursion; and in allusion to this and similar visits, he told the people, after the

* "*Barn*," in Scotland, *bairn*, for CHILD; an expression very common with Samuel, in his addresses to both rich and poor, old and young.

commencement of missionary meetings, that he had "been a missionary many years, and had preached to white heathens in Lancashire." Mrs. P. was confined in child-bed, and Mr. P. himself—being without servant—was preparing breakfast for the children—eight or nine in number—such a breakfast as is commonly used by the lower classes of society, in Lancashire and the west of Yorkshire. Samuel cast an alternate look at this minister of God, and at his poor children: his compassion was moved—it was more than he could support himself under—he retired—walked about the ground adjoining the house—sighed—wept—prayed. He knew the price of provisions was high, and board wages low: he saw the effects. He had but two guineas in his pocket; he returned, divided the sum—and gave Mr. P. a guinea. On his arrival at home, he gave his wife the history of his journey, together with an account of the manner in which he had disposed of his money, stating, among other particulars, that he had "lent the Lord a guinea at Rochdale." Martha remonstrated with him, supposing, as others would have done, that he had scarcely acted with prudence in his generosity, telling him that, in his circumstances, "half a guinea would have been very handsome." Samuel replied in his usual way, with the feelings of a man delivered of a burden, and with strong anticipations of the future, "Bless thee, my lass, the Lord will soon make it up to us," which was actually the case a few weeks afterward, and made up, it may be added, *fourfold.* He seemed to have none of those *secondary* or *intermediate* sentiments and impressions, which are often fatal to better feelings—the creature interposing between the Creator and the soul; and hence it is that we perceive the spring of most of his movements: he considered himself, in all his charities, as acting immediately *under* and *for* God—as *receiving* from HIM, and *giving* to him:* furnishing a standing, a living exemplification of his faith in, "*I* was a hungered, and ye gave *me* meat: inasmuch as ye have done it unto one of the least of these *my* brethren, ye have done it unto *me.*"

There was still a degree of mystery hanging around the benevolence of Samuel at Rochdale, for which Martha was unable satisfactorily to account, as she had only allowed what she deemed the adequate expenses of the journey. But Samuel, supposing he was pinioned a little too closely for the occasion, paid a stolen visit to his friend Mr. Rhodes before he set off, requesting the loan of a guinea, as he had frequently done, saying, "We can set it straight, you know, at Christmas, when we settle." When Martha came to a knowledge of this,

* It was a fine sentiment of the benevolent Reynolds, of Bristol, in reply to a lady who applied to him on behalf of an orphan. After he had given liberally, she said, "When he is old I will teach him to name and thank his benefactor." "Stop," said the good man, "thou art mistaken: we do not thank the clouds for the rain. Teach him to look higher, and thank HIM who giveth both the clouds and the rain."

she remarked, that she had often thought that Mr. Rhodes's payments appeared but small when compared with the work which had been done.

In addition to this mortgage-like source, to which he fled on special occasions, he had a secret place in his shop, where he was accustomed to deposite a little cash for regular use. Living by the side of the great north road from London to Edinburgh, he was constantly receiving visits from objects of distress. On their appearance, he went to his hoard, and relieved them as his feelings dictated, and his funds allowed.

On one occasion he even put his friend Mr. R. upon his metal, in the race of charity. The Rev. J. P., finding that the debt upon the Pontefract circuit pressed heavily on the spirits and pockets of the stewards, resolved to have it either reduced or entirely liquidated. He accordingly went to Mr. R. among the first, as a person of property, in full expectation of meeting with encouragement and support. After looking at the case, and hesitating some time, Mr. R. dryly said, "You may put me down five shillings." The reverend applicant's spirits seemed to drop several degrees; and with his horizon overcast in the outset, he began to conclude, that the debt was not soon to be removed. Samuel was standing by, employing his ears and his eyes, but not his voice; and Mr. P., turning to him, asked despondingly, "How much will you give?" "Put me down a pound," he returned. Mr. P.'s spirits suddenly rose—Samuel stood unmoved, apparently watching the effect—while his wealthy friend stared with astonishment, saying, after a short pause, and in as graceful a manner as possible, "You will have to put me down the same, I suppose." So much for the influence of example.

He was an utter stranger to the feeling of giving "grudgingly." His was, in poetic language, a "burning charity;" like concealed fire, constantly enlarging, till it actually tears away the surface of the earth, to let loose the imprisoned flame. It only wanted an object upon which to expend itself; and as he rarely gave with discretion, the first applicant generally fared the most bountifully. He was returning from the pit one day with a load of coals: a little girl seeing him pass the door, ran toward him, and asked him for a piece of coal, stating that her mother was confined, and the family without fire. He stopped the horse—went into the house—made inquiry into their circumstances—found the tale of the child correct—brought the cart to the door—and poured down the whole of the load free of cost. Having no money upon him to pay for an additional load, and being apprehensive of a lecture at home for the *abundance* of his charity, he returned to the coal-pit, where he knew he had credit for twenty times the quantity, refilled his cart, and returned home with his soul hymning its way up to heaven, like the lark breasting the morning breeze, and gladdening the inhabitants below with its first song.

To him it was of no importance what was the nature of the want; if it *were* a *want*, it was sure to be met by him with the first object calculated to supply it, to which he had any legal claim; and met too with the freedom nd sudden gush of a fountain breaking from the side of a hill, giving forth its streams till its sources are exhausted by its impetuosity. Of this, his conduct to some soldiers on a march, during the late war, affords perhaps as fine a specimen as any that can be selected. It was what is termed a "forced march," and in the height of summer. The regiment being on its route to the south, a party halted at Micklefield early in the morning; the village inn could accommodate but a small portion of them, and the remainder took their seats on the heaps of stones by the side of the road. Samuel, as usual, was up early, and sallying out of the house, he had presented to his view these veterans in arms. A thrill of loyalty was felt in his bosom, as every thing connected with his King, to whom he was passionately attached, was calculated to produce. He instantly returned to the house, and placed before the men the whole contents of the buttery, pantry, and cellar—bread, cheese, milk, butter, meat, and beer went, and he himself, in the midst of the men, as happy as a king living in the hearts of his subjects. Though in the very heyday of enjoyment, he looked with tenderness upon the men, who were about to take the field, and dismissed them with his blessing. But he had part of the reckoning still to pay with his partner. Martha came down stairs, and after engaging in other domestic concerns, proceeded to the buttery, to skim the milk for breakfast. All had disappeared. Inquiry was made; and when she found how the things had been disposed of, she chided him, saying, "You might have taken the cream off before you gave it to them." Samuel replied, "Bless thee, *barn*, it would do them more good with the cream upon it." The officers of the regiment having heard of his conduct, called upon him to remunerate him for what he had done; but he thanked them for their intentions, stating that what he had given, he had *freely given*, and that the men were *welcome* to the whole. The tale of Samuel's bounty was handed from company to company, and lastly from regiment to regiment: and on the plains of Waterloo, some of the brave fellows, when nearly exhausted through excessive toil, were heard to express a wish by some who had heard the story, and knew Samuel, that they again had access to his milk and beer. Little was he aware that he would be borne in British hearts from his native shore, and triumph in those hearts in his deeds of charity, upon a field and in a struggle that decided the fate of Europe,—be recollected as the warrior's solace, in the hour of peril!

Though Samuel received occasional lectures from his good wife on account of his charities, it was not owing to a want of generous feeling in her, but to a greater share of prudence; and it was a fortunate circumstance for him, that he had such a *curb* at hand; otherwise he would have been often seriously involved in his circumstances, and through charity alone, might either have enlarged the list of bankrupts in the Gazette, or been led to the workhouse to subsist on the charity of others. In this, though in the character of a *drawback*, she was in reality a *help-meet*; and by *prudently* looking forward, was enabled to *foresee* the possibility of an *evil* day of want, and to *hide* both herself and the children from its calamities, by a little timely provision. It was not surprising to find Samuel plunging occasionally, yet innocently, when the reins were drawn a little more tightly than he wished. An amusing scene of this kind took place in the domestic circle. He was going out, and had attired himself in his better garb for public appearance. Not knowing what demands of justice or of mercy might be made upon him before his return, he asked his daughter, then at home, and who frequently acted the part of purse-bearer, for a few shillings. Martha, whose hearing was unusually quick on those occasions, was on the look out. The two hands were stretched out—that of the daughter to give, and that of the father to receive—without either of them being aware that another eye was upon them. Martha, unperceived, glided up to them like an apparition—passed her arm between them—and, placing her hand beneath the one containin the silver, gave it a sudden jerk: up flew the contents, which suddenly descended in a shower on the house floor, when Martha, out of seven or eight shillings, secured a dividend of four.

These little incidents show *the man*, as well as the necessary restraints imposed; nor could he be seen without them: and however sensible the biographer may be of their want of dignity, and sometimes even of gravity, there is a greater solicitude in "hitting off the likeness," than in securing fame by the chaste and classical execution of the work. Samuel, to be known, must be threaded through every path of private as well as public life; and into one of the former he may again be traced, and beheld with interest, if not admiration.

He was in the habit of visiting the sick; and as he was no respecter of persons, he attended people of every persuasion, and in every rank of life, to whom he could find access. Among others, he visited the wife of old William Hemsworth, who died in 1820. William and his sons, having united themselves to the Wesleyan society, were in the habit of accompanying Samuel to different places in his religious excursions. She, being a rigid Roman Catholic, looked upon Samuel as a heretic, leading them astray from the true faith. Affliction, at length, overtook her, on her route to the grave: and what was not a little singular, she sent for Samuel to pray with her. His prayers were effectual—her heart was smitten—the clouds of ignorance and superstition rolled off in succession from her understanding, like mists from the face of a landscape before the morning sun. On the arrival of the priest, under whose guidance she had been for a number of years, he was shown to her apartment; but instead of waiting for instruction, she upbraided him for not having inculcated upon her the necessity of the "new birth," stating, at the same time, that she derived "more good from Sammy Hick's prayer, than from all that" she "had heard before, and that if" she recovered, she would "go among the Methodists." The daughter asked the priest to pray with her mother; but supposing her too far gone in heresy for recovery, he retired, saying, "I have done with her." It is pleasing to add, that the woman died in possession of "perfect peace."

Another person of the same persuasion, and nearly at the same time, resident at Micklefield, was visited by Samuel. The priest and Samuel accidentally met in the sick man's chamber at the same time; and in order to effect either the withdrawal or expulsion of the latter, the priest told the family that he could "not do any thing while Samuel" was present. This was a point which required some deliberation; and no one appearing forward in the business, the reverend gentleman took it upon himself, to order Samuel to walk out of the house. Samuel, supposing he might be serviceable on the occasion, observed, "Two are better far than one:" but the priest not according with this sentiment, and the mother of the poor man declaring, intoxicated meanwhile with liquor, that she could not *say her prayers for Sammy Hick*, he was obliged to leave. So much for bi otry and intoxication, linked on the occasion like a wedded pair!

He was more useful in visiting a poor aged widow. After encouraging and praying with her, he put sixpence into her hand—the sum total, it is believed, he had upon his person at the time. She appeared overpowered with gratitude, and he was deeply affected with the manner in which it was expressed. It suddenly occurred to him, and he internally accosted himself—"Bless me! can sixpence make a poor creature happy? How many sixpences have I spent on this mouth of mine, in feeding it with tobacco! I will never take another pipe while I live: I will give to the poor whatever I save from it." From that hour he denied himself. It was not long, however, before he was seriously indisposed. His medical attendant, being either inclined to try the strength of his resolution, or supposing that he had sustained some injury by suddenly breaking off the use of the pipe, and therefore would derive advantage from its re-adoption, addressed him thus:

Phys. "You must resume the use of the pipe, Mr. Hick."

Sam. "Never more, sir, while I live."

Phys. "It is essential to your restoration to health, and I cannot be answerable for consequences, should you reject the advice given."

Sam. "Let come what will, I'll never take another pipe: I've told my Lord so, and I'll abide by it."

Phys. "You will in all probability die, then."

Sam. "Glory be to God for that! I shall go to heaven! I have made a vow, and I'll keep it." His medical adviser found him unflinching in the face of danger and of death; and as he recovered from his illness, he more readily attributed the prolongation of life to the honour which God had conferred upon him for his self-denial, than to the most efficacious medicine that could have been administered.

This fearlessness, for which he was indebted both to natur and grace, produced on one occasion a happy effect. He had been at Askern Spaw with Martha, some time in 1816, and on his return home, took occasion to stand up in the cart, before he reached Norton, to throw his great coat over her in order to prevent her from taking cold during her exposure to the open air. Just at that moment the horse took fright—Samuel lost his balance—fell backward out of the cart—and pitched upon his shoulder. He sustained considerable injury, and when raised from the ground, was unable to stand erect. He was conveyed with some difficulty to the village; on reaching which, a medical gentleman was sent for, who deemed it advisable not to bleed him, though urged to it by him. "I am very ill, sir," said Samuel, "and must be bled." The surgeon replied, "If you are bled at present, you will die." "Die—die, sir," was returned, "What is death to me? I am not afraid of dying. I have nothing to do but to make my will; and I can make it in two minutes; there are plenty of witnesses. My money shall be disposed of so and so," naming, in a few brief sentences, the manner: then stretching out his great arm, as he did on a subsequent occasion, he said, "Live or die, I will be bled." The gentleman, hoping the best, opened the vein, and took a basin of blood from him. Not satisfied, Samuel stretched forth the other arm, and said, "I will be bled in this also." His attendant again complied with his wish, and took from him a second basin full. "When he did this," Samuel observed, "the pain went away as nice as *aught*." On the bandages being properly adjusted, Samuel said, "Now, doctor, you have been made a blessing to my *body*; I will beg of God to bless your *soul*." So saying, he knelt in his usual hurried way, and devoutly prayed for his benefactor. The surgeon, on rising, remarked, "I never had such a patient as you in the whole course of my practice:" and then inquired his name and place of abode, to which Samuel distinctly replied, hitching in at the close, "I come here to preach sometimes." This led to an invitation to the house of the surgeon, the next time he should visit the village, to which Samuel readily acceded, stating afterward to a friend, that he was "glad of it," for he "wanted a good inn there." Accordingly, the next time he was appointed to preach in the village, he rode up to the surgeon's door, was hospitably entertained, and had both the surgeon himself and his family as hearers. The house in which he preached was exceedingly crowded; and on returning with the family, he accosted his host,—"You see, doctor, how uncomfortable we are. We ought to have a chapel. The stone is the Lord's—the wood is the Lord's—and the money is the Lord's." The gentleman took the hint; and with a heart as ready to improve upon it, as he had acuteness to perceive it, offered a subscription to set the work in motion; Samuel instantly proceeded to solicit subscriptions from others; and out of this misfortune arose a Wesleyan Methodist chapel. In that chapel Samuel had the pleasure of holding forth the word of life. It may be added, that so much delighted was the gentleman with the patience, fortitude, and conversation of Samuel; and connecting with it his intention to leave home two or three times before he was sent for, but still unaccountably detained, without being able to assign any reason, till Samuel's messenger arrived, he was led to acknowledge a supreme power, and to perceive a vitality in the influence of religion upon the heart, which he had neither previously known nor confessed.

Prodigal as Samuel was in some of his charities, toward persons in great need, and who were likely to make a proper use of them, there were seasons when he seemed to be vested with a discretional power, beneficial to the recipient. A poor man had lost a horse by sickness. Samuel, who was "a servant of all work," in the begging line, went around the neighbourhood, and collected money for the purchase of another. This amounted to a guinea more than the value of the animal,—a sum of less than twenty shillings being sufficient to purchase another equally poor to replace it. The man himself, though a professor of religion, was less entitled to Samuel's confidence than his benevolence: and to show how low he stood, by the small degree of prosperity he was capable of sustaining, Samuel, speaking of him to a friend, said, "I did not give him the guinea all at once; I gave it him as I thought he needed it; for bless you, *barn*, you see he could not bear *prosperity*." The notion of "*prosperity*" being appended to so small a sum, is worthy of being preserved as a memento emanating from a mind which was itself stamped by it as a still greater curiosity.

Benevolence of heart, though connected with slender personal means, is often of greater value to a neighbourhood, in such a man as Samuel Hick, than the opulence of others. A female who resided about a mile from his house was extremely poor, and hastening, through consumption, to an invisible world. When her case became known, he went to Aberford—applied to several respectable people—stated her circumstances—and solicited a variety of things which he deemed suitable for her relief and support. Aware of the honour which God puts upon faith, agreeably to the declaration of our Lord to the blind man—"According to your faith be it unto you," he provided himself beforehand, in the strength of his confidence, with a basket; which, together with his pocket, was replenished on his return, having between twenty and thirty shillings in one,—muffins, bread, butter, sugar, and a shoulder of mutton in the other. Careful Martha, who was never backward in rare cases, as has been perceived, and would have done more in such as were less necessitous, had she not known that Samuel's benevolence was more than sufficient for both, added her half-crown to the moneys collected; and Samuel, with his basket by his side, set off to the cottage of this daughter of affliction, and was received like the angel of plenty in time of famine.

"His heart always melted," says Mr. Dawson, "at the sight, or on hearing the tale of wo. He could not hear of persons in distress, but he wept over them; and if they were within his reach, he relieved them according to his ability, applying also to others more affluent than himself to assist in such works of mercy. If ever a person answered the character of the liberal man, who devises liberal things, Samuel Hick was the man. The highest luxury that he could enjoy was, to deal out bread to the hungry, to bring the poor into his house that were cast out, to cover the naked, and to satisfy the afflicted soul. Then it was that he felt the full truth of that sentence, 'It is more blessed to give than to receive.'"

But if one object of charity was more paramount than another in his affections and exertions, it was that of Christian missions;—a charity on the broadest scale, which blends all the miseries of time with the glories of eternity, alleviating the one by the contemplation of the other;—a charity which looks at the *whole man*, in all the relations of life;—a charity whose object is the destruction of *sin*—that which, like a pestilential vapour, blights the whole harvest of human hope and comfort, and, carrying the seeds of destruction into every source of prosperity, reduces society to the condition of a tree withered to the root;—a charity, in short, occasioned by "Paradise Lost," and which will never know cessation in its doings till the fact is ascertained of "Paradise Regained." So far back as the period when the late Dr. Coke commenced what has been termed the "drudgery of begging," Samuel gave him half a guinea for the support of the missions; and this, considering the scanty means he had then at command, and the small number of missionaries employed, would not have disgraced the "Reports" of modern times. But it was not till the *public meetings* commenced at Leeds,* and elsewhere, that his soul, as

* The biographer has had too deep an interest in these meetings not to recollect the influence of their beginnings upon his own mind. It is difficult precisely to determine at this distance of time with whom the first thought originated, or what was the first sentence that led to them. Mr. Scarth, of Leeds, repeatedly remarked to Mr. Dawson, *before* Dr. Coke took his departure for India, "The missionary cause must be taken out of the doctor's hands; it must be made a

though it had been in bondage before—for such was the change—bounded off, and expatiated at full liberty. Here he had ample scope for the finest, the fullest, and the deepest philanthropic feelings of his heart; and for many miles around his own homestead it was rare not

public—a common cause." It is not impossible that this may have been the *germ* of the whole. The Dissenters had a public meeting in Leeds, a few months previous to the first public one among the Wesleyans. This having been held in the course of the summer, Messrs. Scarth and Turkington visited the conference, and expressed their views on the subject to the Rev. George Marsden, stating that *something* should be done in a more *public* way for the missionary interest belonging to their own body. With their views Mr. M. perfectly coincided. When the embarrassed state of the missionary fund came before the conference, there appeared to be no alternative between reducing the preachers at home or the missionaries abroad. There was too much zeal and liberality in the body to permit either. The subject was one of deep interest; and did not die at conference. Mr. Morley, the Leeds superintendent, thought, that if the *Dissenters* could raise a MISSIONARY MEETING, the *Methodists* might also; and accordingly suggested the subject to his colleagues, Messrs. Bunting and Pilter, who zealously entered into his views. Not satisfied with commencing this "*new thing*" in Methodism on their own responsibility, they were desirous of knowing how far the proposal of a public meeting would meet with the countenance of others of their brethren. Bramley having been then but recently divided from the Leeds circuit—a close union still subsisting between them—and being contiguous to each other, these gentlemen proceeded thither, with a view to deliberate with the Rev. W. Naylor and the biographer, who were then stationed on the Bramley circuit. No persuasion was requisite; the propriety, necessity, and practicability of the measure were manifest at once. The Leeds and the Bramley preachers thus took the first decisive and active step in the work, which has since been carried on to such an extent. A corresponding chord was soon found to vibrate with pleasure in the breasts of the Rev. Messrs. R. Watson and J. Buckley, of the Wakefield circuit; and they were followed by Messrs. Reece and Atmore, of the Bradford and Halifax circuits, to see his face turn up in the crowd, like the image on a favourite medal, which is the pride and boast of the antiquary, and fixes the eye of the spectator much sooner than most of the others which adorn his cabinet.

CHAPTER VII.

His patriotic feeling—High price of provisions—Differs with Mr. Pawson for prognosticating evil—Letter to the Rev. Edward Irving on prophecy—Threatened invasion of Bonaparte—An address to the king—Samuel's loyalty—M. A. Taylor, Esq.—The suppression of a religious assembly—A defence of a religious revival—His interview with Mr. Taylor—Obtains a license to preach—An allusion to him in a parliamentary debate.

A MAN like Samuel Hick, whose mind was so thoroughly imbued with divine grace, was not likely to be defective in what is termed *nationality*, and the still more Scriptural principle of loyalty. Never did a Jew, by the rivers of Babylon, reflect with greater tenderness upon Judea, "in a strange land," than he

who both exulted in the prospect of so ample a harvest of good. Mr. Bunting organized the first plan—Mr. Watson wrote the first address—Mr. Buckley preached the first sermon on the occasion, at Armley, a place belonging to the Bramley circuit—and the first public meeting was held in the old chapel, at Leeds,—T. Thompson, Esq., M. P., in the chair. The meetings were at first beheld by some of the brethren as the dotage of enthusiasm, and as the forerunner of a marriage union with the world. But they became so productive, and were so instrumental in producing good to the contributors, that the most sturdy opponents were not unfrequently found afterward in the *chair* delivering their recantations.

did upon his country, which he was in the habit of designating, "*our* island"—"*our* England," always considering himself as having a personal interest at stake in all its affairs; and never did a subject in any realm pour out with greater sincerity and fervour the prayer of—"God save the king."

During one of Mr. Pawson's appointments to the Leeds circuit, Samuel observes, "Corn was very dear. The poor people went around our town with a half guinea in their hands, and could not get a *stroke** of corn for it. Mr. Pawson came to Sturton Grange to preach, and while preaching, he told his congregation that there would be a famine in our land, and that he had seen it coming on for twenty years." Such a prophecy, from such a prophet—a man whom, like all other Wesleyan ministers, he considered an apostle of God—and in reference to his own land, "of every land the pride," could not but awaken in him strange emotions. Without attempting to endue Mr. Pawson with the gift of prophecy, it is probable that he might intimate to his congregation, that he had sighed over the extreme wickedness of the wicked—having been touched by it—that from the poignancy of his feelings, he foreboded some manifestation of the divine displeasure—and by way of improving the subject, in order to lead

* *Strike*, a bushel. In the west of Yorkshire, a *strike* is *two pecks* or a *half bushel*; hence the high price of grain at the period referred to, when poor people could not obtain a *half bushel* for a *half guinea*.

the dissolute to repentance, prayer, and reformation, might lay hold of passing events in such a way as to lead Samuel, inapprehensive of his meaning, and not taking in the whole of the connecting links of thought, to draw the inference stated.

Samuel returned home reflecting on what he conceived to be Mr. Pawson's view of the subject; and the following extract will show the acuteness of his feelings, his simplicity, and his piety. "I began," says he, "to be very miserable; and as my children were small, I thought it would be a sore thing for them, my wife, and myself to be pined to death. When I got home I went into my closet to inquire of the Lord, whether there would be a famine or no; and while I was pleading I got as fair an answer from the Lord, that there would be no famine, as when he pardoned my sins and cleansed my soul. I saw that there was plenty of corn to supply till harvest. But this did not satisfy me. I told my wife that I could not rest till I went to inform the preacher that there would be no famine in our land. I set off for Sturton; and when I got there, I told that dear woman of God, Mrs. Ward, my errand." Here Mrs. W. very properly interposed, not only on account of the lateness of the hour, which appears to have been on the same evening after preaching—but by delicately suggesting the impropriety there would be in his "pretending to dictate to one of the first preachers in the connection." But Samuel was not to be repulsed by either *first* or *second*, whether the claim instituted referred to priority of *time* or superiority of *talent*. He had his one argument at hand—"Thus saith the Lord;" and proceeds, "I told her not to blame me, for it was the Lord that had sent me. With a deal to do, she let me into the room; and I told our brother Pawson, that the Lord had sent me to inform him that there would be no famine in the land." Mr. Pawson, whose forebodings were scarcely removed, replied, "Well, brother, I shall be very thankful to the Lord to find it not so." Samuel, taking a little credit for the correctness of his own judgment and impression in the case, and still firm in his belief in the actual prediction of a famine, adds, "So we see how good men may miss their way, for there was no famine." To persons whose feelings are not immediately interested, it is sometimes amusing to hear well-meaning men, without a prophetic soul, guessing against each other for their Maker. In the present case, Samuel's conduct in going to "inquire of the Lord," manifested a spirit worthy the most simple, the purest, the best part of patriarchal times; and as they were chiefly his *own* fears that had to be allayed, the impression that effected their removal was so far—all prophecy on the occasion apart—an act of mercy—mercy manifested in the exercise of prayer.

He availed himself of this supposed prophetic failure of Mr. Pawson, February 28th, 1826, when he addressed a letter to the Rev

E. Irving, who had then reached the acme of his oratorical attractions, though not of his theological reveries, and who, as Samuel had been informed, had been prognosticating national calamities, because of national wickedness. The original, which is in the writer's possession, is a curiosity, and would, if printed as it flowed from his pen, exemplify the estimate given of his mind in the preceding pages. With the exception of a few transpositions, retrenchments in verbiage, and the occasional substitution of a word, the following may be considered as an allowable copy :—

"Dear Brother Irving, the Prophet in London :

"I am informed that you have prophesied that this island is *bown* to come to desolation ; but I think you should put a condition in your prophecy, viz., that if the people humble themselves, pray, and turn from their wicked ways, then God will hear from heaven, will pardon their sins, and will heal the land. When the Prophet Jonah went to preach at Nineveh, the whole of the people of the city humbled themselves, and prayed to God ; and God heard their prayer, and saved them from destruction. If there had been ten righteous souls in the cities of Sodom and Gomorrah, when they were destroyed, in which there were so many thousands of men, women, and children, they would not have suffered : and I fully believe, that if Abraham had pleaded on, the Lord would have saved the cities for his servant's sake ; but he gave up pleading, and then they were consumed.

"But I have to inform you, sir, that there are more than ten righteous men in a city; for the little one has become a thousand, and the small one a strong nation. We have our Moseses, and our Elijahs, and our Daniels in our island, who are all pleading. We have thousands of children training up to fear God and honour the king; we have Bible societies, missionary meetings, and tract societies. These four institutions are the Lord's; and this island is the Lord's nursery, in which he raises up plants to plant the gospel in all the world, in order to be a witness unto all nations. Then the wickedness of the wicked shall come to an end—all shall know the Lord from the least to the greatest—nations shall learn war no more—and the whole earth shall be filled with the glory of God.

"The pope prophesied, in years past and gone,* that he should get back the inheritance of his forefathers, be set upon the British throne, and have all the churches restored: but that will never come to pass; God will never suffer the pope to govern his nursery or plantation. We shall be governed by peaceable governors.

* Samuel met with a man, in one of his journeys, who avowed his belief in the Roman Catholic creed, and his faith also in the restoration of our cathedrals and churches to the papal state. The public mind was considerably agitated at the time with the Catholic question, and the impression produced by both led him, probably, to introduce his holiness to Mr. Irving.

We shall have peace and plenty. The year that has passed has been a plentiful year for temporal food; and I trust before we see the end of this we shall find it to have been one of the best we ever had for spiritual food—that many will be brought to the knowledge of God—and that we shall see the downfall of infidelity.

"I have known good men miss their way in my day, by their prophecies. The prophets foretold that there should be wars and rumours of wars in the latter days, and that nation should rise up against nation. These prophecies have been fulfilled. Nation has been up against nation. There has been such destruction as never was before. But these days were to be shortened for the elect's sake." Then follows his account of what he denominated Mr. Pawson's prophecy, appending to it the case of another person, who, he observes, "prophesied that our island would be covered with war and bloodshed," and as a precautionary measure, "took his family to America, where he purchased a large estate. But," continues Samuel, "these were foolish prophecies, and false prophets, and I firmly believe yours will prove to be like them. While we continue to honour God, by sending the gospel to the poor perishing heathen, by keeping up our noble Bible and tract societies, and Sunday schools, we shall neither have pestilence nor famine, nor shall the sword be permitted to go through the land. And although there is at present a great stagnation of trade and commerce, yet there is a remedy for us, on certain conditions. It is not a prophet, nor an archangel, but the God that made the world, and all that therein is, who says, 'If I shut up heaven that there be no rain, or if I send a pestilence, if my people that is called by my name will humble themselves, and turn from their wicked ways, I will pardon their sins, and will heal their land.' This is the case. Persons are turning from their sins every day. Judgment is mixed with mercy. England is one of the first islands in the world. We have liberty of conscience—we have peace—and I hope trade and commerce will again revive, and that the suffering poor will have plenty of work, to enable them to earn bread for their families."

There is not the slightest intention in the writer to bring the "Village Blacksmith" into the arena of controversy, with a view to place him in polemic array against Mr. Irving; nor need Mr. Irving be ashamed of the association, as a few of Samuel's positions are as tenable as some of those with which he has favoured the world in his more recent publications. Proceeding on the correctness of Samuel's information, which is only assumed for the occasion, his suggestion relative to the propriety of annexing *conditions* to threatening, and the support which he professes to derive from this suggestion from the case of Nineveh, is worthy of respect. His application of the subject to Britain, which he illustrates by the case of

Sodom and Gomorrah, showing the superiority of the one over the other—Britain with her multitude of intercessors actually engaged at the throne of grace, her Christian philanthropy, as exhibited in her institutions, and the probable increase of conversions to God through the instrumentality of Sunday schools —and the cities of the plain without their "ten righteous" characters—deducing from the whole the probability of our safety, shows that he was in possession of correct Scriptural notions, though they often radiated in different directions, like so many scattered rays of light, being unable to employ them to the best advantage, and therefore not always falling with fulness on the point to be illuminated. The act, too, of pressing the late revolutionary wars into his service, which he considered to be no other than the "rumours of wars" mentioned in Scripture, by way of showing the difference between ancient and modern prophetic pretensions—the one having been fulfilled, and the other remaining unaccomplished—and his attempt to rescue the prevailing commercial distress out of Mr. Irving's hands, that he might not avail himself of it in support of his predicted judgments, intimate a quickness of intellect, though unequal to that which precedes. But the letter is given chiefly with a view to show the manner in which his thoughts moved, when venturing beyond the precincts of a few brief sentences; and for this purpose, too, as well as that of honouring the feelings of his heart, his address to his majesty George III. may be introduced. At the time when Bonaparte threatened to invade England, there were great "searchings of heart." Samuel was among the sufferers in spirit. When fear was at its height, he retired into the fields, like the prophet to the summit of a solitary mountain, to intercede with his Maker; and he there received what set his own mind at rest—an assurance that our shores would never be either printed or polluted by the foot of the enemy. From that period he went on his way rejoicing, and in the strength of his confidence, his patriotic and loyal feeling, he wrote the address just alluded to, the substance of which is as follows:—

"O king, live for ever! Let not your heart be troubled, nor your countenance be changed; for that God whose church and cause you have defended, will also defend you, and deliver you from the lion and the bear, and also from this uncircumcised Philistine; for he shall never set his foot upon English ground. And if your majesty the king wants a regiment of life-guards to defend your person, your property, or your nation, God will raise them up from the church of Christ, and I will go in the forefront; and like Gideon's army, with their lamps in pitchers, one of these will chase a thousand, and two will put ten thousand to flight. And if your majesty the king wants any money to support or defend your person, your property, or your nation, I am now possessed of £600, and your majesty shall have every shilling of it. When I began the world, I had not a penny, nor a bite of bread to put into my mouth, and I will again begin the world as naked as at first. And that God whom I love and serve will never suffer the crown to be taken from the head of your majesty, till he shall crown you with immortality and eternal life."

Whether the letter ever reached his majesty is doubtful, not only because of the medium through which it was conveyed, but from the known character of that venerable monarch ; as it is more than probable, that, from the novelty of the occasion, he would have condescended, not to accept the offer, but to pay respect to the generous emotions which emanated from the bosom of such a subject ; and the more so, as the name of *Hick* was not unfamiliar to the royal ear. Samuel had a brother-in-law,* who was groom in the stables at Windsor, and to whom his majesty paid personal attention. Having been absent from his post through indisposition, his majesty, on perceiving it, inquired, in his hasty manner, "Where is Hick? Where is Hick?" When informed that he was ill, the royal inquiry was, "Has he had medical aid?" instantly adding, "if not, let him have it immediately." But the sufferer died ; and Mr. Dawson observes, "I have been informed, that his widow was the object of his majesty's attention and bounty." Samuel, by means of his brother-in-law, had acquired that knowledge of his majesty's private character which inspired

* His wife's brother, whose maiden name was Hick.

him with veneration. This feeling led him to Windsor, during his last visit to the metropolis; but of all the objects presented to the eye of a stranger, nothing fixed his attention so much as the house of his God; and in that house, not any thing yielded such rapture as the cushion upon which the royal personage had been accustomed regularly to perform his devotional exercises. On *that* cushion Samuel devoutly knelt; and as he could throw his whole soul into that prayer, "Give the king thy judgments, O God;" so he could as heartily add, "and thy righteousness unto the King's son:" and hence it was, that when George III. resigned his crown, he transferred his loyal affection to George IV.

While the letter shows the piety, the loyalty, and the liberality of its writer, together with the occasionally beautiful adaptation of Scriptural language and Scriptural metaphor to the subject in hand, for which he was sometimes so happy, and which, in some instances, could not have been more felicitously introduced by our first divines, we are not less impressed with his contracted views, and amused with his notions of generalship. For though Roman history has familiarized us with an instance of one of its first characters having been summoned from the plough to figure in arms, yet we are not quite prepared to see Samuel throwing aside the leathern apron for regimentals—to see him brandishing the sword, heading a troop of soldiers, and cutting his way through the ranks of the enemy. His hand was better adapted to the grasp of the hammer than the musket, and his heart—which would have sickened at cruelty to a beetle—would have sooner led him to heal than to wound. The estimate he formed of his prowess was what would have suited his state when he silenced the clergyman in the presence of Mr. Burdsall. He would now have much sooner stripped, and turned up his shirt sleeves, in front of the anvil, to beat swords into ploughshares, and spears into pruning hooks, than have girded himself for the fight: and it is questionable whether he had any intention in the case, besides that of appearing like the monks of Bangor before Ethelfrith, accoutred, not with "carnal" weapons, but with "the whole armour of God," which, in his estimation, was more fitted for "the pulling down of strong holds," than any other instrument that could be invented, whether by a Congreve or an Archimedes. If he had any views beyond those of combating the assailants with the weapons of *faith* and *prayer*, we can only marvel at the difference between him and John Nelson, whom he heard preach at Aberford cross, who, when impressed for a soldier, said to those who were decking him in military attire, "You may array me as a man of war, but I shall never fight." But whether Samuel had taken the field or not, he would have given the £600 as cheerfully as he ever gave sixpence to a destitute widow.

Leaving the great continental field, where

the thunderbolt of war was seen turning up the soil like a ploughshare, and where the military tempest appeared to be gradually clearing the air and settling the political atmosphere—with which events it would have appeared ridiculous to name such an insignificant being as Samuel, had it not been for his loyal address—we shall direct our attention to a slight skirmish of another description, nearer his own homestead, and see how he was skilled in the military tactics requisite for the occasion. "I remember," he observes, "a great outpouring of the Lord's Spirit at Ledstone, near where I resided; and in that town there lived a parliament-man, who was a justice of peace." This "parliament-man" was no other than Michael Angelo Taylor, Esq., who has distinguished himself in the senate on several measures for the melioration of the metropolitan police, and different other questions. One evening during the revival referred to, Mr. T. was passing the place, which was licensed for preaching, and in which the people were met for public worship. On hearing an unusual noise, he stepped up to the door; and not being over and above skilled in the science of salvation, or having his ear tuned for the music of penitential groans, he, according to the testimony of Samuel, "stamped and swore," declaring he would have them "all taken up," calling out meanwhile for a "constable."* Mr. T. addressed a farmer who

* The reader is referred to a note at the close of these pages for some remarks which appeared in a respectable

acted in that capacity, and told him he would have no such disturbance in the parish. A good sister, who was present, began to pray for Mr. T., repeating several times, "Lord, bless him." Mr. T., on the other hand, elevating his voice to an unusual pitch, told her to cease her noise: "but she," says Samuel, "like the blind man, cried out the more." Mr. T., however, at length succeeded in "breaking up the meeting." This was a severe trial to Samuel, who says, "I went home, but could get very little rest. The next morning I went to our class-leader, and told him that I could not rest till I went to Mr. T. to inform him he had broken the laws of our land." His class-leader was Mr. Rhodes, who, partly to deter Samuel, from an impression of the possibility of the case, hinted that Mr. T. would commit him to the house of correction. Samuel replied,

periodical, a few years back, when the writer found it necessary to defend the same cause from an attack made upon it, in an article in the "British Critic," and also in a separate treatise, written professedly against the Wesleyan body. The closing observations, which have been since added, may not be characterized by that gravity which a more solemn and literary biographical subject would—to preserve it in proper keeping—have demanded; but being in character in these pages, it has been judged proper to insert them. The writer, however, wishes it not to be understood, that he comes forward as the *advocate* of noise, but rather as an *apologist* and *expositor;* for though he would find it difficult, in every instance, to tune his own ear to a love of adverse sounds, he thinks that his feelings ought to be under the guidance of his judgment—that the subject has been much misunderstood—and that great forbearance is due to inexperience, or, in other words, to religious childhood

"I have the Lord on my side, and the law on my side, and I do not fear the face of a man." His firmness gave confidence to Mr. Rhodes, who agreed to accompany him. They both set off, and arriving at Mr. T.'s before he had come down stairs in the morning, were ushered into the "servants' hall." There they remained, till summoned into the presence-chamber. Mr. T., on descending to breakfast, had been informed of their visit. On entering the room, he had, says Samuel, "a very stormy countenance." The substance of the conversation, as left on record, is as follows:—

Mr. T. "Well, Hick, what do you want?"

Samuel. "I want, if you please, to worship God under my own vine and fig-tree, no man daring to make me afraid, or disturb me in the worship of God. And, sir, I am come to inform you, as one of his majesty's *peace*-makers, that last night you broke the laws of the land, and that the law stands in force against you. But we, as a body of people, do not love law. We are determined, however, to have the liberty our king grants us. The place which we were worshipping in is from the king, as it is licensed: and I believe there is a double penalty for your breaking the law."

Mr. T. "I know you very well; you are in the habit of travelling from place to place to preach: but I have the outline of a bill, which will be brought into parliament, and which will at once put a stop to all such fellows, and prevent them from going about. I will make you remain in your own parish, and go to your own church."

Samuel. "Bless the Lord! sir, you cannot stop us. It is the work of God; and unless you can prevent the sun from shining, you cannot stop it. You say you will make us go to our own parish church. It is more than three miles off. It is true, we have a chapel of ease; but the minister comes to it only twice in the year: and we cannot live, sir, with such food as this:" that is, with so small a portion.

Mr. T. "What, have you only two sermons preached in the year?"

Samuel. "No, sir; and he would not come then, only he cannot get his Easter dues without coming."

Here the servant in attendance, and Mr. Rhodes, could support it no longer, but burst into a fit of laughter, and left the room. Mr. Taylor, who appeared not to have known that the place was licensed in which he was the night before, and to have assumed the character of sternness for the purpose of drawing Samuel out into conversation, called upon Mr. Rhodes to enter the room again, asking why he went out. Mr. R. apologized, and stated, that he could not refrain from laughing, and withdrew to avoid a breach of good behaviour. Mr. T. accosting him, said, "You know, Mr. Rhodes, the old man wants a license to preach. This I cannot grant in my individual capacity. But he and you may go to Bradford next Thursday; ask for the clerk of the court, and tell him you want a license for a dissenting minister. He will there receive it; and if, after that, any one should disturb either of you, inform me, and I will defend you." This was too much for Samuel to bear in silence; and without suffering Mr. R. to reply, he permitted that chord of the heart which had just been struck, to give out its fullest and wildest tones, saluting Mr. T. with, "Bless the Lord! they give you a sore character in our country, but I think you are not so bad as they say you are." This, by a thousand men, would have been taken, as it might have been given, as an insult. But Mr. T., as he knew Samuel, had the good sense to give to it its real value, and passed it off in pleasantry. "After this," proceeds Samuel, "I believe he would have granted me any favour. He sent down to the farmer also, in whose house the meeting was held, and told him, if he was in want of any thing from his house or gardens, it should be at his service. So we see, when a man's ways please the Lord, he makes his enemies to be at peace with him."

Samuel went too far in considering Mr. T. an *enemy;* for had he really been such, he would have pursued a different line of conduct. Simple, however, as the whole of this occurrence was, sufficient matter arose out of it to attract the attention of the British senate; for as the "*two sermons*" per annum, in a "chapel of ease," led, from the *easy* character of the labour, to an investigation of other instances of gross neglect, so it gave Mr. T. an opportunity of stating in the house the necessity there was for the ecclesiastical authorities to inquire, whether the different places belonging to the establishment were properly supplied with religious instructers, noticing the case of which he was informed by Samuel, arguing from thence, that it was not to be wondered that a "*blacksmith*," in Yorkshire, should apply to him for a license to authorize him to preach as a dissenting minister. When one of the newspapers was handed to Samuel, in which the fact was stated, and the allusion made, he was not a little elated, and in his simplicity could even connect with the circumstance, in a way in which no one besides himself could do, the "government churches," which were soon afterward erected, and would have as soon—for such was his knowledge of the politics and ecclesiastical history of the day—attributed every new edifice to *that*, as to any other cause. Though some of these goodly structures were not very well attended, he was far from viewing them as useless: "They will be ready," said he, "for the millennium, when it comes; for we shall want them then:" not that he really wished any other religious body to enjoy them; but he was confident they were not erected in vain. He generally spoke respectfully of the Church of England, and indulged a pleasing hope that she would rise to be more holy, active, and useful, than she had ever been.

CHAPTER VIII.

His power in prayer—Divine impressions—An afflicting providence—Remarkable answers to prayer—Familiar expressions in prayer to be avoided—Encounters a blacksmith—His usefulness—His meekness under persecution—Singular method of self-defence against the aspersions of a clergyman—Musical festivals—Mr. Bradburn—Lovefeast—Perfection—Seasonable remarks—The doctrine of sanctification maintained in opposition to a clergyman—Cheerful disposition—Indiscretionate zeal in a meeting of the Society of Friends.

THAT which imparted real elevation of character to Samuel was, his strong faith, and his power with God in prayer: and here it is that he was seen rising out of the habiliments of the blacksmith, surrounded by the visitants, stunned with the din, and enveloped in the smoke of the smithy, like a being belonging to another world, gradually unfolding himself, or suddenly breaking upon the spectators in the true spirit of an angel of light. A few instances have been adduced of his power in prayer on his own behalf; but he still has to be viewed in the character of a successful *intercessor*.

He had an impression upon his mind one day, that he ought to go to the coal-pit, for what he termed "a load of *sleck*."* But having a tolerable stock in the smithy, he hesitated and attempted to suppress it. The impression was renewed, and—"Go, go," was reiterated, as by a voice from within. "I'll pray about

* The refuse or smaller part of the coal, used in furnaces, &c.

it," said he to himself. But "go" was still the language which he seemed to hear, while engaged upon his knees. He rose and told his wife he was going for a load of "sleck." She, as was natural, opposed him, pointing to the heap in the smithy, as a substantial reason why he should stop at home. But his argument was in his heart, and to this he attended, yoking the horse to the cart, and driving off to the pit, without any thing to support his conduct, except the naked impression specified. On reaching the spot, a person exclaimed, in a state of great trepidation, "Ay, Sammy, you are well come; such a one (mentioning the person's name) has been nearly killed, and we want you to pray with him!" The poor sufferer had just been brought up from the pit, when he arrived; and the persons around him were about to extract a piece of wood, which had fallen upon him, penetrated his shoulder, and forced its way, like the spear of Abner, through the opposite side of his body. On perceiving their intentions from their conduct, Samuel said, in a hurried tone, "Do not take it out; if you do, he will die in a moment."* The spirit of

* How he became possessed of this opinion, or whether he had entertained it any length of time, is difficult to state; but it is not a little singular to find, that it is in consonance with the notions and practices of some of our ancestors, who, in tournaments and ancient combats, frequently permitted the shaft of death, which had been propelled through the body, to remain there for a short time, with a view to stanch the blood to a certain extent—when the wound was deemed mortal, till the person should be enabled to express his last will in the settlement of his affairs.

prayer was the element in which he breathed; and for such employment he was always ready. He knelt by the side of the poor man, wrestled with God for his salvation, and obtained satisfactory evidence of an answer to the petitions he presented at the throne of grace. "I now saw," says he, "for what it was that I had to go to the pit." And yet, with this result, there are persons professing the Christian name who would denounce the impression as enthusiastic, and who would, together with the calamity, insert his being at the pit at that precise period in the chapter of accidents, which occupies, in their estimation, so large a share of the business of human life. Only preserve religion in the back ground, or abstract it entirely from the subject, and these persons will talk both seriously and poetically of the mind being darkened, like the sunny landscape, by a sudden cloud, auguring a coming tempest: and of such impulses deserving attention as being the hints of our guardian spirits that danger is impending. All this is allowable in verse, and the poet is admired for the sentiment; while the heathen philosopher is permitted to descant upon it in prose: but the moment the man of God asserts the fact—from whom the others have received it, either directly or remotely, and afterward marred by lowering it—he must be sent through the world with the brand of an enthusiast upon his forehead!

A circumstance not less remarkable occurred at Pontefract—a place where Samuel was highly respected, and where he deeply interested himself in the erection of a new chapel. It was agreed, in order to aid the collection at the opening, that each collector should deposite a sovereign in his box, and that the collectors should be changed each service. Samuel entered into the plan with his native ardour, and promoted, in various instances, its accomplishment. On recollecting the names of friends, who were likely to afford aid, he immediately proceeded to their residences, and accosted them: "Why, the friends are *bown* to open a new chapel in Pontefract: you intend to be there, don't you, and to be a collector?" To this exordium, he appended the plan, closing it with a personal application,—"You approve of it, don't you?" In cases of approval, accompanied with a doubt, whether there would be an opportunity to attend, he generally relieved them, by observing, "I will tell you what you must do; you must give me a sovereign, and I will get some one to collect for you." Such was his success, by this mode of procedure, that, on the day of opening, he handed over to the treasurer nearly twenty pounds. On the morning, he took his seat previous to the commencement of the service in a pew near the pulpit. He had promised himself much enjoyment, and was just sipping of its streams, while glancing upon the collecting worshippers, when he suddenly became unaccountably discomposed. He vacated his seat, and taking up his hat, directed his steps to the gallery, where he placed himself by the side of a young lady in one of the front pews. It was instantly suggested, "Thou hast done it now,—perched in the front for every body to look at thee,—they will think it is nothing but pride that has led thee here." The chapel was now exceedingly crowded; and no sooner was his soliloquy ended, than the congregation was thrown into a state of the utmost confusion by an unfounded alarm respecting the safety of the building. The young lady who sat next him leaped on the top of the pew, and was in the act of precipitating herself into the body of the chapel, when Samuel, with a promptitude equalled only by his composure, prevented her, by taking her in his arms, exhorting her at the same time to "be still," saying, "I would rather die in a Methodist chapel than anywhere else." He now saw, as in the case of the poor collier, a reason for the feeling which induced him to leave his first seat, and occupy another of such prominence. An immortal spirit was in all probability saved, in the first instance, from perdition; human life, in the second, from a premature grave. The female is still living, and a member of the Wesleyan Society.

In the course of a summer of excessive drought, a few years back, when the grain suffered greatly, and many of the cattle, especially in Lincolnshire, died, Samuel was much affected. He visited Knaresborough, at which place he preached on the Lord's day. Remaining in the town and neighbourhood over the sabbath, he appeared extremely restless in the house in which he resided, during the whole of Monday. He spoke but little—was full of thought—now praying—now walking about the room—next sitting in a crouching posture—then suddenly starting up, and going to the door, turning his eyes toward heaven, as if looking for some celestial phenomenon—when he would again return—groan in spirit—and resume his seat. The family, being impressed with his movements, asked him whether any thing was the matter with him, or whether he expected any person, as the occasion of his going to the door so frequently. "Bless you, *barns*," was his reply, "do you not recollect that I was praying for rain last night in the pulpit? and what will the infidels at Knaresborough think, if it do not come? if my Lord should fail me, and not stand by me? But it must have time: it cannot be here yet; it has to come from the sea. Neither can it be seen at first; the prophet only saw a bit of cloud, like a man's hand: by and by it spread along the sky. I am looking for an answer to my prayer—but it must have time." He continued in the same unsettled state—occasionally going out, and looking with intensity on the pure azure over his head; for a more unclouded heaven was rarely ever seen. Contrary to all external signs of rain, and contrary to the expectations of all, except himself, the sky became overcast toward evening, and the clouds dropped the fatness of a shower upon the earth.

His very soul seemed to drink in the falling drops. The family grouped around him, like children around their father, while he gave out his favourite hymn—"I'll praise my Maker while I've breath;" and after singing it with a countenance all a-glow through the sunshine of heaven upon his soul, he knelt down and prayed. All were overpowered: it was a season of refreshing from the presence of the Lord.

If this relation had concerned another man than the subject of the memoir, the biographer would have been incredulous enough to have suspended his judgment,—possibly to have doubted,—and would have been led to inquire, whether, by some particular signs, the person might not have prognosticated a change. But Samuel was too artless to be suspected—too sincere to practise impositions—and his knowledge was too circumscribed to subject him to the charge of being "weather-wise." He was unable to see so far as Columbus, who, in another case, astonished and preserved a portion of the inhabitants of the new world in awe, by being able to foretel, through his astronomical knowledge, a meteorological appearance. Samuel had no weather-glass upon which to look except the Bible, in which he was taught to believe and expect *that* for which he prayed; nothing on which he could depend but God, and *his faith* was *set* in God for *rain*. This, like some other instances which have been noticed, is a beautiful exemplification of the simplicity of Christianity, as it exists in its effects in an uncultivated mind; the person receiving every fact of Scripture history as an undoubted truth of God, given for the encouragement, the conviction, and the instruction of all future ages, whether it refers to the improvement of the mass of mankind, or the individual.

In perfect character with the preceding remarkable fact, connected with the element of *water*, is another, respecting the element of *air*, both of which may yet be attested by *living witnesses;* and which ought not to be beyond the reach of credibility, if we believe there is a God—that he has power over the works of his own hands—and that he employs the elements, not only as general sources of felicity, but on particular occasions unbinds them in their operations, and lets them loose upon man, either as a special blessing or a special scourge, in order to prevent common good from being looked upon with an eye of indifference. Samuel was at Knottingly, a populous village in the neighbourhood of Ferrybridge, in 1817, where he took occasion to inform his hearers, that there would be a love-feast at Micklefield, on a certain day, when he should be glad to see all who were entitled to that privilege. He further observed, with his usual frankness and generosity, that he had two *loads** of corn, and that they should be ground for the occasion. These comprised the whole of the corn left of the previous year's produce. When, therefore, he returned home,

* A *load* of corn at Micklefield, signifies six *strokes*, or three bushels.

and named his general invitation and intention, Martha, who had as deep an interest in it as himself, inquired very expressively: "And didst thou tell them, when all the corn was done, how we were to get through the remainder of the season, till another crop should be reaped?" "*To-morrow*," alas! rarely entered into Samuel's calculations, unless connected with the church. The day fixed for the love-feast drew near—there was no flour in the house—and the wind-mills, in consequence of a long calm, stretched out their arms in vain to catch the rising breeze. In the midst of this death-like quiet, Samuel carried his corn to the mill nearest his own residence, and requested the miller to unfurl his sails. The miller objected, stating that there was "no wind." Samuel, on the other hand, continued to urge his request, saying, "I will go and pray while you spread the cloth." More with a view of gratifying the applicant than of any faith he had in HIM who holds the natural winds in his fists, and who answers the petitions of his creatures, the man stretched his canvass. No sooner had he done this, than, to his utter astonishment, a fine breeze sprung up—the fans whirled around—the corn was converted into meal—and Samuel returned with his burden, rejoicing, and had every thing in readiness for the festival. A neighbour who had seen the fans in vigorous motion, took also some corn to be ground; but the wind had dropped, and the miller remarked to him, "You must send for

Sammy Hick to pray for the wind to blow again."

Few circumstances, perhaps, can be adduced, more characteristic of Samuel, than a remark which he made in reference to the man who "went down from Jerusalem to Jericho, and fell among thieves." After commenting on the situation of the poor sufferer—for all was real history to Samuel, he glanced at the conduct of the Priest, the Levite, and the Samaritan. Speaking particularly of the priest, he endeavoured to apologize for him as far as he conscientiously could, by intimating that he might have been "poor," in consequence of priests not having such "big livings" then, as in the present day. Turning at length, however, upon his piety, he quaintly and pointedly remarked, "Bad as the Levite was, the priest was the worst of the two; for admitting him to have been without money, he might have said to the wounded man, 'Come, we'll have a bit of prayer together!'" There is a volume contained in this single sentence, on the habit of devotion, which Samuel constantly carried about with him; and had it been a scene of real life, and himself one of the actors, he would have been seen sidling up to the sufferer, whether on the highway or at the market-cross, —afterward devoutly kneeling—and with uplifted hands and heart, pleading with the Most High for healing and strength.

His prayers were not restricted to man. He saw as great propriety in praying for the restoration of cattle that might be afflicted with any particular distemper, as in soliciting the divine blessing upon the fruits of the field, and the seasons of the year. Thus it was, on a particular occasion, that he associated his own horse with the cow of a friend, in his devotions, both of which were unwell;—in *every thing*, in supplication and prayer, making his request known to the Lord.

There were instances, however, of familiarity of expression, which, though not criminal in him, ought to be avoided; and also something in his manner, which was calculated to disturb the solemnities of domestic worship. He was in a friend's house, where he was introduced to the company of a minister, the Rev. A. L., who, he had heard, was paying his addresses to a young lady, and to Mr. U., a solicitor. On Mr. U.'s name and profession being announced, he looked askance at him, as upon an object for which he might be *charged* for the bestowment of a passing glance, quickly turning away his head, and muttering, "Hem, *a torney!*" He was soon absorbed in thought; and when urged to help himself to a glass of wine, he took it up, and, on applying it to his lip, as if the apparition of Mr. U. had shot quickly past him, he said, "From *tornies* and lawyers, good Lord, deliver us!" Mr. U., who knew to what reflections the profession was subject, avoided any observation. The case, however, was not dismissed: Samuel was called upon to go to prayer. After generalizing his petitions he took up each case separately, praying that Mr. A. L. might be happy enough to obtain "a good wife," as the marriage state was "the best." He next prayed for the *conversion* of Mr. U., saying, "Lord, save this *torney*. What he is thou knowest,—I know not; but when he is saved, he will not charge folk so much money for their jobs. Thou hast saved an attorney at Longpreston, and he gets as good a living as any of them. Lord, save this man." After this, he proceeded to pray for the family, mingling, as is too often the case, *rebuke, exhortation, &c.*, with prayer. This is not the most "excellent way:" besides, *cowards* very often avail themselves, under the guise of devotion, of letting off their bad feeling against their fellow Christians in this "way," by praying *at* them, instead of supplicating mercy *for* them. In Samuel, it was a weakness inseparable from his nature. Ill will had no place in him; and his native courage never failed him, as the following circumstance goes to prove.

A person of his own trade, who resided a few miles from Howden, entered the place where he was preaching, in a state of inebriation, and made some disturbance. Samuel, and some of the people, expostulated with him, but without effecting any good end. Finding that gentle means failed, he went up to him, and by his own masculine grasp, forced him to the door. But this, alas! was a greater expenditure of peace, than a display of strength. He felt "something wrong within," he observed, and could find no rest, on his return from worship. He made his case known to God, and wrestled—as though he had been the greater criminal of the two—till he recovered his peace. This being obtained, he retired to sleep. The subject, however, was not dismissed from his mind. When he rose in the morning, he found that he could not be perfectly composed in his spirit, till he went to the man, to ask pardon; for though he had settled the dispute between God and his conscience, he knew there was something due to the sinner, who might draw unfavourable inferences from his example. The man was ashamed of his conduct, and could not but admire the spirit of Samuel, who embraced the opportunity of seriously conversing with, and praying for him. Not only were good impressions made upon the mind of the aggressor, but his wife, who was under deep conviction of sin, entered, during that prayer, into the glorious liberty of the children of God.

When he only was concerned, and the interruption of others was out of the question, Samuel could, on the other hand, sustain any hardship, any insult, with exemplary meekness and forbearance; and his strongest graces were often put to the test. A young lady, who had been known to him from her childhood, and whose palfrey had lost a shoe, called at his shop to have it replaced. She appeared delicate. He looked compassionately upon her, and asked, "Dost thou know, *barn*, whether thou hast a soul?" Startled with the question, she looked in return; but before she was permitted to reply, he said, "Thou hast one, whether thou knowest it or not; and it will live in happiness or misery for ever." These, and other remarks, produced serious reflections. Her father perceived from her manner, on her return home—her residence being not far from Samuel's dwelling—that something was preying upon her spirits. She told him the cause: "What," he exclaimed, "has that old blacksmith been at thee, to turn thy head? but I will *whack* (beat) him." So saying, he took up a large stick, similar to a hedge-stake—left the house—posted off to Samuel's residence—found him at the anvil—and without the least intimation, fetched him a heavy blow on the side, which, said Samuel, when relating the circumstance, "nearly felled me to the ground," adding, "and it was not a little that would have done it in those days." On receiving the blow, he turned around, and said, "What art thou about, man? what is that for?" Supposing it to be out of revenge, and that religion was the cause of it, he made a sudden wheel, and lifting up his arm, inclined the other side to his enraged assailant, saying, "Here, man, hit that too." But either his courage failed him, or he was softened by the manner in which the blow was received; beholding in Samuel a real disciple of Him, who said, "Whosoever shall smite thee on the right cheek, turn to him the other also." He then left him; and Samuel had the happiness of witnessing the progress of religion in the daughter. Some time after this, the person himself was taken ill, and Samuel was sent for. He was shown into the chamber, and looking on the sick man, he asked, "What is the matter with thee? art thou *bown* to die?" He stretched out his arm to Samuel, and said, "Will you forgive me?" Not recollecting the circumstance for the moment, Samuel asked, "What for? I have nothing against thee, *barn*, nor any man living." The case being noticed, the question was again asked, "Will you forgive me?" "Forgive thee, *barn?* I tell thee I have nothing against thee! But if thou art about to die, we will pray a bit, and see if the Lord will forgive thee." Samuel knelt by the side of the couch, and the dying man united with him: and from the penitence, fervour, and gratitude which he manifested, there was hope in his death. The daughter continued an object of his solicitude; she grew up to womanhood,—became a mother,—and he afterward exulted to see her and two of her daughters members of the Wesleyan Society. Four conversions are here to be traced, in regular succession, and attributable apparently to a word fitly and seasonably spoken, by one of the *weak things* of this world, becoming mighty through God.

Samuel appeared, in many cases, to have the power of *accommodating* his *conduct* to the *characters* and *occasions* which demanded his attention, and that too in a way which his mental faculties would scarcely warrant; for while he would employ muscular force in a case where the intellect was inspired by the abuse of intoxicating liquors, and bear with meekness the arm of flesh upon himself, for righteousness' sake, he would at the same time defend himself against the tongue of slander, and subdue, by Christian means, any improper feeling he might perceive in the professors of Christianity themselves. A singular instance of self-defence occurred, in the course of one of his journeys. He was returning home by way of Aberford, in a stage coach. A clergyman, and some ladies of fashion, were his companions. They were on their way to the grand musical festival held in York Minster. The clergyman expatiated on the delights of the occasion, the innocence* of such enjoyments,

* An article in the Christian Observer of 1821, p. 250, of which the following is an extract, demands attention; and the more so, as, from the medium of publication, it shows the view which the evangelical part of his brethren take of the subject:

"It appears to me that it is not lawful for Christians to attend a concert of sacred music in a church for charitable purposes, either as respects the performances, the performers, or the place. Music is, *strictly speaking*, 'sacred' only when employed in the worship of God, of which the song of praise and thanksgiving forms one of the most delightful parts. Its animating and elevating influences many Christians can abundantly testify, who have sometimes, when joining a large congregation in one united chorus, been almost ready to imagine that they caught the faint echo of those immortal strains which cherubim and seraphim pour forth in honour of the celestial King. But of the performers of these public oratorios it seems almost impossible, even for that charity which hopeth all things, not to fear, that with them the prayer of penitence, or the glow of gratitude, the rapture of hope, or the triumph of faith, are nothing more than idle words—a solemn mockery of Him who demands the homage of the heart, and declares that he 'will not hold and the benevolence of the object. He observed, that he knew of no class of persons who would venture to hazard an objection against such amusements, except a few "canting Methodists." He then took occasion to launch out some violent invectives against the body, insisting on their incapacity to form a judgment in such cases, from the circumstance of the members belonging to the lowest classes

him guiltless that taketh his name in vain.' *Their* object is gain, and that of their auditors amusement.

"The worship of God is not for a moment in the thoughts of the assembly: yet for this express purpose, and this alone, was the house of God prepared. It is written in the Old Testament, and the obligation of the precept is confirmed by the authority of our Saviour in the New, 'My house shall be called of all nations a house of prayer:' and did he who once drove the buyers and sellers out of the Jewish temple now dwell among us in a human form, we can, I think, scarcely imagine that the votaries of pleasure would be regarded by him with a more lenient eye than the lovers of gain. To buy and sell is lawful, and so may music be; but it is not lawful to desecrate the sanctuary of God by applying it to any secular purpose whatever.

"To the inquiry, 'Is it lawful for Christians to attend a performance of music of a moral tendency, mixed with sacred or of sacred only, within the walls of a theatre?' I again answer, No. If in the former instance the performance be a profanation of the place, in this the performance is polluted by the place. And the most strenuous advocates for theatrical exhibitions cannot deny that they are inseparably attended by a fearful train of incidental evils, all of which remain in equally active and equally destructive operation, whether the audience be attracted by the genius of Handel or Shakspeare.

"The natural tendency of music is, to cheer the spirits when oppressed by study or fatigue, and to soothe the temper irritated by the little vexations of life. It supplies a never-failing source of innocent recreation, and generally proves an additional bond of family attachment. Every advantage, however, which music has to bestow, may be obtained in *private*. Should it therefore be conceded, that it of society, finally denouncing them as a set of hypocrites and vagabonds. Samuel, who had hitherto avoided obtruding his remarks upon the party, could brook it no longer. He considered himself implicated in the general charge, and his spirit rose indignantly at it: "Sir," said he, "I am a Methodist. I am going to the place where I was born, and where I am well known; and I will make you prove your words,

is *lawful* for Christians to attend the concerts of miscellaneous music performed in the Hanover-Square rooms or elsewhere, I think it must be maintained that it is by no means *expedient* to do so.

"If it be possible that these musical entertainments rank among those 'pomps and vanities' which we pledged ourselves by our baptismal covenant to renounce—if they have any tendency to make the every-day duties and occupations of life comparatively insipid—if by this indulgence we tread upon the frontier line which separates the lawful enjoyment from the unlawful compliance—if by thus advancing to the brink of a precipice, we become liable to fall headlong in some unguarded moment—or though we can tread the dizzy height in safety, should others, following our example, stumble and fall—where is the Christian that can hesitate an instant between the gratification of an hour and the risk of incurring any one of these awful possibilities? It is always dangerous to be conformed to this world—always safe to deny ourselves, to take up our cross and follow our Redeemer. It would be less inconsistent for the philosopher to covet the toys of infancy, than it is for the member of Christ, the child of God, and the inheritor of the kingdom of heaven, anxiously to desire even the most elegant and refined of the pleasures of sense. He should ever remember that he is not his own. His fortune, his time, his talents, his influence, his example, must all be devoted to the glory of God. Remembering the exhortation of our Lord, 'Watch and pray, lest ye enter into temptation,' he desires not to widen the narrow path which leadeth unto life eternal, but to obtain grace to pursue it with patient perseverance; knowing that so only shall 'an entrance be administered unto him abundantly of his Lord and Saviour Jesus Christ.'"

sir." The clergyman was a little confounded by this sudden burst of expression, and had no expectation of being so suddenly and unceremoniously subpœnaed to appear as a witness in his own defence. It was in vain to attempt the hackneyed method of parrying off the reflection by exempting the present company. The character of the body was as dear to Samuel as his own; and he continued to bore the reverend gentleman, till the coach stopped at the door of the inn at Aberford. The innkeeper was in immediate attendance, when Samuel and the clergyman alighted, the latter being little aware—as under a contrary impression he would have probably retained his inside berth—that the subject would be again agitated. Samuel accosted the master of the house, with no common earnestness and gesticulation, saying, "You know me, don't you?" and before he had time to receive a distinct reply in the affirmative, pressed nearly into the same breath, the grand question, of which the other was only the precursor,—"Am I a hypocrite or a vagabond?" "No, Samuel," was the reply: "you are known all around here, as an honest, hard-working man." To this Samuel responded, "I work for all I have, pay every body their own, and get nothing for preaching." He then pointed to the clergyman, and recapitulated what he had said. The innkeeper, not knowing the cause of Samuel's interrogatories before, and seeing a probable customer in the clergyman, was not very anxious to proceed with his answers; and the clergyman, unwilling to confirm his delinquency by retiring, stood a short time. Samuel's earnest appeals in the mean time attracted attention; the people thickened around them, in front of the inn; he proceeded to dwell on the charges, and to point to the clergyman, as going to spend his time and his money at the concert. The clergyman found himself so much annoyed by the looks, the jokes, and remarks of the crowd, who encouraged Samuel in his zeal for character, that he was glad when the horses were changed, and he found himself safely seated by the side of the ladies, reaping instruction, no doubt, from the event, though not much enamoured with the uncourteous manner in which his fellow-traveller had defended himself.

Though the clergyman's opinion of the low-bred character of the Methodists was not likely to be much improved by the specimen with which he had just been favoured, yet it was only the rougher side of Samuel's integrity of which he had a view, and which his own rasping had raised. Samuel was much better qualified to repress and correct improper *feeling*, than to combat erroneous notions. He attended a lovefeast in the Wakefield circuit, when Mr. Bradburn was stationed there. Several of the good people were in the habit of giving out a verse of a hymn before they narrated their Christian experience, by way of tuning their spirits for the work. This was prohibited by Mr. Bradburn, not only as a reflection upon himself, being both authorized and competent to conduct the service, but as an improper appropriation of the time which was set apart for *speaking*. Samuel, either forgetting the prohibition, or being too warm to be restrained within its limits, gave out a verse. Mr. Bradburn was instantly in his majesty, and with one of his severest and worst faces, looked at Samuel, who stood up in the congregation and sung alone, no one daring to join him—prefacing his rebuke with one of his singularly extravagant remarks,—"Where is the person that would not come out of a red hot oven, to hear such a man as you sing?" then proceeding to make such observations as he thought proper. Samuel, supposing the rebuke to have been given in an improper spirit, went into the vestry after service to settle matters. Offering to shake hands with Mr. B., who was not in one of his most complacent moods, he was saluted with—"What, are you the man that persisted in singing, after I peremptorily forbid it?" "Ye—ye—yes, sir," said Samuel; "but I hope you will forgive me, Mr. Bradburn:" and without waiting to see how the request was taken, he was in an instant upon his knees among the people. Those around followed his example, and last of all, Mr. B. knelt by his side, who found that it would scarcely look decorous to stand alone. Every heart was touched with Samuel's simplicity and fervour; and when he concluded prayer, Mr. B., with a full heart, and with all the magnanimity and generous flow of spirit he possessed, stretched out his hand, familiarly saying, "There, my brother; this is the way—to keep paying off as we go on."

Though he often overcame opposing feelings by prayer, for which he was better qualified than for holding a long parley on opinion; yet on subjects proposed by a querist, he would change two or three sharp rounds on a controverted point. "I have often been struck," says Mr. Dawson, "at the promptness and propriety of his replies to persons who have proposed objections and questions to him upon particular subjects, and in peculiar cases. He manifested some astonishing gleams of sanctified satire, when directed to a person or a subject, which penetrated deep into the heart; while sparkles of holy wit would touch the risible faculties, and thrill a delight through the soul of the hearer, which neither debased his understanding nor his affections. A ray of light would sometimes dart from him in a moment, which would instantly scatter the shades and remove the scruples from an inquiring mind. Of this peculiarity of talent he himself was insensible: all was spontaneous and natural." While this citation comes in as evidence of what has been stated, it may be further illustrated by other striking instances of quickness of perception, discrimination, and point.

Having business to transact which bore hard upon his patience, and seeing the person who was agent for him in the transaction going about with the utmost deliberation, with countenance and temper as serene as the unruffled lake, he seemed uncomfortable in the presence of such superiority; and yet, unwilling to unchristianize himself, as well as sensible of the kindly feeling he possessed toward the persons who were the occasion of his exercises, he said, "We are both perfect; you are *perfect* in *patience*, and I am *perfect* in *love*." Though the theology of this is questionable, as a general position, yet in its particular application to Samuel, there is more truth in it than at first might appear; for if he excelled in any one branch of "the fruit of the Spirit," it was in love.

To a gentleman labouring under great nervous depression, whom he had visited, and who was moving along the streets as though he was apprehensive that every step would shake his system in pieces, he was rendered singularly useful. They met; and Samuel, having a deeper interest in the soul than the body, asked, "Well, how are you getting on your way to heaven?" The poor invalid, in a dejected, half-desponding tone, replied, "But slowly, I fear;" intimating that he was creeping along only at a snail's pace. "Why, bless you, *barn*," returned Samuel, "there were snails in the ark." The reply was so earnest, so unexpected, and met the dispirited man so immediately on his own ground, that the temptation broke away, and he rose out of his depression. It was a resurrection to his feelings; inferring, that if the snail reached the ark, he too, "faint, yet pursuing," might gain admission into heaven.

Perhaps one of his happiest conquests in oral controversy was obtained over the Rev. —— K., of Leeds, a gentleman of great shrewdness and learning. They were both on board a Selby steam-packet, going down the river toward Hull. Samuel was walking the deck, and humming over a hymn-tune, which appeared to attract the attention of Mr. K., who abruptly opened out upon him on the evils of Methodism, suspecting him to belong to that body, from the character of the music. He insisted on the mischief it had done by the tenets it propagated, particularly instancing the doctrine of *sanctification*, for which, he contended, there was no foundation. Though Samuel did not appear to be personally known to Mr. K., yet Mr. K. was not unknown to him; to whom he instantly returned, "See that you never read the Church Prayers again, for I am sure there is *full sanctification* in them." "No such thing," was the reply. "What," said Samuel, "do you not pray that the Lord would *cleanse* the *thoughts* of the *heart* by the *inspiration* of the Holy Spirit? See that you do not read that, sir, next Sunday." Mr. K. finding himself pressed from this high quarter, and partly conceding the principle, by flying to what he deemed its effects, asked, "What good has the doctrine done?" gliding, as a diversion of the subject, into the general topic of Methodism again; demanding, "What have the Methodists effected? Bad women are on the increase; Leeds is swarming with them." "How is that?" inquired Samuel: "I was in Leeds the other week, and never met with one." "I know," rejoined Mr. K., "that there never were so many as there are at present." "Happen so," replied Samuel, as though he had reached the end of both his patience and his thoughts: "it may be that you are better acquainted with them than me, sir." This was *quantum sufficit*, and Mr. K. left him to hum over his tune to the remainder of the hymn. Pungent, however, as the last remark may have seemed, it would have been found, if Samuel had been interrogated upon it, that there was as much of concession intended for superior knowledge, as there was of any indirect reflection upon moral character; and ten minutes would scarcely have elapsed, till—from other subjects occupying his thoughts—he would have been as insensible to what had passed as though he had never exchanged a syllable with the gentleman that spoke to him.

Singing was one of his favourite employments, both in company and alone. Engaged thus, as he was riding along the road once, in company with Mr. Dawson, and another friend or two, he seemed lost occasionally to the society of his fellow-travellers. He had got hold of a tune which was in use among the *Ranters*, so called. This he continued to hum over, in the same way as when he walked the deck, exclaiming at short intervals, "Bless the Lord for a fine shower!" The rain continued more copious in its descent;—his companions buttoned up, and turned their sides to the weather, sinking the lower part of the face into the collars of their coats ;—Samuel sung on, sensible only of his mercies, again exclaiming, "Bless the Lord for a fine shower!" One of his companions, as much annoyed with the tune as by the rain, objected to it as an indifferent one. "Sing a better, then," said Samuel, turning his head as suddenly from him as he had directed it toward him, still singing and keeping time to the amble of the horse, facing the weather, and praising the Lord for watering the earth. The friend again complained of the tune, and again solicited another. "Sing yourself," said Samuel. "I have no voice for the work," was the reply. "Don't complain," rejoined Samuel, "of what you cannot mend," again directing his face to the shower, and his mind to the Giver of it, absent every now and then to all companionship, and as happy, though saturated with the teeming contents of the clouds, as if he had been sheltered under his own roof.

Though he possessed the power of occasionally accommodating himself to existing circumstances, and particular companies, isolated instances occurred, when he was perfectly lost to the respect due to the habits and feelings of others. He was led by inclination to a public meeting of the Society of Friends, and took his seat in the midst of them. This was an ordinance, and an assembly, for which he was the least fitted, either by nature or by habit; and although he had often sung—

> "A solemn reverence checks our songs,
> And praise sits silent on our tongues,"

he never till now knew what it was to live under the *restraint* of praise. "The songs of Zion" were in his heart, in which he was singing, and making melody to the Lord, as many of the worshippers around him might have been employed: but having read of Paul and Silas, under less agreeable circumstances, adding to the music of the *heart* the variations of the *voice* and the motion of the *lips*—rising in their strains till "the prisoners heard them," and embracing the notion that praise only receives its perfection in utterance, he either so far forgot himself, or was otherwise glowing with such an intensity of feeling while musing, that the long silence observed in the commencement became insupportable. He took his hymn-book from his pocket, and starting on his feet—his huge figure receiving elevation from the seated and lowering position of those around him, said, "Come, let us sing a verse or two." Neither the voice nor the language belonged to the place; a number of eyes were instantly fixed upon him; and strange feelings were stirring, till a venerable man arose, who knew him, and accosted him, saying, "Samuel, sit thee down, and *wait*." The mandate was obeyed, without reply or murmur; and all was suddenly as still as before. After waiting some time in silence, during almost every minute of which Samuel expected some one to rise and address the assembly, but no attempt being made, he again bounded from his seat, under an impression that prayer might be more acceptable than praise, and said, "Let us kneel down, friends, and pray a bit." Just as he was in the attitude of kneeling, the same venerable man stood up, and with great solemnity again addressed him, "Samuel, sit thee down, and wait till the SPIRIT *moves* thee." Less docile than before, Samuel returned, "We Methodists think it very well, if we can have the Spirit for *asking*;" referring with great readiness to that passage of Scripture, "If ye then, being evil, know how to give good gifts unto your children: how much more shall your heavenly Father give the Holy Spirit to them that ask him?" Though Samuel was correct in doctrine, he was *here* erroneous in conduct, and had forgotten his own dislike of interruptions in divine service, when worshipping God agreeably to the dictates of his conscience, under his own "vine, and under his fig-tree."

CHAPTER IX.

His self-denial—Sympathy for the poor—Gratitude for mercies—Early rising—Singular band-meeting—The best way of beginning the day—His conduct in the families he visited—Bolton—Ratcliffe Close—Often abrupt in his manners—His views of proprietorship—A genuine Wesleyan—An attempt to purchase him—His character as the head of a family—Gives up business—Preaching excursions—Visits Rigton—Providential supply—His public addresses—Delight in his work—E. Brook, Esq.—Denby Dale—Prosperity of the work of God—A new chapel—Samuel visits Rochdale—Rises superior to his exercises—takes a tour into different parts of Lancashire—Great commercial distress—Liberality of P. E. Towneley, Esq.—Meeting for the relief of the poor—Samuel's return home—Visits different parts of the York circuit—Revival of religion—Persecution.

As Samuel had obtained the grace which enabled him to "rejoice evermore," he seemed to create a paradise in every circle in which he moved. Whenever he was oppressed—which was rarely the case—it was either on account of the wants and miseries of others, or occasioned by an overwhelming sense of his own mercies. Thus, on being urged to take more food at table, he has been heard to say, in seasons of commercial and agricultural distress, "O no: I cannot take more while I think of so many around me nearly starving for want of bread."

So, also, on being entertained out of the ordinary line, in the house of a friend, his gratitude, like the thermometer, rose to the highest point. He was at Pontefract during the bustle of an election, and was lodged in the house of

Mr. M., a member of the Society of Friends, whose family was strongly attached to Samuel. He was honoured with the best fare, the best room, and the best bed, the last of which was unusually high. On being asked the next day, how he liked his lodgings, he said, "Why, *barn*, I have been crying half the night; I never was in such a bed before; I had to take a chair to get into it. O how I wept; for I thought my Lord never had such a bed as *that*." This was properly "the joy of grief." Samuel dwelt much upon his Saviour; the "*servant*" and the "*Lord*" afforded him some amazing contrasts, and drew forth the finest feelings of his soul.

But he had his "songs in the night," and his morning carols, as well as his tears. "He was in the habit," Mr. Dawson observes, "of rising very early in the morning, (about four o'clock,) and of partially dressing himself, when he bowed his knees before his divine Father, praying first for the church in general, next for particular characters, and lastly for special cases. He then sung a verse of a hymn—retired to bed again—and after a short time arose, and began the day with praise and prayer." The occasion of this systematic proceeding is known to few. Samuel had a *band-mate*, with whom he met for some time, and to whom he was much endeared. Four o'clock in the morning was the hour of meeting; and this was selected, not only because of its tranquillity, but because it prevented self-indulgence. His companion died, and he mourned his loss like the stock-dove, whose mate had just sat by his side on the same bough, and had dropped off through the hand of the fowler. The hour and the ordinance were held sacred by the survivor. He rose at the appointed time—sung—prayed—unfolded the secrets of his heart to God, as he was wont to do with his Christian friend—thus going regularly through the service, as though the dead were still alive, and by his side, holding converse with him. This is one of those mementos of Christian friendship which rarely occur in the same form; but while its singularity excites the surprise of some, its piety will secure the admiration of others, and amply atone for any peculiarity in its manner. Those, only, perhaps, will indulge the laugh, who, nevertheless, have their *anniversaries, &c.*, but support them in another way, by toasting each other over the maddening bowl, and cheering each other with the speech and the song, till they become objects of pity, rather than subjects for imitation.

The summary account of his matins, as given by Mr. Dawson, is exemplified by a particular case, as recorded by the family of P. Rothwell, Esq., of Sunning Hill, Bolton, in whose house Samuel at one time resided for the space of nearly three weeks. "He frequently rose," it is remarked, "in the night to pray. On one of those occasions he was heard singing a hymn, after which he pleaded with God that he might enjoy a closer walk with Jesus, and his prayer was soon turned into praise. He repeated several times, 'O that I could praise thee! O that I could praise thee as I would!—but I shall praise thee again when I pass over Jordan! Glory! glory! glory!' He then prayed for his family, the family he was visiting, the church of God, and for the world at large. He appeared to feel much while pleading for sinners, and then was borne away in transport for redeeming mercy. Some time after he rose from his knees, his language was, 'Glory! glory!'" He has been known on some of these occasions to indulge in a sublimity of thought of which at other times he was incapable, and which—taken in connection with the whole man would have fixed upon him, by some gifted beings, had they overheard him, much more appropriately than ever was applied to Goldsmith, the epithet of "an inspired idiot," and he would have stood a fair chance of being deified among the Mohammedans.

Such a beginning was an excellent preparation for the duties, the exercises, and the mercies of the day; and it will be generally found, that its close will correspond with its commencement. The man who permits God to *hear* his *voice* in the *morning* will not himself be silent, nor yet mourn an absent God in the evening. These "morning communings" secured attention to "stated times" for retirement through the day, when he entered into his closet before his Father, who sees in secret, and rewards openly; and this is the secret of that charm which was thrown around his spirit and demeanour in social life. He came forth in the morning, like the sun from his chambers in the east—refreshed and refreshing. Happy in himself, he chased away melancholy from the soul, and lighted up a sunshine in the countenances of those with whom he conversed. "No family," said a friend, in whose house he had been resident some weeks—"No family could be miserable with whom he lived, because he laboured to make every person around him happy." Mrs. Bealey, of Ratcliffe Close, near Bury, in Lancashire, a lady well qualified to appreciate real worth, whether religious, moral, or intellectual, and under whose hospitable roof Samuel was entertained nearly two months, observed to Mr. Dawson, "That he interested himself in the welfare of the whole family, as though he had been united to them by the tender ties of nature. He participated in all their pleasures, as well as increased them, and was rendered truly useful to the men and children employed in the works. He sympathized also with persons with whom he was acquainted, in their losses in cattle or trade, as though he had been the loser himself." It was the love and joy within, which, as is remarked elsewhere by Mr. Dawson, "gave a beam to his eye, a smile to his countenance, a tone to his voice, and an energy to his language, which melted and attracted every heart that came within the sphere of his influence."

This attractive influence was not always sudden, but it was rarely otherwise than certain. On his first visit to the residence of a gentleman in Lancashire, to whom till then he was personally unknown, he was directed to the house accidentally. He rode up to the door of that gentleman, and after having seen his horse put under the care of his servant, he entered the house, where he was introduced into the parlour. Without either letter or person to introduce him, and with no other passport than the connection of the family with the Wesleyan body, he took his seat in the domestic circle, where he sat, unconscious as innocence or infancy of any other prerequisite for social enjoyment, than the religion of his Saviour. The habits of the gentleman, and the society in which he moved, rendered him at first uncomfortable; and he was equally at a loss to know what to do with, and what to make of, his new and unexpected guest. A short interlude assisted in relieving the first feeling. The sitting-room door was opened, and a person stepped in, with whom the master of the house had to transact a little business. Samuel's presence added to the poignancy of his more delicate feelings. However, he was *there*, and the person was at liberty to suppose, if he judged proper, that Samuel was on business as well as himself. He sat in silence, and appeared to take no notice of either party. When the transaction was closed, and the person rose to retire, Samuel started on his feet, as though he had been awakened from a trance, "Stop, sir, let us pray a bit before you go: you seem full of the world, and we'll try to get it out of your heart." This rendered the occasion of his visit desperate; and nothing but violence could be done to the feelings of his host to render such conduct supportable. But there was no time for excuse or remonstrance; Samuel's voice was the warning clock—no sooner heard, than on his knees. The effect of this may be as readily conceived as expressed. Yet notwithstanding the coy beginning on the part of the gentleman, he was soon led to place the highest value on Samuel's piety and presence, and continued to entertain both man and horse for some time; and so much regard did his homely visiter gain from himself and his family, that they parted with sincere regret.

Even in families where religion was not professed, his simplicity of manner, and general good character, gained him unhesitating access. When the Rev. A. Learoyd was on the Knaresborough circuit, he went to preach at a neighbouring village, and on entering the house of a friend, he found Samuel seated, who had just arrived. "Where have you put your horse, Samuel?" inquired Mr. L. "I have left it at the other end of the village," was the reply; adding, "will you go with me to the house?" Mr. L. being aware that the family had no connection with the Wesleyan body, asked, "Why did you go there?" "I saw plenty of hay, and good stables," returned Samuel, "and I thought it would be a good home for Jackey." The singularity of the visit led Mr. L. to accede to his wishes; and on being seated in the family circle, Samuel proceeded to interrogate his host on the state of his soul. Considerable fluency characterized the replies: but Samuel, being suspicious that very little religion was enjoyed, proceeded to speak more plainly, exhorting him to apply to Christ for converting grace. The word of exhortation was well received, and he was pressed to remain the night with them: the invitation was accepted, and he acted the part of a *priest* in the family. "Let me," said he to the servant-maid, "have a dry bed;" and to the servant-man, "You must give Jackey plenty to eat:—take good care of him, for he is the Lord's horse;—the hay and the corn are the Lord's also." Abrupt as was his introduction here, and little as such freedoms are to be recommended, either in Samuel himself or as examples for others, yet the family were much pleased with his visit. Such *leadings* and movements, in irrational creatures, would be attributed to *instinct;* but Samuel was *girded* and *carried* often, like Peter when he was old, by "another" than himself; and he was more indebted to the Spirit and providence of God for his introduction and reception than either to his sagacity or the formalities of modern manners.

His representation of "the hay and the corn," as belonging to the Supreme Being, arose from a settled principle in his creed, and included a certain exclusiveness, not generally recognized by the professors of Christianity.

His own crops were viewed in the same light; and his mind was so imbued with this notion, that all delegated or personal right, in reference to man, seemed frequently annihilated. He was going to preaching one sabbath morning, when he was met by a person who knew his regard for the sanctity of that day. There had been a great deal of rain, which proved fatal to the "*line*" or flax crops. The following is the purport of what passed between them on the road:—

Neighbour. "Where are you going, Sammy?"

Samuel. "To preaching."

Neigh. "More need you get your line in, now that God is giving you fine weather."

Sam. "He does not give fine weather for us to break the sabbath."

Neigh. "Why, you see others making hay while the sun shines: they will get their line in to-day, and yours, if you let it lie till to-morrow, and it should be wet, will be spoiled."

Sam. "I have none to spoil, *barn*."

Neigh. "Is not yon, lying down (pointing to it) yours?"

Sam. "No."

Neigh. "What, is not yon your close?"

Sam. "No, it is the Lord's: he has a right to do with it what he likes; and if he have a mind to spoil it, he may: it is his own, and no one has any business to quarrel with him for it. It is the Lord's day too, and I will give it to him."

A brief dialogue, also involving the same

principle, took place in the neighbourhood of Ferry Bridge, when Samuel was journeying from thence homeward. A gentleman was passing with a little boy, and having his attention drawn to some sheep that were grazing in a field adjoining the road, he accosted Samuel:

Gentleman. "Do you know, my good man, to whom those sheep belong?"

Samuel. "My Lord, sir."

Gent. "They are very fine ones; I do not recollect ever having seen their equal."

Sam. "They are a fine breed, sir."

Gent. "I thought they might probably belong to Mr. Alderson, of Ferry Bridge."

Sam. "No, sir, they belong to my Lord; don't you know, that the earth is the Lord's, and the fulness thereof; and that the cattle upon a thousand hills are his?"

Gent. "You are right—you are right, old man."

Samuel's reply would have been a mere play upon words in the mouth of many other persons; but he was sincere; and the gentleman's attention was suddenly and unexpectedly elevated from earth to heaven, without his being offended by the manner in which it was done.

With regard to "Jackey," who occupied such a prominent place in Samuel's esteem, and who is only noticed as bearing upon his master's history, it may be remarked, that on one occasion Samuel displayed a feeling respecting the treatment of the animal, which was not at all common to him. One of the young men belonging to a family at whose house he stopped, withheld the meat from "Jackey," and otherwise failed in his attention as groom. It came to Samuel's knowledge, and for a considerable length of time he utterly refused to go near the place again. In process of time he went back, but he would never take his favourite with him; thus showing, that while he entertained no resentment—by his own return—the only feeling remaining was that of distrust in reference to his horse.

Wherever Wesleyan Methodism was respected, Samuel was sure to be loved. He was a genuine believer in its doctrines, a living witness of its experimental truths, an example of its purest morals, a firm supporter of its discipline, and a warm friend of its ministers. Of the latter, he ever spoke with respect and affection; and if his holy indignation was at any time kindled, it was when persons endeavoured to lower their character, by cold oblique hints, in the eyes of the world, and when an apparent delight was taken in sowing discord among brethren. Satisfied with his privileges, he avoided such as were given to change. He was accustomed to say, "I am determined to remain in the *old ship*. She has carried thousands across the ocean, and landed them safe in glory; and if I stay in her, she will carry me there too."* Speaking once of a person

* Samuel was not without his inducements to leave the body. Mr. Sigston, who has taken such a prominent part in the late division at Leeds, became offended in 1803, and

who had acted in the capacity of a local preacher, but had afterward united himself to another society, he resorted to his favourite figure of the "*old ship*," and inquired why he had left *her*, after she had borne him so long in safety? The simile was taken up by the other, who intimated that she was in danger of foundering. Samuel returned, "You should not have been such a coward as to leave her, but should have remained on board, either to help to mend her, or prevent her from going to the bottom. But you have forsaken an old friend; I know she is sound at heart, and as safe as ever." "My wife and I," said he to another person, "are sailing together in her. Some of our children are with us; we are getting stronger;" and then, with a fine glow of feeling, would exclaim, "We shall all sail to heaven together—I know we shall." This figurative mode of expression was rendered very popular in a sermon preached

formed a small society, whose members received the appellation of Sigstonites. They held their meetings in a room which was taken for the purpose in Kirkgate. The head of this small party was known by a few of the friends belonging to the Pontefract circuit, among whom two exhorters, and two accredited local preachers, espoused his cause, the latter of whom were never very remarkable for submitting to rule. These took with them about thirty members of the society, and occupied a school-room in Knottingly, erected about ten yards from the Methodist chapel, by a person who, though not in society, took unspeakable pleasure in promoting the division. Samuel was earnestly importuned to unite himself to the Knottingly dissentients, and was told, as an inducement, that he should have a certain sum presented to him as a compensation for his labours, wherever he preached. It argued an ignorance of Samuel's character to think that he was to be bought by gold.

by the late Rev. Joseph Benson, on schism, about the time of Mr. Kilham's defection from the body; and it was one of those figures which Samuel could work without much danger of being wrecked in its management.

The religion which he carried into the families of others, and recommended in his public walks, was not without its influence at home. Though Martha and he could not always see eye to eye, in money affairs—and it was fortunate for him that they could not—yet he was an affectionate *husband*, as well as a tender *father*. He moved before his family more, perhaps, in the character of a *priest*, to *pray* for them, than a *prophet* and a *king*, to *instruct* and *govern*. He was fitted for the one rather than the other; and such was his attention to the FAMILY ALTAR, such his prevalent intercession before it, that his incapacity for the two latter appeared to be greatly counterbalanced by the hallowed character of the former. He bore his partner and his children constantly before God, in the arms of faith and prayer, and lived in full confidence that the whole would be saved. If any of his opinions, more than others, bordered upon extravagance, it was upon the certain salvation of the children of praying parents. The possibility of perdition, in the case of any of them, was beyond endurance.

Though he took excursions to different places, from the period of his becoming a local preacher, yet it was not till the latter part of 1825, or

14

the beginning of 1826, when he gave up business, that he took a more extensive range, and considered himself as doing the work, and therefore entitled to the name and honours of a HOME MISSIONARY. He was then possessed of what he deemed sufficient for the support of himself and his aged partner, during the evening of life. Being now at liberty from the trammels of business, he was invited into several circuits in Yorkshire and Lancashire, all of which he visited, preaching in the different towns and villages, and in many of which he was not only useful in the conversion of sinners, but in raising pecuniary supplies for the support of foreign missions, the erection and relief of places of worship.

While gratifying the benevolent feelings of his heart, in obeying the calls of the people, he not unfrequently suffered various inconveniences, notwithstanding the kindness of friends. An instance which occurred a short time prior to this part of his history, but which it would not be well to omit, betokening great absence of mind on the part of the persons on the spot, presents him under very unpleasant circumstances. He attended a missionary meeting at Rigton in the Forest, a place belonging to the Otley circuit, about three or four miles from Harrowgate. "We had a blessed meeting," said Samuel: "I was very happy, and gave all the money I had in my pocket." After the meeting was concluded, he mounted his horse to return home. And in what aspect is he to be viewed? Without any one offering to pay his expenses—not the value of a farthing in his pocket—advanced in life—a slow rider, and not a very sprightly horse—near the end of October, when the season was breaking up—in the night—alone—and about twenty miles from his own house. He became the subject of temptation. It was suggested—"No money to procure a feed of corn for thy horse, or refreshment for thyself—and friends who might receive thee are gone to bed!" The struggle was short; and the victory was obtained in his own way. Satan found no place in him for either repining or distrust. "I shaped him his answer," observed Samuel, "and said, 'Devil, I never *stack* fast yet.'" With his confidence invigorated by a recollection of past mercy, his happiness returned, and he remained the only nightingale of Christianity on the road, till he reached the village of Harewood. Then a gentleman who knew him took his horse by the bridle, and asked him where he had been. He gave him, in reply, an account of the meeting; from which the gentleman glided into the subject of his temporal concerns, in order to ascertain apparently how far a report was correct, which he had heard respecting some property out of which Samuel had been wronged. Samuel told him that he had "had two thousand pounds left" to him, but had "been deprived of it."* "I am very sorry for you," was the re-

* The report heard by the one, and the language employed by the other, would scarcely comport with the subject, if

joinder. Samuel replied, "Though I have been deprived of this, it has never deprived me of an hour's sleep. I never had a worse lot for it. I have not wanted for any good thing, and could always say with Job, 'The Lord gave, and the Lord taketh away: blessed be the name of the Lord.' Though he took Job's, he has not taken the whole of my property: I still have all my children." The gentleman asked, "Can you read?" "Yes," returned Samuel, "if I had my spectacles out of my pocket." "There," replied the gentleman, holding a piece of paper in his hand, which was rendered visible by the glimmering light of the stars—"There is a five pound note for you. You love God and his cause; and I believe you will never want." Samuel's eyes were instantly filled with tears, and his heart with gratitude. "Here," said he, "I saw the salvation of God. I cried for joy all the way as I went down the lonesome lanes; and when I got to a public house, I asked the landlord if he could change me a five-pound bill; for I told him I could not have any thing for myself or

applied to a particular event which took place. Martha's brother, who had a considerable sum of money on interest in Royd's Iron Works, near Leeds, expressed a wish to live and die with Samuel; proposing to allow the interest for his maintenance during life, and the principal at his death. The proposal was accepted—her brother resided with them—the Company at the Iron Works failed—the whole of the property was swept away—Samuel's hopes were blighted, yet he generously kept him in his own house till the day of his death, and thus prevented what must otherwise inevitably have ensued—his going to the workhouse.

my horse, unless he could change it. He said he could, if it were a good one. So I got off my horse, and ordered him a good feed of corn, and had some refreshment for myself. This was a fair salvation from the Lord. When I got home, I told my wife; she *brast* (burst) into tears; and we praised the Lord together." This was viewed by Samuel somewhat in the light of a triumph over Martha, who had chided him in the morning for taking so much money from home with him, to a missionary meeting, to which he gave his time, his labours, and expenses. He therefore added, by way of making his path more open to the purse in future, "You see, we never give to the Lord, but he gives in return."

His addresses in the pulpit rarely extended beyond half an hour. This afforded time to engage in the work which was his favourite employment—*a prayer meeting;* and these meetings furnished him very often with a knowledge of the progress of the word of life, as the benefits received under preaching were more fully developed in them, as well as cherished by the intercessory prayers of the faithful. Having the unction of the Holy One—an anointing which he received from him that abode in him—he was enabled to proceed in the work with cheerfulness, and very often carried with him a commanding authority over the feelings and conduct of others. He was frequently under high excitation; so much so, indeed, as sometimes to overpower his physical energies. "O," said he to his friend Mr. D. once, after a missionary meeting at Howden, in which he had pleaded the cause of the heathen on the platform, till he was nearly exhausted—"O," said he, "I am so happy. I shall surely die some of these times!" On another occasion, when at Pontefract, he remarked to a friend, after the meeting, with ecstatic feeling, and in his own peculiarly expressive language, "I felt as though I should have *swelted* (melted) away to heaven." This is no common thought—not even to be exceeded by Pope's "DYING CHRISTIAN," whom he represents as *languishing into life.* It is only in cases like this that we feel the force of Coleridge's remark in the motto selected for the memoir; and feel, too, a disposition to subscribe to the sentiments of a critic, in a number of Blackwood's Magazine, where he observes, "That the knowledge that shone but by fits and dimly upon the eyes of Socrates and Plato, whose eyes rolled in vain to find the light, has descended into various lands as well as our own—even into the huts where poor men lie; and thoughts are familiar there, beneath the low and smoky roof, higher and more sublime than ever flowed from the lips of a Grecian sage, meditating among the magnificence of his pillared temples." Though the expression, "pleading the cause of the heathen," may be a little too argumentative in its character, when applied to the speeches and addresses of the "Village Blacksmith," and may excite the laugh in those who employ the *head*, to the exclusion of the *heart*, in such work ; yet Samuel's honest and pathetic appeals very often touched the feelings and raised the "cash accounts"—raised perhaps with a smile—when the dull spirits, sapless speeches, and tedious readings of those who could see a greater curse in a little incoherence and hilarity than in lukewarmness, produced only listlessness and a yawn.

A still more expressive sentiment was employed by him, when preaching once in his own neighbourhood, on "The Spirit and the bride say, Come. And let him that heareth say, Come. And let him that is athirst come. And whosoever will, let him take the water of life freely." He expatiated on the value and uses of water, as far as common observation allowed him to proceed,—passing from that element to the "water of life," which formed the prominent feature of his text,—urging the freedom with which it was offered,—and finally impressing his hearers with the importance of the subject. He told them, in speaking of its value, that he himself was unacquainted with it,—that he doubted whether any of his hearers knew how to appreciate it,—that he doubted whether there was a person upon the face of the earth who knew its worth,—nay, further, that he did not believe an angel in heaven could enter into its merit,—that, in short, he never heard of but one who knew its real value, and "that was the rich man in hell, who would have given a world for a drop of it." The climacterical manner in which he thus worked his way up to the point which he wished to gain—like St. Paul's light afflictions and eternal weight of glory—the amazing contrast between a world and a drop—that drop solicited by a tongue of fire—and the eternal destinies of his hearers suspended on their acceptance of offered grace, to prevent the untimely knowledge of its worth by its loss in perdition, would have done honour to the first orators, in the best days of classic Greece and Rome.

During some of his moments of inspiration, he would manifest considerable impatience, when he was likely to be deprived of an opportunity of giving vent to the overflowings of his mind. A speaker at a missionary meeting, who prosed a good deal, inflicted a heavy punishment upon him in this way. Long before he had concluded, Samuel appeared extremely uneasy. "Sit still, Sammy," said the chairman in an under tone, being near him, and on terms of intimacy. "He is too long by the half," returned Samuel. After sitting awhile, with his hands clenched, and fixed between his knees, as in a vice, he again manifested symptoms of restlessness; when again the chairman endeavoured quietly to impose silence, and inspire a little long-suffering. Various rounds were exchanged between them, one requesting the other to "be still," and the other requesting that the speaker, who was unconscious of what was passing in the rear, might be told to "give over." The good brother continued prosing, without the least sign of coming, in any moderate length of time, to a close. Samuel, at length, started up—who, by the way, spoke only the feelings of others, who possessed more self-command and prudence, though less courage, and said, turning to the chairman, "Sir, that brother does not love his neighbour as himself; he does not take the Scriptural rule of doing to others as he would that others should do to him, for he will let no body speak but himself." Here the business dropped between the parties; the speaker being left to take the credit of having pleased all except Samuel, and Samuel brushed up his better feelings to engage the attention of the people during the few moments allotted to him, as the seconder of the resolution. Being coupled on another occasion with a popular speaker, Samuel turned to him, and said, "They have paired us like rabbits."

The Rev. J. Roadhouse, having heard either that he had actually declined business, or was on the eve of it, invited him, in the beginning of October, 1825, to pay the friends a visit at Cross Hills, a place in the Addingham circuit. A few weeks passed over, and not having heard from Samuel, the invitation began to wear away from recollection. About the middle of November, Samuel one day unexpectedly made his appearance, mounted on "Jackey." The latter was cheerfully provided for by a friend, and Samuel took up his abode with Mr. Roadhouse. He generally accompanied Mr. R. to the different places of preaching—commenced the service with singing and prayer—spoke from ten to twenty minutes—and then gave place to Mr. R. to conclude the service. On one of these occasions, he broke off his address rather abruptly, and suddenly stepping back in the pulpit, said, "Brother R. will now preach to you, for two sermons are better than one." A good feeling having been excited, Mr. R. commenced his address, by an allusion to the words of the Jewish monarch, "What shall the man do who cometh after the king?" Samuel, before any application could be made, exclaimed, "Do! you will do well enough, only go on." The service terminated much better than this unexpected interlude at first promised. Two persons were deeply affected with his public address; and at another place five persons were brought to a state of penitence.

The great commercial depression which distinguished the close of this year was just beginning to be experienced. Many of the poor people in Addingham and its neighbourhood sold part of their furniture, and whatever they could spare of other things, in order to procure food. Samuel visited them; and after having given all the money away which he had deemed sufficient for his journey, a poor boy entered the door-way of a house where he was sitting. The weather was cold, and the boy was without neckerchief. Samuel pitied him—asked for a pair of scissors—took his handkerchief from his own pocket—cut it into halves—and tied one of them around the neck of the poor little fellow—rejoicing in the opportunity afforded of clothing the naked.

He remained here nearly three weeks; and just as he was leaving Mr. Roadhouse, to proceed to his friends at Grassington, he thanked him for his kindness toward him, and then with tears said, "You must let me have some money to pay the toll bars, and get Jackey a feed of corn." Till now, Mr. R. was not aware that he was pennyless; and yet, in the midst of it, he seemed more mindful of his horse than of himself. After having spent a short time at Grassington, he visited Skipton, where he remained three weeks, and was rendered very useful in different parts of the circuit. Miss Lister of Colne, (now Mrs. Howarth of Clithero,) having heard much of his zeal, and power with God in prayer, sent an invitation to him to spend a few days at her house. Here also he tarried nearly three weeks, taking occasional rambles into the Burnley circuit. Some of the persons who were brought to God through his labours during this visit have reached the goal, and others are pressing toward the *mark*, in order to obtain the *prize*. From Colne he proceeded home, where he remained but a short time, yielding to other invitations.

We find him in the neighbourhood of Huddersfield and Denby-Dale, in the latter part of January, 1826, with E. Brook, Esq., as his companion in labour. His attention to others led him to neglect himself; and the latter, finding him without a proper winter covering, purchased an excellent top-coat to preserve him from the cold. But though he was thus equipped, and could speak of "plenty of coals" and "good fires," the "cold storms" which howled around him, and the heavy "snows" which fell, kindled the sensibilities of his nature toward Martha, whom he had left at home, and whom he addressed in his letters, as his "dear bosom-friend." In a letter dated January 24th, from Denby-Dale, he exhorted his daughter to do all in her "power" to "make" her "dear mother comfortable"—to "keep her well happed up by day and by night"—to "give her a little wine to nourish her"—assuring her that she should "be recompensed"—requesting her to write immediately should any thing untoward take place—and telling her, that he bore them all up, "both in public and private, at a throne of grace." He solicited a "long letter" in return, informing him how they were "going on in the best things;" whether or not "Mrs. Porter" was dead; and then, with the fondness of a grandfather—the cherub forms twining around his heart, and romping about in his imagination—he adds, "Let me know how my dear grandchild does," and say whether she can yet "run," holding out "her bonny little hand." This is a stroke of pure nature. The autumn of life turns away from the gloom of its winter, and seems to be perpetually reverting to the freshness, and bloom, and loveliness of its spring, as though anxious to live it over again in the innocent child, or by feeling after it, and catching hold of some of its joys, it experienced a kind of resuscitation, and went forth with renewed vigour.

While in this quarter he spoke of having "plenty of work, and good wages"—the wages of "peace, joy, and love,"—of sinners being "saved,"—of "backsliders" being healed,—of God placing "the ring" on the finger, and "the shoes on the feet" of the returning "prodigal." His mind, he observed, was "kept in perfect peace;" and such was the joy he experienced, such his "prospect of glory," when he arose one morning, that he concluded that the Lord was either about to "fit" him "for some trial," or to grant him instant preparation for his "glorious inheritance." He had been engaged in the course of the week in which he wrote in begging for a chapel, "the ground" of which, he observed, was given to him by "Mr. D., of Highflats," a member of the Society of Friends; and the week after he purposed going to "Penistone," to assist in begging for another chapel in that place.

In his perambulations among the sick and the poor, he entered the house of a woman with seven children, who had only had one pound of animal food for the family for the space of about four weeks. Her tale of distress required no embellishment to find access to the ear and heart of Samuel. As soon as he heard it, he gave her some money to procure "a meat dinner" for herself and children the following day.

After "finishing his work," as he termed it, in that neighbourhood, he returned home, where he again remained but a short time. He set off for Rochdale in February or March, taking Bradford on his way, at which place he was pressed to remain from Tuesday to Thursday, preaching at Great-Horton and Low Moor, and holding prayer meetings. On reaching Rochdale, where he had some family affairs to settle, he found ample ground for the exercise of his patience, through the nefarious conduct of a female and some others, who had appropriated to themselves the wearing apparel and other property which was left to his wife by her sister, Mrs. L., denying at the same time such appropriation. His want of confidence in the gentlemen of the law made him decline all legal measures; and his faith in God led him to believe that things would work around to a proper point, in the order of Divine Providence; and though tried at first, he soon lost all sense of wrong, in the means of grace in which he was constantly engaged, the prospect of a visit to Manchester, and the services connected with the opening of a new chapel at Rochdale, stating the amount of the collections and subscriptions "to be nearly two thousand pounds," and exhorting Martha to make progress in piety, and to solace herself with the thought that though she was deprived of her right in her sister's wardrobe here, she should hereafter receive "a white garment," one that would "never grow threadbare." With what kind of grace Martha received the exhortation and encouragement, is not for the writer to state: but she must have viewed it as a poor apology for indifference in his own cause, as well as an inadequate protection from the cold of winter. Muffled up in his "new top-coat," and forgetting his advice to his daughter, to "hap" her "mother by night and by day," he now, with the opportunity before him, of adding to her attire, seemed to act on the comfortless principle of "Be ye warmed," or as though she had been all *spirit*, and the bare mention of a future state was sufficient to kindle a fire that would warm the whole system. But Martha found she had a body as well as a soul: however, she knew he meant well; and this was only one case among many in which she had to bear with him, and to look for "treasure in heaven," as a substitute for a little more upon earth.

Though he rose superior to the trials of this case, when immediately engaged in preaching and visiting, yet there were moments when its hardships returned upon him, so as to lead him to dwell upon them in conversation with his friends. Mrs. L., one of Martha's sisters, was possessed of £600 on her marriage. The interest of this, should she die first, was to be enjoyed by her husband, and then the principal was to revert to her own family on his demise. Contrary to the original agreement, £500 of this was made over by the husband to a member of his own family, and Martha was cut off with the remainder. To secure this, she was obliged to visit Rochdale, in order to sign the writings; and being extremely infirm, the expense, added to the difficulty of conveyance, rendered the journey painful and tedious. Samuel thought, on coming to the whole of this property, that he would be able to devote more of his time to the public service of his Saviour. Looking back upon the expense, trouble, and disappointment, he observed to Mr. Dawson once, "I have prayed to the Lord, that he would send me no more miser money." Mr. D. very significantly returned, "I dare say your prayer will be answered, Samuel."

Having received invitations to different places, and being generally mounted on his blind, but favourite horse, "Jackey," whom he esteemed for his works' sake—having carried the heralds of peace for some years around the York circuit—he was enabled to extend his circle. It was in the course of this journey that he left, as previously promised, his MS. life with the writer at Manchester. He extended his circuit to Bolton, Clithero, Colne, Addingham, Grassington, Burnley, Padiham, Bacup, Rossendale, Bury, Ratcliffe Close, and many of the adjacent and intermediate places. The absence of the Rev. W. M'Kitrick from the Burnley circuit, who had been called to Leeds to attend to some family arrangements, led Samuel to remain longer in Burnley and its neighbourhood than in some other places, being requested to attend to Mr. M'K.'s appointments. The effects of the "general panic," so called, were still experienced, both by the manufacturers and their men; and few districts suffered more than the one from fifteen to twenty miles around the circle in which he laboured. The sick and poor were the objects of his constant solicitude; and many were the scenes of distress he witnessed, as well as the cases he relieved. Writing to a friend, he remarks, "I have seen much suffering and many privations since I saw you. The sufferings of the people have been neither few nor small. I have been in the midst of them for three months; and I believe my dear Lord and Master has sent me here. What with praying with the people, and what with begging for them, I have had full employment. I was so affected one night that I could not take my rest." Though he took a fair sum of his own money into the neighbourhood with him, it was soon exhausted. The friends were kind to him in granting him supplies; but he was always poor; for no sooner were his resources recruited, than he flew to the haunts of wretchedness, prayed with the people, conversed with them, and wept over them. One circumstance which affected him more than almost any other which came under his observation was the case of a poor child, whom he saw sitting and satisfying the cravings of hunger by devouring some grains which had been brought from a brew-house.

On finding the demands made upon his benevolence pressing him beyond what he was able to endure, he asked some friends whether something could not be done by way of public subscription. He was answered that the bulk of the people were poor, and that the manufacturers were equally distressed with the persons they had employed, and were obliged to dismiss, because of a want of trade and public confidence. He was informed, however, that there was one gentleman in the neighbourhood, of great opulence, who was capable of imparting seasonable and adequate relief—only, the informants intimated, that he was a member of the Roman Catholic Church, and might not be quite accessible to persons making Protestant appeals. "No matter what he is," returned Samuel, "the people are not to starve." Addressing the same friend in the letter just referred to, he observes, "I asked them to go with me, but they refused, because of his religion. I told them, that the Lord had the hearts of all men in his keeping, and that he kept the hearts of the Roman Catholics also. I went to the Lord and asked him to go with me." It was too late in the evening for him to present the case; but he was up betimes the next morning, when, mounted on his favourite horse, he proceeded to Towneley Hall, near Burnley, the residence of Peregrine Edward Towneley, Esq. He knocked at the door, and the knock being answered by a servant not in livery, whom he thought sufficiently gentlemanly in his appearance to be the master of the domain, he asked at once, "Are you Mr. Towneley, sir?" Being answered in the negative, he inquired, "Can I see him, sir?" The servant replied he could, and showed him into a room. Mr. Towneley soon appeared, and with his usual promptitude, frankness, and condescension, inquired the errand of his visiter. Mr. T., though perfectly gentlemanly in his manners —which the biographer knows from personal interview—yet happens to be one of those characters who prefer their real worth to be brought to the test of the understanding and the heart, rather than in the show of fashion and finery to the eye; his attire, therefore, being somewhat less prepossessing than that of the person who opened the hall door, Samuel had recourse to his old question, to ascertain the fact—"Are you Mr. Towneley, sir?" This point being settled, he proceeded with his "tale of wo"—stating what he had seen, heard, and done, finally bringing the subject home to the bosom and to the coffers of his auditor. "I am come, sir," said he, "to relate to you the suffering state of the poor in Burnley. I have been a month in the neighbourhood; and my employment has been to visit them. Many of them are without religion. It affects my mind that I cannot help them. I have given all the money I had; I am now between fifty and sixty miles from my own home; and if I had a turnpike-gate to go through, I have not a penny to pay it with. If something is not done for the poor, they will be pined to death, and it will bring a judgment upon our island." "The poor," returned Mr. Towneley, "must be relieved; but how is it to be done?" Samuel replied, "The best way will be to call a meeting of the respectable inhabitants of the town, and to form a committee; and then present relief will be given." Mr. T. was affected with his simplicity, and being convinced of his integrity, observed, that if any measure could be devised to promote the public good, he would with great pleasure accede to it, and would set the example of a public subscription. He further added, that he would be glad to meet a committee of gentlemen, at the earliest period, and at any hour of the day. Samuel proceeded, "This noble man sent the next morning, by his steward, £150 for the sufferers." A public meeting immediately followed for the purpose of taking into consideration the distress of the poor; and if the "Village Blacksmith" had not the credit of entirely originating—of which perhaps few will be disposed to rob him—he was, at least, the cause of hastening it.

Suffering in this case, as in many others, led to violence. "But," said Samuel, "my soul was kept in perfect peace in the midst of all. Our friends would not let me leave them till the disturbances ceased. I prayed for the people, and warned them of their danger. I told them, that if they did not drop it, they would be cut off; and the Lord stayed the wrath of man. When the Lord works, he works like a God.* He stopped the way of the wicked."

The writer attended a missionary meeting at Clithero, in the course of the spring, at which Samuel was present, and at which he spoke. Samuel preached on the occasion, early in the morning, and improved the case of the jailer at Philippi, recorded in the Acts of the Apostles, taking for his text the 31st verse. Many of the thoughts were original—some of them touching—not a few pertinent—but, as a whole, without connection.

Though his addresses, from a want of classification, might be brought under the general appellation of TRUTH AT RANDOM, still it *was* TRUTH; and as such, God, in the aboundings of his mercy to the sinner, and in condescension to the instrument, honoured it with the stamp of

* A poor, but pious negro-woman, being addressed by her teacher on the goodness of God, was asked, whether she was not astonished at his mercy in giving his Son, and his condescension in giving that Son for her. She replied, she was not. Supposing she was not sufficiently impressed with the subject, and defective in the fine feeling of gratitude, he continued to expatiate on the vastness and freedom of his love, giving additional emphasis to his language, and colouring to his subject, closing again with the question, "What, are you not astonished at this?" "No, massa," was still the reply. Turning upon her with a degree of impatience, "And why are you not astonished?" he inquired. "Why, massa, me no astonished, because it be just like him!" The simplicity and sublimity of this sentiment, which borders upon that of Samuel Hick, but leaving him still in the rear, both for originality and beauty, is rarely to be equalled by the sayings of persons in educated society, and fills us with regret to think that the body of a mind so fit for freedom, should be in bondage to one probably many degrees her inferior in intellect.

his own signet. A person but indifferently skilled in incentives to vanity, asked Samuel one day, how it could be accounted for, that while some of the most polished and systematic discourses of some preachers fell pointless upon the hearts of the hearers, *his* homely addresses took such effect. "Why," returned Samuel, "their preaching is like a line; they go straight forward, and only hit one; but mine goes out and in—to the right and to the left, and running this way and that way among a crowd"—as though he had a cracker running riot in his imagination, thrown among the spectators from the hand of a person displaying fire-works—"it is sure to strike some." He employed the same metaphorical language, on another occasion, to the Rev. James Wood, only varying it in his application. "I cannot," said he, "go straight forward in preaching; but when I miss my mark in going, I often fell them in coming back again." Another friend, urging upon him the propriety of employing something like system in his addresses, told him to divide and subdivide them like his brethren. He was not aware apparently of Samuel's want of the power of classification, or of his peculiar views of preparatory composition. Listening to his adviser, with his face toward the ground, as was sometimes his habit, he turned his view upward, on the closing sentence, and with an expressive look, as well as peculiar tone, both indicative of a belief that the speaker was not very well versed in the grand secret of useful preaching,

"Why, bless you, *barn*," said he, "I give it them hot off the bakestone!" indirectly intimating, that the spiritual "bread" provided by many of the systematizers was very often cold, in consequence of the time employed in preparation, before it reached the people. He had long wished the Rev. R. Newton to preach at Micklefield; and, as an inducement, proposed to give two of his own sermons for one by Mr. Newton, which he thought—with equal sincerity and simplicity—would be an equivalent, both in actual labour and probable usefulness. This, in Samuel, was not the language of pride and self-sufficiency: he "spoke as a child."

It appears, that during this tour to "the west," the "laborious work," as he expressed himself, through which he had to pass, was such as to reduce his physical strength. But in the midst of it he could sing, "Labour is rest, and pain is sweet;" and then would exultingly exclaim, "God has been with me; if I have lost weight in body, I have gained it in soul. He has given me strength according to my day." Horton, Wakefield, and other places, were visited on his return. At one of them he took for his text 1 John i, 7, and was rather pleased than otherwise to find that a gentleman had taken his sermon in short-hand; and still more so, to know that he had been benefited by it, though not a little surprised to be presented by him with half a sovereign at the close of the service. While in the Pately-Bridge circuit, which was another of the scenes of his labour, in the course of this excursion, he wrote from Mr. Bramley's, Brown Bank, and in his letter observes, "I am where my soul and body rest in peace—peace that the world can neither give nor take away—a peace that is constant." The body and soul resting in peace, has all the quiet about it of a saint silently waiting in the grave for the morning of the resurrection; and it was this feeling that rendered the "laborious work" just referred to easy, like St. Paul's "light affliction."

Home had still its attractions, but his zeal permitted it to become only a partial resting-place. Passing over some other fields of labour, we find him toward the close of July, as appears from his letters, exercising his talents at Stamford-Bridge, Copmanthorpe, Acomb, and other places in the York circuit, and pressed to pay another visit to Bolton. One part of his business was to beg for a chapel; and "for every sovereign" received, he observed, "God gave his brethren and himself a soul." But though "plenty of money" was obtained, "no small stir" was made by the enemies of religion when they witnessed the grace of God in the new converts. In the neighbourhood of Stamford-Bridge, especially, persecution showed its odious front, in the steward of a gentleman of landed property, who threatened to turn the farmers off their farms, if they persisted in attending the ministry of the Methodist preachers. Samuel "thought this a very hard case," and proceeded at once to the fountain head for redress—to the landed proprietor himself. He told the gentleman that he came to "beg a favour." On being asked the purport of his request, he replied, "To ask you to let your tenants have the same liberty the king grants his subjects." Though partly alive to the subject, the reply demanded farther explanation; and Samuel added, "To let your tenants go to the Methodist chapel." The gentleman, with considerable warmth, interposed his interdict, stating, that they should not. Samuel continued to urge his plea, by affirming that the tenants objected to were the best "church-goers" in the neighbourhood—that there was service in the Established Church only in the forenoon—and that they wished to hear the Methodists in the afternoon. The threatening of the steward, which now appeared to be only the echo of the master's voice, was repeated and confirmed; and one of the reasons assigned was, that the "Methodists" were "a disaffected people." This was a tender point. "Sir," said Samuel, "you do not know them so well as I do. I have known them fifty years. They are the most loyal body of people living, and they are doing more good than any other people upon earth: and, sir, I think it is very hard that you should attempt to prevent your tenants from praying to God, who is sending his judgments abroad in our island, when prayer is the only weapon that can turn them aside." Samuel, alas! was dismissed without obtaining the object of his petition: but he still exulted in the firmness and perseverance manifested by the persons against whom the threatening was directed, and over whom it hung like an angry cloud; rejoicing especially in one whom he claimed as a "*name-sake*."

He paid another visit to York, and Stamford-Bridge, in March, 1827; and in a letter, like a song of triumph, observed that he was in his "element"—had "lived to see good days"—never "saw such a revival before"—that if the Lord would only grant him the desire of his heart, a "general revival," he would then "say, with old Simeon, Now, Lord, let thy servant depart in peace, for mine eyes have seen thy salvation"—that he had been "assisting to hold a lovefeast," and though he had been "a Methodist for so many years," he never experienced such a lovefeast in all his life—that the sum of "eleven pounds had been collected in it for the poor"—that the "family increased" so rapidly, another chapel would be necessary —that the "friends in York liked" his "doctrine of sanctification"—that several had obtained "liberty" while he was preaching in St. George's chapel—and that "some had been sanctified;" then turning upon Martha, whom he was addressing, he proceeded, "I hope you are getting hold of the hem of our Lord's garment. You shall be made whole. I know you once enjoyed sanctification.* The fountain is

* Martha deprived herself of an occasional blessing, through the natural warmth of her temper; and the great difference in Samuel, between his converted and unconverted

still open. The Spirit and the bride say, Come."

In the course of this visit, a young man heard him preach, who stood rebuked before God under the word. Nature and grace had a powerful struggle in the onset: he was so exasperated at Samuel, as to avow, if he ever went again to hear him, he would "take a rope and hang him with it." Still the subject of conflicting feelings, he went once more; but the lion no longer shook his mane for the contest: a little child might have led him. The same voice which roused his fury, allayed it: he became calm—heard with attention—mixed faith with hearing—believed—and was saved.

state, is perceptible in the effect he permitted it to have upon his mind. In the first instance, he either rebelled or fled from it; in the second, he was all meekness, exhortation, and anxiety, to see her enjoying the perfection of the dispensation under which she lived. On one occasion, prior to his conversion, he left the house with an intention never to return. A friend asking him why he relented, Samuel replied, "Why, *barn*, as I was crossing the field, I saw the bonny white lambs playing; they looked so innocent and happy, that I thought I could not leave them, and to went back again." He was a mere child of nature, and nature here, with its innocent gambols, laid a firmer hold of his heart, than the recollection of his vows before the marriage altar. But now, as Martha had often to bear with him, so, uncomplaining, he bears with her; and mutual good is the object of both. Samuel's is not the first heart that has been smitten with tenderness at the sight of a lamb; and than the first glance of the first lamb of the season, there is scarcely any thing more calculated to awaken the sensibilities of our nature. The associations are too obvious to be insisted upon; and a heart so susceptible of the tender and the innocent, is capable of being led in any direction, and wound up to any pitch.

CHAPTER X.

His first visit to London—Dialogue at an inn on the road—Wesleyan Missionary Meeting—Preaches at Southwark—Exalts divine truth at the expense of human knowledge—Persons benefited by his addresses—His notions of nervous complaints—His second visit to the metropolis—Mrs. Wrathall; her character, experience, and affliction—Samuel's general views and feelings, as connected with his second visit—Pleads strenuously for the doctrine of sanctification—Is both opposed and supported in it by persons of the Baptist persuasion—Receives a gentle admonition from Martha—A specimen of one of his public addresses, when in one of his most felicitous moods.

His visit to the metropolis, which has only been incidentally noticed, deserves to be introduced distinctly and at large. He was there twice; and though a period of eight years occupied the space between, they are here classed together, not only because of the affinity of subject and place, as has been observed in other cases; but because of the nonimportance of the one compared with the other, rendering a distinct notice less necessary.

It appears in a communication from Mr. Wrathall to the writer, that Samuel's "first visit to London was in May, 1819," on which occasion "he remained somewhat more than a month." Though he had a daughter in London, then housekeeper to Mr. W., and other relations in the neighbourhood, a more powerful spring was found in the general annual Wesleyan Missionary Meeting, to give an impetus to his movements toward the metropolis, than either in friendship or relationship. On this trip, he remarks, "I had a very pleasant journey, as I had the Lord with me; and the weather being fine, made my way very comfortable. I sung hymns in the night to keep me awake." On the coach arriving at Retford, time was allowed for the passengers to take refreshment, when Samuel and the other persons on the outside alighted, together with four gentlemen from within. Samuel, having as usual beat "quick time," suddenly disappeared. One of the inside passengers inquired pleasantly of the coachman where the man was who "had been so merry on the top," and was answered, that he had "gone into the kitchen." A request was immediately sent, inviting him into the dining-room, with which he complied. The room, the table, and the provision, at first surprised him. To the occasional and alternate interrogatories of each, he replied; the substance of part of which is as follows, and for the brevity of which every coach-traveller will be able to furnish an answer, having been repeatedly saluted with the horn, when his appetite has urged him to stay.

Gentleman. "We have sent for you, to ask you to sit down at table with us."

Samuel. "I am obliged: but I have ordered the waiter to draw me a pint of ale, and I have plenty of beef and bread with me."

Gent. "You have been such good company, we have agreed to treat you with your supper."

On this he sat down, and partook of their

hospitable cheer; the four gentlemen and himself constituting the party.

Gent. "How far may you be going this road?"

Sam. "To London."

Gent. "How far have you travelled?"

Sam. "From Micklefield, near Ferry Bridge."

Gent. "What business calls you up to town?"

Sam. "I am going to a noble missionary meeting."

Gent. "Don't you think you have a poor errand?"

Here an armistice was instantly proclaimed between Samuel and his supper, and looking expressively at the speaker, he said,

"Sir, I would not turn back, if you were to give me five pounds for doing it."

Gent. "Perhaps not. Who pays your expenses?"

Sam. "I pay my own, sir. I have plenty of money; and if you dispute it, I will let you see it."

Such a confession, in some societies—as he had upward of £170 upon him—would have been prized, and his ignorance of the world might have been improved upon; but he was in honourable company. On his offer being declined, another of the gentlemen struck in—

"There is a great deal of money spent upon the heathen. If we are to suppose that the Lord will never send them to a place of punishment for not believing in a Saviour of whom they have never heard, would it not be much better to let them alone?"

Sam. "The Lord has declared, that he will give his Son the heathen for his inheritance, and the uttermost parts of the earth for his possession—that the gospel of the kingdom shall be preached in all the world—and that then will come the end, when all shall know him from the least to the greatest."

He could not enter into the subtleties in which the question was involved, and with which it has often been perplexed by the selfish, and unbelieving, and the designing; but he cast anchor in God's designs, commands, and promises, which were the general notions he wished to express—his design to save, his promise to give, and his command to preach to the heathen; and there he remained riding in safety: what God commanded he considered himself bound to perform, and what he had promised, he knew he was faithful to fulfil.

Gent. "Do you intend to deliver a speech on the occasion?"

Sam. "O no: I expect there will be a number of gentlemen at the meeting, from all parts of the world, and I hope to have the pleasure of hearing them make their noble speeches."

Gent. "If you will promise to make a speech, we will come and hear you."

The conversation was interrupted by the announcement of the horses being ready to start. Samuel resumed his seat and his song, and arrived in safety the next day in London. At the public meeting he found his way to the platform; and to his great surprise, one of the gentlemen who had regaled him with his supper at Retford took a seat next him, and presented him with an orange; but he was still more astonished, when the gentleman's name was announced as R. F., Esq., of Bradford, Yorkshire, who was called upon to second a resolution.

The first chapel he preached in was that of Southwark, and the second, Hinde-street. On the first occasion he took one of his favourite texts, James i. 27. A gentleman accosted him after the service, in a frank way—"My good old Yorkshireman, though I could not understand the whole of your language, part of which might have been Danish for any thing I know to the contrary, yet I have had my soul blessed under your sermon." Samuel replied, "It makes no matter, sir, what the language is, if the soul only gets blessed."* The gentle-

* This circumstance was afterward related and improved by Samuel in a missionary meeting, in a way equally expressive of his ignorance and his piety. Some observations had been made on the labour requisite to acquire the languages, before a missionary could be able to address himself to the heathen, so as to be understood. Samuel, who was always impressed with the notion that he was called to be a missionary, and took his *visionary voyage* to the West Indies, noticed in a preceding page, as an intimation of it, not only saw his own way more clearly to go abroad, but believed he perceived a much shorter cut across the field of labour and travel for others. The Southwark gentleman was produced by him as an example of the power of truth to bless, without a knowledge of the language in which it was conveyed. This case seemed to impart new light—removed every impediment—set a missionary immediately upon his work; and in its

man invited him to spend a day at his house, stating, on Samuel observing that, as a stranger, he would not be able to find his way, that he would send his servant to conduct him thither. While he was yet in the vestry, taking a biscuit and a glass of wine—a treat with which he had been but rarely indulged in small country places—a lady entered, inquiring, under strong feeling, whether she could see the minister. Samuel supposing the inquiry to be for one of the preachers on the circuit, who was present, kept his seat. The preacher went up to the lady, and requested to know whether it was the person that had been preaching she wished to see. Casting a glance around the place, and seeing Samuel, she exclaimed, "O yes: *that* is the person." Samuel sprang from his seat, with his wine and biscuit in his hand, saying, "What do you please to want with me, madam?" "O, I wish to tell you, sir," was the reply, "what I felt while you were preaching.

novelty, Samuel appeared to have lost sight of the apostle's observations on an "unknown tongue." His error lay, not in a distinction—had he been able to comprehend it—between truth in the *spirit* and truth in the *letter*—between human language as addressed to the ear, and the power of God as felt in the heart—between sound and sense—between what a man may hear and what he may feel;—but in taking it for granted, that it was *that* portion of the address which the gentleman did *not* understand, rather than that which he *did*, which was so beneficial to him—in taking it for granted that a special case might be applied as a general rule—and in supposing that the use of the understanding would be suspended rather than the word should return void, and the work of grace should not go on. He now, in his simplicity, added to his *call*, his *qualification*—the latter founded on an erroneous view of the overwhelming power of God.

A trembling came all over me, and I could not hold a limb still." Samuel, who had but *one cause* for all these things, and happened to be correct in this instance, as well as in many others, said, "It is the work of the Spirit of God, and we will return the Lord thanks for it." The proposition was accepted; and he observed, "Though she was dressed in fine silks, which crackled again, she knelt down on the vestry floor, and, while pleading, the Lord blessed her soul."

Another case came under his observation, which was more obstinate than that of the lady, and assumed to him an air of novelty. He was sent to pray with a gentleman, whose affliction was stated to him to be a "nervous complaint." His own nerves being of a wiry make—living in a neighbourhood of health—and moving generally among that class of people whose nervous system is kept continually braced by labour and by the breeze, he had to take both his head and his heart to school on the subject. The malady assumed an awful appearance to him; for when he entered the room, he remarked, that the person "was sunk so low, that he lay on the sofa like a dead man." As he had but one cause for the stirrings of the human spirit, so he had but one cure for most of our maladies. Faith in Christ was his *heal-all*, and was his grand specific here. He spent nearly a whole day with the gentleman, either praying with him, or sitting by his side, singing hymns, relating his experience, exhorting him to the exercise of faith. In his addresses he told him, that it was only "holy medicine" that "could cure" him, and that "all the doctors in London could not cure a nervous complaint, for it was a soul-complaint." On parting, the gentleman entreated him to repeat his visit, and added, "I would freely give all I possess to be as happy as you are." This case made a deep impression on Samuel's mind, and in his reflections afterward, he remarked, "I pity any one who is troubled with this dreadful complaint; but I believe many fall into it for want of faith. They reason with themselves, and with the enemy, instead of reasoning with God, who says, 'Come, and let *us* reason together.'" Little as honest Samuel knew of the subject, he might have been farther wrong, than in supposing that mental agony will induce physical debility. While we cease to wonder that the gentleman should look upon his state as enviable, we are convinced that no one, except a child in spirit, could have sat and sung hymns by the side of so much misery—of one whose spirit was tuned only for a "dark-woven lay."

The principal part of his time was occupied in visiting the sick, and in attending the ordinances of God; and thus engaged, he might well say, "I was very happy all the time I was in London." Business requiring his presence at home, he remained only a month in the metropolis.

His second visit was in 1827, but the day and the month when he set off are uncertain;

a correspondent connected with the family stating it to have been in May, while a letter written by himself bears testimony of his having been in Yorkshire in the month of July. The memory might have possibly been depended upon in the first instance; and the first visit having been in May, might have been the occasion of the error. His daughter Rosamond had entered the marriage state with Mr. Wrathall, in the interval of his visits. This took place in 1824; and it was on account of her long and severe indisposition that he took the present journey. The following brief narrative of this excellent woman, whom it may be proper here to introduce, was published in the obituary of the Wesleyan Methodist Magazine, by the Rev. Richard Reece.*

"Mrs. Rosamond Wrathall was daughter of Mr. Samuel Hick, of Micklefield, Yorkshire; a man generally known, and highly esteemed for his usefulness among the Methodists for nearly half a century; and who, with his pious wife, considered it their duty to impress upon the minds of their children the great truths of the gospel. Early indications were given that the heart of Mrs. Wrathall was under the influ-

* 1828, p. 499. A curious "Prospectus for publishing the Life of the late Samuel Hick, of Micklefield," issued from the press in the summer of 1830, which promised to "contain the experience and happy death of Mrs. RATHALL of London, daughter of the deceased, who died while he was in London." It is presumed that the late Mrs. WRATHALL was intended by the author, and that, through his ignorance of the subject, he adopted another name.

ence of divine grace. At the age of seven years her mind was enlightened to see the evil nature and dreadful consequences of sin. Although she was humble and teachable, and very dutiful and affectionate to her parents, yet she felt the need of pardon, and of the purification of her nature. The period at which she received the blessing of justification through faith in the merits of Christ is unknown; but it must have been at an early age. During the whole of her Christian course she was an ornament to her profession, and was greatly attached to the Methodist connection. She refrained from evil speaking, and used her influence to restrain the practice of it in others. She put on the ornament of a meek and quiet spirit, which is in the sight of God of great price. Her disposition was naturally generous; and after her conversion she was constantly devising liberal things. She spared no labour nor expense to alleviate the necessities of the poor, and lead them to Christ. She was a pattern of integrity and piety. At the commencement of her long affliction, she was deeply convinced of the need of a farther work of grace upon her heart; and desired that her excellent father might be sent for, that she might enjoy the benefit of his counsel and faithful prayers."

Samuel, after a safe journey, alighted at the Saracen's Head, and proceeded to the house of his son-in-law. He found Mrs. W. very much indisposed. The blessing she sought had been the subject of his preaching and conversation for many years, as well as the experience of his soul; and his child's anxiety for it led him to dwell upon it more than usual, in public and in private, as also in his correspondence during his stay in London. "Her mind," continues Mr. Reece, "became more and more calm and stayed upon God; she received the blessing of entire sanctification, which she so much desired, and continued in the exercise of prayer and thanksgiving to the end of her life."

During Samuel's second stay in this human ant-hill, whose swarms are always in motion, and whose streets gave him the notion, in his own language, of a constant "*fair*," he laboured under the impression that a great work was to be done—done instantly—and that he was to sustain a share in the toil and in the glory. He sighed over the irreligious part of the community, composed, as he stated, of "Jews, Turks, Infidels, and Barbarians," all of whom might "believe" in the existence of a "God," but "lived as though there were none;" concluding, that if it were not for the "few righteous" to be found in the city, it would at once be "destroyed like Sodom." With these views, and with a heart thus affected, he embraced every opportunity of rendering himself useful, and could speak of having "plenty of work"—of being often "tired *in* it, but not *of* it"—of "preaching in chapels and in the open air"—of making "collections for chapels and for schools"—of "visiting the sick"—attending "lovefeasts"—assisting in "prayer meetings"—dining and praying on board some of the vessels on the Thames—and, in the midst of all this, of having "plenty of friends," and of being "hearty and happy." One of the vessels having to perform only a short voyage, and having reached her destination before he left town, returning with *fruit* and *spice*, he took care devoutly to connect with his notice of her safety, the prayer meeting which he himself and some friends held "in the cabin," before her departure; and also to exhort Martha, who was not likely to be benefited by any part of the cargo, to make progress in piety, and both he and she would hereafter be indulged with a taste of the "grapes" of the kingdom, and with "wine on the lees, well refined." It was here that he not only attempted to moralize, but to philosophize; stating it to be his opinion, that if the Lord had not "sent the tide through the city, to sweeten the air, a plague" would have been the result; as though the tide had followed rather than preceded the foundation of its walls. But Samuel was a Christian, not a philosopher; his head was less the receptacle of knowledge than his heart was of grace. While he laboured as though the immortal interests of the whole of the inhabitants of the city rested upon him, he cast a glance of solicitude toward home, telling Martha, that it was not "out of sight, out of mind:" and requesting to be informed how she was "in body and soul;" repeatedly forwarding her not only "parcels," but what he knew she "liked"—a "cheap letter." His letters indicate also deep anxiety for the prosperity of the work of God at Micklefield; and, among others, an ardent desire for the salvation of a "Mr. Coulson." Nor did he forget his "old servant Jackey," whom he wished to be attended to, and preserved in his blindness from falling into the "bogs."* His desire to be useful led him to request Martha to enlarge his "furlough;" intimating at the same time his readiness to return on the first notice of his being "wanted at home."

The only personal indisposition of which he had to complain was a slight attack of cholera morbus, which he believed he had caught from one of the young men resident in the house, and which he therefore characterized as "*smittle*."† One of the most relieving considerations

* His partiality to this animal arose chiefly from the circumstance of its having carried the Rev. David Stoner around the York circuit, to whom he was warmly attached, both as an eminent servant of God, and as having been born near his own home. And yet, for this very attachment, Samuel might have stood rebuked by his own words. Being at Aberford fair once, and walking with his friend Mr. Dawson among the crowd, he was met by an acquaintance. "You look cast down," said Samuel; "what is the matter with you?" "I have lost a fine horse," was the reply, naming its value. "Why, bless you, man, you made a god of it, and worshipped it: I worshipped a fine ewe once, and God took her away from me." Such was Samuel's consolation under loss, and such his occasional views of improper attachments.

† A provincialism, denoting any thing *contagious*. He was not a little delighted with what he considered a triumph over the ignorance of some of the metropolitans, who had consulted the English Dictionary for the term, he having told them in the course of his sermon, that "sin was *smittle*"—exhorting them to keep at the utmost distance from it.

to his mind under it was—and this shows his anxiety to be useful—that it had not been permitted to "take" him from his "work." The sudden death of a female—the affliction of his daughter—and the daily funeral processions along the streets of the city, produced a quickening influence upon his soul, and furnished him with seasonable preaching and conversational topics, grounding on the whole the necessity of a constant preparation for another state of being.

His peculiarities in manner and dialect attracted attention; and among others with whom he conversed, and who were induced to hear him preach, were some persons of the Baptist persuasion. While a few of these contested the doctrine of "entire sanctification" with him, others of them admitted its necessity and attainment. One of the latter addressed a letter to him on the subject, which he intended to insert in his "Life." Treating on it in a letter to Martha, he observed, "I have preached ever since I came to London, a full, free, and present salvation; and I will continue to preach it while I have life and strength. Thousands have heard me. I have told them, that if the king were to make a decree, that the man preaching this doctrine should have his head taken off, I would at once go to the block, proclaiming as I went, with a loud voice, that HOLINESS belongeth unto the house of the Lord for ever, and would there die for it like a martyr."

Preaching in one of the chapels, on "Blessed

are the pure in heart, for they shall see God," a female who had heard him, professed to have received the blessing, after having sought it for the space of seventeen years. A young man also bore the same testimony, in one of the lovefeasts. Some of these cases were entered into his home epistolary correspondence, adding to the narrations, "You see what a poor instrument the Lord can work with!—either by a ram's horn, or by the crowing of a cock. But he shall have the glory; he will not give it to another; he has purchased it with his blood." These intimations led Martha to look upon his state with a little jealousy; and on furnishing him with a portion of ballast—a labour of love for which she was well qualified and always ready—he replied to her, "I am thankful for your advice; and I hope God will keep me in the dust. I assure you, I have often to cry out, 'Lord, enlarge my heart, and fill it.' I sometimes think I shall sink under the weight of love: and if I should be called away in such a state, O how sweet it will be to fall asleep in the arms of Jesus!"

While urging his hearers to seek holiness, he broke out on one occasion, somewhat in the following strain:—"If any of you had a sum of money left to you by a friend, you would put in your claim and prove the will. Jesus Christ has made his will; and his will is your sanctification. You may put in your claim for the blessing by simple faith. The property belongs to every believer. Our Lord made a just will.

He left all his children share and share alike; the youngest the same blessing as the oldest. 'The weakest believer that hangs upon him' may have it. It is faith that lays claim to it. Faith says, 'It is my property.' Faith has two hands. It takes hold of the blessing with the one, and continues to hold it fast by the other. Stretch out the hand of faith then. Take the property your dear Lord has purchased for *you*, and for *all* believers." This is truth in russet costume: and yet, homely though it be, it is not only more dignified in its character, but the imagery is better selected, as well as more consistently supported, than that which has been sometimes employed by doctors and dignitaries.*

What gave him peculiar pleasure, in reference to his favourite theme of sanctification, was, the circumstance of receiving an invitation to take tea with two of the preachers, at the house of a lady who had travelled the path of holiness upward of half a century, and who had entertained the venerable founder of Methodism. With this Christian matron he compared

* In a sermon preached at *court*, the celebrated DR. SOUTH remarks, in speaking of the delights of a soul "*clarified*" by grace, "No man, at the years and vigour of thirty, is either *fond of sugar-plums or rattles*." Another observation is, "No man would preserve the *itch* on himself, only for the pleasure of *scratching*."—*Sermons*, Serm. I, Prov. iii, 17.

Archbishop TILLOTSON, in his thanksgiving Sermon before the king and queen, October 27th, 1692, on Jer. ix, 23, 24, speaking of his majesty's preservation in the field of battle, says, "I do not believe, that from the first use of *great guns* to that day, any mortal man ever had his shoulder so *kindly kissed* by a *cannon bullet*."

notes; and remarked, "She has enjoyed pure religion ever since Mr. Wesley's day; and the best of all is, she enjoys it now. It is natural for us to talk about that which we love. Her experience is just the same as mine. I am glad when I find any one that enjoys the blessing."

CHAPTER XI.

Continues in London—An epitome of a week's labour—Mrs. Wrathall's religious enjoyments—Samuel meets with one converted Jew, and attempts the Christian improvement of another—Preaches out of doors—Visits Michael Angelo Taylor, Esq.—Farther account of Mrs. Wrathall—Samuel's usefulness—His love of Yorkshire—Enjoys a ride into the country—Goes into Kent—Tent-preaching—Is reproved for loud praying—His views of death—Spiritualize a thunder-storm—An African—Mrs. Wrathall's death—Samuel visits Windsor—Is rendered a blessing to the people—Returns to London—Is called into Yorkshire to preach a funeral sermon.

In following Samuel during his residence in the metropolis, it will furnish some variety, if special cognizance be taken of the more incidental part of his history. His life was one of incident: every motion, like scenic representation, told on the eye and the ear of the bystander, unfolding his habitudes and feelings. Though no regular journal was kept, the following may be considered as nearly in the order, with two or three exceptions, in which the occurrences and conversations took place.

July.—Persons visiting the metropolis, like

those who cross the line for the first time, are obliged to conform to certain ceremonies, if not of dipping, at least in dressing. Samuel's raiment was generally plain, both in cut and quality; and when not employed in the smithy, extremely clean. His coat was rarely permitted to altar its fashion.* The change in London, however, was not so much in the shape, as in the quality—from plain to superfine. "My son," said he to Martha, "has ordered me a suit of new clothes; and your dear Ann, whom you love, has bought me a new hat: I never had such a hat on my head in my life before." This was as much the result of kindness as of necessity. Improved in his appearance, and requested to supply a few places for the Rev. R. Reece, with whose plan he was presented as his credential, during his engagements at the Conference, he traversed the city, in something more than his ordinary character, when at home, at Micklefield; and Martha's lectures on humility were as necessary occasionally to suppress the stirrings of vanity—vanity, however, in some of its least offensive forms, and without much of the consciousness of its presence—as they were kindly taken. His daughter, with a child's fondness, wrote home in one of his letters, in the early part of

* He was once, in the way of compliment, presented by a friend with a pair of handsome new trousers. But they were so ill adapted to his person, habits, and other costume, that when thus adorned, it looked like the last and present century united in the same man; or as though the half of him belonged to some one besides himself.

this month,—"My dear mother, I will give you part of father's weekly work. He went to Southwark chapel on Monday morning, at five o'clock; from whence a young gentleman took him home to breakfast, and kept him the whole of the day. He went to a fellowship meeting at night, and did not reach home till ten o'clock. On Wednesday morning he preached at City-Road at six o'clock, and did not arrive here till tea time. After tea he went to preach at Albion-street; and to-day he has been at Chelsea missionary meeting. It is now ten o'clock, and he has just arrived by coach. I assure you my dear father is in high glee. He tells us that he has had a good time; and that, while he was speaking, the persons upon the platform almost stamped it down.* They all shook hands with him, told him they were obliged to him for his services, and paid his coach-fare. Wherever he goes, the people invite him back again. You see how your husband is beloved."

Though Mrs. W. was pleased with the respect paid to her father—and it would have been strange if a little natural feeling had not escaped—she remained the same humble

* Samuel himself was in the habit of stamping, not only when others were speaking, but when he himself spoke. A singular scene took place some time prior to this, and nearer his own home. Addressing an audience at a public meeting, and being very animated, his ponderous movements shook the whole platform. Just at the moment of applying a subject, and saying, "Thus it was that the prophets went," the part on which he stood gave way, and he instantly disappeared. Fortunately no injury was sustained.

Christian as before; nor was it with Samuel any thing else but the mere ebullition of the moment. Personal piety seemed to include every thing besides, both in himself and in others; and the progress of it was particularly watched in his daughter. "I believe," said he, in writing of her to his partner, "the Lord has sent me to London to learn gratitude from the heart of your own flesh and blood. I never saw such a happy creature, or one more thankful, in all my life. She has often been made a blessing to my soul since I came hither; and not only to me, but to others, who come to see her in her affliction. She enjoys perfect love—that which casts out all fear—and is fit either for living or dying. I often think, if you were to see her in this happy state, it would rejoice your heart. It is above all riches to see a dear child of ours so happy. Her dear husband outstrips all the men I ever saw for affection. She wants for nothing that the world can bestow: and your dear Ann waits upon her with tenderness. They are like a three-fold cord, twisted together in love. We have nothing but peace, joy, and love." These endearments, together with the kindness of friends, and an extensive field of usefulness, led him further to observe to Martha, "I find a noble body of Methodists in this city, and I am very glad I am one of the members of this noble family. If I had you with me, we would end our days here."

As nearly all classes of persons attached

themselves to him in the line in which he moved, so he found himself comfortable everywhere; and hence spoke of having "many homes"—not being "able to supply all" his friends with his society. Among others who clung to him was a Jew; but whether on account of his piety or singularity, is unknown. A Jew, to Samuel, was as great a phenomenon in society as he also was an extraordinary specimen of an adherent of the Christian faith. Of this singular people he knew very little, except what he had collected from the Bible. Impressions of *distance*, both as to *time* and *place*, with him were always connected with their history; and through his associating the holy city and the personal manifestation of Christ among them in all his reflections he could scarcely have been more interested, if the fable of the wandering Jew had been realized in his presence, or if a Hebrew had stolen out of the sepulchre of his fathers at Jerusalem, and, in his travels, had reached England, than the concern he felt in looking upon the person in question. "I was planned," said he, "to preach in City-Road vestry, and I got into company with a converted Jew. He is a fine young man, and is as clear in his experience as I am. I was delighted with his company. A pious lady has sent him over to London to be instructed in divine things. His parents have turned him out of doors for becoming a Christian; but the Lord has taken him into his family. He is going to college, and he asked me to go with him." The young man must either have been extremely ignorant of human character, or disposed to amuse himself with the weaker part of Samuel's nature, in making to him such a proposal. However, Samuel told him that he had been at "Jesus Christ's college," where he had "taken up" his "degrees." He took breakfast and dinner with this young convert, and found a difficulty in parting with him.

The interest this case excited, led him to think more than usual on the state of the Jews; and turning his attention to them, they seemed to multiply in his sight as he passed along the streets. This gave rise to his expression, that the city appeared to be filled "with Jews, Turks, and Infidels." A genuine son of Abraham kept a jeweller and silversmith's shop opposite his daughter's house. He often looked at Samuel while passing his door, with the characteristic keenness and expectation of a London Israelitish tradesman, hoping to benefit by the ignorance of an inexperienced countryman. But his soul possessed superior attraction to Samuel than either his shop or his window; and he was not without hope that he might be of service to him. With unusual caution and deliberation, he paced backward and forward before the old gentleman's door. The morning was pleasant, in which he rejoiced. He had not been there long before the object of his desire made his appearance. They exchanged looks, when Samuel accosted him, "Bless the Lord! here is a fine morning." "It ish, it ish fery fine," replied the Jew; immediately inquiring—as he was old, and could not go into the city to seek it—"Vat pe te besht news in te city?" "The best news that I can hear," replied Samuel, "is, that Jesus Christ is pardoning sinners, and sanctifying believers." "Poh, poh," rejoined the old man, turning up his face, "tuff and nonshensh! it ish all telushion." Samuel was as ill prepared for this, as the Jew had been for what he had advanced, and observed, with a view to produce instantaneous conviction—as he concluded the testimony of his own experience would be every way demonstrative to both Jew and Gentile—"If it be a delusion, it is a *blessed* delusion; for I am very happy in it. No, no, sir: I know better. I have known for the last forty years that Jesus Christ has power upon earth to forgive sins, and also to cleanse from all unrighteousness." Alas, for Samuel, he ploughed only on the rock: the old man turned his back upon him in a rage, as though Samuel had intended to insult him—entered his shop—and shut the door in his face. Samuel looked after him with the disappointment of a fowler, who, having discharged his piece, and expecting the game to drop at a short distance, sees it on the wing and untouched; yet expressed his gratitude, in "not being numbered with unbelievers." It is not a little amusing to find him in the chair of Lavater after this, pronouncing his opinion with the precision of a physiognomist. "I can tell a Jew," said he, "as I pass him on the street; for his countenance is gloomy and dark; not like that of the Christian, which is cheerful and pleasant: and who has such a right to be cheerful as the man that has Christ formed in him the hope of glory?"*

On finding that he could make but little impression upon the Jew, he again turned to the Gentile. The "morning meetings," at five and six o'clock, which were well attended, were among the most salutary he enjoyed. On one occasion, a foreigner, who had attended out of curiosity, was deeply affected, and three persons professed to have received the blessing of purity. After the meetings he was often taken away to visit the sick, and pray with the penitent. One of the persons who came before him he suspected to be affected with worldly sorrow; and this is the more remarkable, as he had more charity than judgment in all cases of

* This was not his first attempt at physiognomy; nor was he peculiar in his views on the subject. He had read Isaiah, who, in speaking of certain characters, says, "The show of their countenance doth witness against them;" and he had a notion that religion would improve the *exterior*, as well as the *interior*, of every human being. These views escaped in prayer once, while he was imploring the blessing of God upon a female who acted in the capacity of cook in a family which he visited. Having heard a little of the person in question, and having inferred, from the peculiar curvature and expression of the face, that she was not blessed with a redundancy of the milder qualities which grace the softer part of creation, he prayed for the subjugation of every improper temper; and as an inducement to her to seek after personal piety, he said he was sure, "if her soul were converted to God, she would look five pounds better than she did then."

distress: another he was called to visit—a stationer—was in deep despair. With a view to attract persons who never attended a place of worship, he turned out into the street, and stood up, accompanied by a local preacher, in a large square. The householders threw open their windows to listen to him, and the people continued to crowd around him, till the congregation might be denominated large. A person, in a state of intoxication, threw a bunch of flowers at him, and was otherwise turbulent. Some of the friends were about to remove him by violence, when Samuel said, "Let him alone; he cannot hurt me, and I am sure I shall not harm him." The man was subdued by the mildness of the address. "The lion's mouth," said Samuel, "was stopped." While preaching he felt great tenderness of spirit. This was soon manifested by the people; for, in the language of Creech, "The melted is the melting heart." He exhorted—he beseeched—he reproved—he wept—the people wept in concert with him—and having forgotten his pocket-handkerchief, he borrowed one of a friend, to wipe away the tears which rolled down his face. The bunch of flowers was hailed by him as a slight expression of "persecution," in the honours pronounced on which he "rejoiced."

Samuel was one who could more readily recollect a kindness than an injury; and considering himself indebted to Michael Angelo Taylor, Esq., for his license, who then resided in London, and viewing him withal, in his own words, as an "old neighbour," he went to White-Hall to pay his respects to him. The statesman expressed himself as glad to see him, inquiring the occasion which had brought him to town. On being informed that it was the affliction of his daughter, Mr. T. signified his regret. Samuel, on the contrary, told him he felt no sorrow on her account, for she was "very happy, and ready for her passage to glory." Mr. T. ordered the butler to give him some refreshment; the apparent kindness, prompting which, was of greater value to Samuel, than the most costly viands.

Samuel remarked toward the close of the month, as Mrs. Wrathall's health still declined, "Our dear child will be safe landed on Canaan's happy shore in a short time. I never saw such a patient creature as she is. She has not much pain, and will have nothing to do but fall asleep. She began to change last week, and grows weaker and weaker." Two or three days after, he observed, "I have just been giving your dear child her breakfast. If you only saw her in her affliction—so thankful, so happy, I am sure it would rejoice your heart. If she is spared a little longer, it will be for the glory of God and the good of those that come to see her. She has many friends: I can scarcely go anywhere but I find them. Your dear Ann is a miracle. She is not afraid of going out to hear me preach. I hope both you and me, and all our children, and even our children's children, to the third and rourth generation, will meet at

God's right hand." On the 30th of the month, he added, "Your dear child is very happy:" then proceeding to generalize, "we are all peace: Ann and I have been taking some refreshment together, and have just been at the family altar. I hope you do not forget this duty; and be sure you do not *pinch* yourself for comforts. I often think of you when I sit down to a good dinner, and wish I had you, my dear, to share it with me. But if we do not sit down at one table now, we shall eat at our Father's table together hereafter. My lot is cast in a pleasant place. When I want to retire to read or write, I have a room to go into. I would not *swap* (exchange) place with the best nobleman in this city."

August.—This month presents but little variety, besides the regular work of preaching, praying, and visiting, with the exception of a quickening influence in one of the prayer-meetings, which was held after he had preached, in which a person of the Roman Catholic persuasion was awakened. Having to go a considerable distance to his lodgings, he departed from the place about ten o'clock at night, leaving, as he expressed himself, "the friends pleading for the slain." Before the close of the month, his Yorkshire phrases, his zeal, and the influence attending his homely addresses, rendered him rather conspicuous among his fellows. To this he was not altogether blind; and remarked in the confidence of a man to his wife, "I am well known in London: the more work I do the more I have to do; and when it will all be done I cannot tell. I have great pleasure in it. The Lord is saving souls." Then, as before, he urged Martha not to *pinch* herself; "for," he added, "I am sure we have as much as will keep you; and as for me, my Master, whom I love and serve, will supply all my needs out of his abundant fulness. The earth is his own property." This was not the language that arises out of satiety from present indulgence, on finding himself seated at the table of his son-in-law, but of confidence in God, who *blesses* the labourer with his *hire*, because *worthy* of it. He had no anxiety on his own account; it only found a place in his bosom for others; and toward these it was generally exercised rather in reference to the present exigencies of any particular case than with a view to the *future* destiny of the individual concerned. His faith in the goodness, power, and veracity of God, would never suffer him to bring the trials of *to-morrow* on those of *to-day*; or by afflictive forebodings to go out and meet his exercises half way: and even "the evil" of "the day," which ought to be deemed "*sufficient*" by all intelligent beings, was deprived of great part of its weight with Samuel, and thus rendered *light* and *momentary*, through the grace by which he was supported, and the glorious hope of a blessed immortality. Nothing but personal piety could have enabled him to overcome parental feeling so far as to give him the appearance of being not only all peace, but covered with sunshine at the gate of heaven, and just on the point of entering, in the midst of a beloved daughter's affliction. At the close of this month, as on that of the preceding one, he had only to report increasing debility with regard to Mrs. W. "Ann and I have been getting up your dear afflicted child. She is very happy in soul, but very weak in body." He waked and watched by her with a solicitude like that of a mother rather than that of a father, and never permitted his public labours to intrench upon the attentions demanded by natural affection.

SEPTEMBER.—Though happy among the persons with whom he associated, his joys were considerably increased on any arrival from Yorkshire, whether it turned up in the shape of a human face, a letter, or a message. Among several persons noticed, no one was viewed with more unmingled pleasure than W. Scarth, Esq., of Leeds, who invited him to take tea at his lodgings—the house of the widow of the late Rev. C. Atmore—"Where," said Samuel, "we spent a little bit comfortable time together." Mr. S. told him that his presence and labours would be required at home: this, with an oral communication from Ratcliffe Close, to pay another visit to that place, where he had been so useful among the Sunday-school children, operated upon him like the promise of a week's work to a poor man, who is overjoyed with the tidings of a second job before the first is finished. His only wish for life arose from his desire to be useful.

Next to a friend from Yorkshire was the delight he experienced in again beholding the face of God's creation, in a view of the country. His eye had been accustomed to rove over the beauty, the wildness, and the freshness of open rural scenery; and though he knew not the sentiment of the writer who said, "God made the country, but man made the town;" yet he felt like a person who saw more of his Maker's hand in the trees and in the shrubs than in a range of buildings—like one whose eye had not only a wider range, but whose lungs had something like fair play, and with whom respiration seemed to be aided. Mr. Knight drove him fifteen miles into the country in a gig. He felt like a child let loose from the nursery. Absence had given additional richness to the verdure. "I was glad," said he, "to see the fields look so green. The Lord is sending us a Michaelmas summer, and a fine seed-time. He is making up for the loss of last year. Bless his dear name! he is very kind to us. After taking the rod to us, he then shows us his salvation. He never does wrong: he does all in love; and it is well done. What we know not now, we shall know hereafter."

He was favoured with a still farther treat, in being taken into Kent, by Mr. Cooper, who married his niece, and with whom he remained a fortnight. On his return he made a collection for a Sunday school; and such was the concourse of people, that he was obliged to preach out of doors. The collection amounted to about double the sum to what it had been on any former occasion.

Mr. Pocock's plan of *tent-preaching*, which had reached the metropolis, presented a novel scene to Samuel; and in one of these he held forth the word of life. But in no meeting, of a purely religious character, did he appear so much in his element as in those he held after preaching, to which there has been such repeated reference. In one of these, in the course of this month, after he had made a collection for a chapel, which had undergone some repairs, he gave the people an account of a plan adopted in the York circuit, during a revival. He told them that the friends "set three *benks*"* (benches,)—one for penitents—another for backsliders—and a third for those that wanted full salvation; and that while they sung a verse or two of a hymn, the people filled the *benks*. They then went to prayer, and the Lord poured out his Spirit upon them. Whether this systematic plan was adopted by the me-

* This appears to be from the Saxon *benc*, a long seat; as *banc*, in the same language, signifies a long heap of earth. It is hence that our *bench* is derived. *Bankan*, a bank; *maingk*, *beinse*, and *benk*, a bench; *bank* and *bench* being one and the same word, signifying a long sitting place, as in the case of the British judges, who sat for ages upon banks instead of benches. It is the same with the Irish *balc*, which answers to the *balc* of the Welsh, and denotes a balk of land, as also does a bench. *Banquet* is supposed to be a slip of the same root. *Banquegeal* is to feast, and *banuez*, *banket* is a feast; the idea being taken from sitting to a table, as *cinio* is a feast; and *ciniau*, *cuynos* a table, from sitting on banks or benches to it, as *banquette*, in French, is at present a small bank in fortification.

tropolitans on the occasion is not stated: but it is affirmed that ten persons were blessed,—some with pardon, and others with the sanctification of the Spirit. He closed the month by attending one of the quarterly meetings, and by preaching at St. George's chapel. His excellent daughter continued to approach nearer and nearer the grand boundary line which divides time and eternity—her fairest prospects on the one side, and her infirmities only on the other.

OCTOBER.—While some of the preachers and friends were characterized by Samuel as "flames of fire," there were others who were less favourable to his mode of proceeding, and of course required more zeal. But having only one straight-forward course, admonitory interpositions were generally fruitless. A female, having been convinced of sin while he was preaching on Rom. viii, 13, was in deep distress in one of the prayer meetings. He knelt down to pray for her; and experiencing unusual freedom, he elevated his voice to an extraordinary height. "One of the London preachers," said he, "came to me, and pulled me by the coat. I asked him what was the matter: and he told me not to pray so loud, as another person was in distress in the chapel, and it produced confusion. But I took no notice of the discharge: I prayed on till the Lord set her soul at liberty, and she declared it in the great congregation." He added, "It is better to obey God than man." He had never learned to sound a retreat: "*Onward*," was his motto in every thing that concerned the soul; and this he was constantly urging upon others, as well as dwelling upon himself. To a friend he observed, about the same time, "I hope, my dear brother, you are still going on in the good old way, which leads to glory and to God. If we get religion to live with, we shall have religion to die with." Then, with no bad attempt at smartness, he asked, "Die, did I say? No, that is a wrong term for a Christian. It is religion to fall asleep with. When David finished his work, he slept with his fathers. The prophets also fell asleep; and St. Paul asks, 'O death, where is thy sting? Thanks be to God, who giveth us the victory, through our Lord Jesus Christ.'" It was the consciousness of preparation which he carried about with him, that deprived death of its terrors, and kept alive the notion of *sleep*—of a person just closing his eyes, and going to rest after the toils of the day.

It was as natural for him to converse on religious subjects as it was to breathe; and almost as impossible for him to see or hear any thing, without connecting religion with it. After a tremendous night of thunder, lightning, wind, and rain, on the 10th of the month, he remarked, "We have been spared from the threatening storm by a kind Protector; but I am afraid we shall hear of many lives being lost on the wide ocean. The rain has washed the tiles and the streets clean. The tiles look as if they were new. My prayer is, that God would send a thunder storm into every sinner's heart, and the lightning of his Spirit, to enlighten every sinner's conscience; and that he would, by the precious blood of Christ, cleanse the hearts of all true believers, as he has washed the tiles and the streets of this city."

He had laboured and prayed much for the heathen; and though divided from them by seas and continents, a circumstance occurred, which appeared to bring them to his own door, in the person of a black, who sat as his hearer in one of the chapels. His hue awakened all Samuel's sympathies for the negroes of the West India Islands. So much was his mind absorbed in the subject, that the whole congregation of whites appeared to be concentrated in this swarthy son of Ham. He told them that God was no respecter of persons—that persons of all nations working righteousness were accepted of him—and that colour, size, and age, made no difference to him, provided they came as penitents to his footstool. Such were the effects produced by his pointed and personal appeals, that the black got up in the midst of the people, and attested the goodness of God personally to himself, in the forgiveness of all his sins. Samuel went home with him—he being in comfortable circumstances—and took supper with him; and was pleased to find that "he had as clear a witness of the Spirit as a white man." The last expression would seem to indicate as though he had been infected with the slaveholder's cant, that negroes are an inferior race of beings, and incapable of improvement; and for the weakest and most innocent minds to receive a taint from the opinion, in its progress through European society, only shows the necessity of mooting it, by opposing to it the stubbornness of fact, in instances of religious and intellectual improvement.

Mr. Wrathall received a letter from Grassington about this time, requesting his presence, on account of the indisposition of his uncle, to whom he was left executor, and who was in fact at the point of death. Mrs. Wrathall's increasing debility rendered the prospect of absence the more painful. However, the certainty of her father's society was an agreeable compensation for the temporary loss proposed. In writing home on the 11th, he remarked, "Your dear daughter Rosamond is much better this morning than she has been for some days past. We thought a few days ago she was about to enter her eternal rest. But the Lord does all things well. She has been made a blessing to many. She expressed her thankfulness for her food this morning, and gave out that verse, 'We thank thee, Lord, for this our food.' I believe I shall have cause to bless God to all eternity for her." Her bodily improvement, alas! was but of short duration; for she died on the 17th of the month, a blessed witness of the power of God to save to the uttermost.

Samuel continued in London after the decease of his daughter, till January, 1828, in the early part of which month he paid a visit to Windsor, partly out of respect to it as the seat of royalty, and partly in compliance with an invitation from some friends; and was escorted thither by a person from town. A pious soldier of the name of Wm. Emmott, a corporal in the Royal Horse Guards, was the only person with whom he had any acquaintance. He preached on the evening of his arrival, and held a prayer meeting afterward. So much were the people pleased and profited, that they requested him to remain with them a few days. Mr. Pollard, the superintendent, wrote to Miss Hick, his daughter, who was at Mr. Wrathall's, January 7th, stating his intention. Part of the note is, "Your father is going to stay with us at Windsor over the next sabbath. He is very happy and useful." Samuel added on the same page, "My dear child, this morning I am in my glory. The Lord poured out his Spirit at the prayer meeting last night. Four souls obtained liberty; and many were blessed. If spared till to-morrow, I am *bown* to see Dr. Clarke. He has sent me word, that he will give me a week's board. There is a great work to do in this place; and you know I love the Lord with all my heart. I have been at the king's stables, where my brother-in-law conversed with his majesty. Our brother Jeb is with me, who will return to-day. God bless you all. You must take me in when I come."

He was shown over the grounds and castle

of Windsor. The road leading up to the palace, the flight of steps, the rooms, the paintings, and the extensive prospect from the summit—presenting, he observed, "a view of twelve counties"—were what appeared to have fixed attention, and left his mind, like a "chamber of imagery," imbued with their various forms. And yet, much as he was impressed with these, they did not excite the emotions of which he was the subject, when he could connect any thing celestial or devotional with what passed in review. Thus the representation of the late lamented Princess Charlotte, with her infant, ascending to heaven, fired his fancy, and melted his heart. "It was," in his own language, "as *naturable* (natural) as life." But fascinated as he was with this, a stronger feeling was produced—only not so permanent—by the sight of the old cushion—to which allusion has been already made—upon which his Majesty George III. knelt during his morning devotions. "The cushion," said Samuel, "was worn through with constant kneeling. I knelt me down upon it, and prayed that the time might come when all his majesty's subjects would wear out their cushions with praying." This "divine breathing," though oddly expressed, was sincere; and few, perhaps, have been the persons that have approached his prayerful example on visiting the royal domain.

The following selections from a letter written just before he left Windsor will show the spirit in which he continued: "Thursday was spent to the glory of God. I preached at Chertsey, about two miles from Windsor, at night, and held a prayer meeting. Many were blessed. Friday was spent in singing and in prayer. We had a prayer meeting at night. Bless the Lord! after a good night's rest, I arose happy in my soul. I had a good preparation for the second sabbath of the new year. Praise the Lord, O my soul, and forget not all his benefits. I preached on the Sunday forenoon, and held a lovefeast in the afternoon. It was a precious time to my soul: and the friends told me they never had such a lovefeast before. After preaching at night, we had a great outpouring of the Spirit of God. This is truly a wicked place. There are many soldiers in it. Methodism is very low; but I hope the time will come when it shall blossom like the rose. Most of the people in the town appear to be going the church-way, blindfold, to hell. The king has his residence at this place; and the people, like the Romans, must worship like their king. But I pray that the churches may be supplied with gospel-preachers; and then they will be filled with gospel-hearers. May the Lord hasten that happy day!"

On his return to London, where it is probable his stay would have been still protracted, he found a summons from Yorkshire, requesting his presence, to discharge a debt of friendship. Mrs. Pullein, of Follifoot, had exacted a promise from him, that in the event of his surviving her, he should preach her funeral sermon. On her demise, the family wrote to Samuel. His friends told him it was not necessary he should go then,—that he should go on purpose,—or even take a journey at all of such a distance, at his age, and during such a season, to preach a single sermon, particularly as there were preachers in Yorkshire who could supply his lack of service. But though they knew the nature of a promise, they felt nothing of its responsibility pressing upon their consciences, and could therefore satisfy themselves with what they were not personally called upon to discharge. Samuel felt it in all its weight, and connected with it all the solemnities of the occasion, and said, "When I meet Mrs. Pullein in the morning of the resurrection, and she asks, 'Sammy, did not you promise to preach my funeral sermon?' what shall I say? I have promised, and must go." He obeyed the call. He took for his text Numbers xxiii, 10, "Let me die the death of the righteous;" on reading which he closed the Bible, and said to the people, "Now, if you will live the life, you shall die the death of the righteous; and much more than this I cannot tell you, if I were to preach to you ever so long." Though he had travelled upward of two hundred miles to preach this occasional sermon, he only spoke about ten minutes.

His warm and kindly feelings, and the utter intractability of his nature to bend to the becoming gravities, whether real or assumed, of funeral occasions, would sometimes disturb the serious aspect of a whole company. As he knew no feelings, except those which he ordinarily carried about with him, so he had but one face, one attitude, one mode of expressing himself, whatever might be the event or the circumstances in which persons might be placed. His sincerity, and his ignorance of all etiquette, would admit of nothing else. Thus, several years prior to this, he was invited to attend the funeral of Mrs. W., of Garforth, on the occasion of whose death a sermon was preached, and afterward published, by the Rev. J. Wood. A cold collation was provided for the friends on the day of interment, which, as the company was large, was served up in a malt-kiln, where one party succeeded another, returning, when refreshed, to a large room. Samuel, with others, had made preparations for a funeral sermon. His text, he told the friends, was given to him in sleep; on which occasion he had roused Martha, as he had done in reference to the dream which sealed his call to the ministry, and to which she paid equal attention, when the information was communicated. The text was, "I was a hungered, and ye gave me meat." But honest Samuel, not being favoured with a concordance, was unable to advert to the book, the chapter, and the verse, where it was to be found, and therefore had to institute an inquiry among his friends for his farther satisfaction. He had a heart to receive the impression which truth made upon it, and memory sufficient to retain the sentiment, and often the form of expression; but, like many others, of much more reading, the common-place book of his recollection could not in every instance carry the penman's title and his page. The mind being set at rest, as it regarded the text, and the excellences of the deceased being the subject of conversation, Samuel wept, and in the midst of his tears, sent forth a smile of joy at the thought of another soul having weathered the storm of life, and obtained firm footing on the opposite shore, where the heaving surges are smoothed down to a "sea of glass." He intimated his intention to preach a sermon on the occasion of her death, in one of the chapels; and stated further, with his usual artlessness—not aware that the disclosure would subject him to a little concealed pleasantry—that he had penned his thoughts on the subject, placing his hand to his pocket, with a still farther intimation that he had the MS. with him. Some of the friends, who were less the subjects of sorrow than the immediate relations of the deceased, perceiving that he only required an invitation to bring the production to light, and knowing the singular character which his thoughts assumed in the dress in which they were generally arrayed, requested him to read what he had penned to the company,—hoping withal, that some gems might turn up that would interest the hearers. Samuel took hold of his pocket with one hand, and the MS. with the other, and drew it forth, a good deal sullied and cramped, as though it had been forged in the smithy, and lain in his pocket with other things since it had been written. He sprung from his chair—proceeded across the room—placed his glasses in order—turned his shoulder to the window, and the MS. to the light—looked and looked again—occasionally contracting his eyes, and adding to the adjustment of his spectacles. Not succeeding to his wishes, he turned the other shoulder to the window—permitting as much of the light to fall upon the paper as possible,—hemming, and stammering, and shuffling—till at length, in a fit of impatience and disappointment, and without being able to work his way through a single sentence, he threw it down on the table before the Rev. J. Wood, saying, "There, Mr. Wood,—I cannot read it—take it, and try what you can do with it," smacking his glasses into their case, like a sword into its scabbard, and stalking across the room again to his seat. When it is remarked, that this was too much for the gravity of Mr. Wood, the reader is left to conjecture the effect produced upon others. Yet, with all this, Samuel was left the subject of weeping, smiling, unsuspecting simplicity.

CHAPTER XII.

Takes a tour through different parts of Yorkshire—Low state of the work of God at Warter—Gives the preference to vocal music in a place of worship—Goes into the Snaith circuit—Goole—Meets with old friends—Is affected with early recollections, on visiting the scene of Martha's juvenile days—Prayer meetings—Returns to Yorkshire—Labours in the Easingwold circuit—Is again cheered with the sight of old associates—His increasing popularity—Meets with a serious accident by a fall from his horse—His conduct when under medical attendance—Is visited by Mr. Dawson—His partial restoration to health—Visits the West Riding—Proceeds into Lancashire—Is attacked by an infidel while preaching out of doors at Bolton—Is summoned by letter to Grassington—Becomes seriously indisposed—Witnesses the happy death of his niece—Returns home—Declines rapidly in health—Attends to some funeral arrangements—His state of mind—His triumphant death—The general sympathy excited on the occasion—Conclusion.

On his return home, he continued with the same diligence, which had previously distinguished his conduct, to benefit his fellow-creatures. The great religious institutions of the nineteenth century were styled by him "the seeds of the millennium;" and every act of his own was viewed as an effort to force the shoots;—a tree this, which will throw its mighty shadow over every nation under heaven.

The year (1828) was begun in the spirit in which its predecessor had closed—a spirit purely devotional. Having been at home a short time, he again left it, and went into the Pocklington circuit, tarrying a night on the road, at the house of his old friend, Mr. Peart. One of the travelling preachers being indisposed, he was requested to supply a few places. At Warter, in the neighbourhood of the Wolds, which was the place where he opened his commission, he found but little of that fermented feeling which he had seen manifested in the neighbourhood of York. He found preaching here, he remarked, "as hard work as labouring at the anvil." The word seemed to rebound upon himself, and so to "return void." "There was as great a difference in the climate, for religion," continued he, between the district he had left, and that upon which he had entered, "as between summer and winter." But he "claimed," as he stated, his "privilege of having a prayer meeting after preaching," and requested those who were desirous of pardon, "to come up to the *benk*." The wife of a blacksmith was one who acceded to the proposal; and, having been some time under religious awakenings, was prepared for the consolations of the Spirit of God, which she obtained through the exercise of faith in Christ. At Pocklington, Elvington, and Sutton-upon-Derwent, he was exceedingly happy in his work.

From hence he proceeded to Selby, and attended the March quarterly meeting. Here he was hospitably entertained by Mr. B. Clarkson. His congregations were large, and the blessing of God attended his labours. He was especially delighted with the singing. "I never heard such singing before," he remarked: "they have no instruments—no fiddles—no organs. They sing with the spirit, and with the understanding also. I thought when I heard them, if our friends at Leeds would only use their voices to praise the Lord, it would not only be more pleasing to him, but they would be more blessed in their souls; for *singing is worshipping God.*" This is the common-sense view of the subject; and the last sentence falls with the weight of a destructive hammer upon every instrument of music in a place of Christian worship. He spoke of peace and prosperity in the Selby circuit, and hoped that the time would soon come, when, in other places, "party zeal would be driven to its own hell."

The port of Goole, a place in the Snaith circuit, had, in the space of six years, increased in its population from two hundred to nearly one thousand inhabitants. A Wesleyan society had been established for a number of years, and the place in which they worshipped latterly was a temporary erection, raised at the expense of the Aire and Calder Canal Company, and in which a number of Sunday scholars were taught. The place being small and uncomfortable, the friends agreed to build a chapel, toward which Mr. Hamer, who was the first to enter his name, subscribed £50. On the same day, and in the course of a few hours, upward of £100 was promised. One of the Snaith friends, having heard of Samuel's success in different instances, requested that he should be invited to aid them. He was accordingly written to, but the letter not reaching him immediately, if at all, he did not proceed thither till one of the circuit preachers had personally expressed to him their wish.

He proceeded, therefore, from Selby to Snaith, and its adjacencies. In the earlier stage of the visit, April 13th, he observes, "I am now at Goole. I have to preach every night; and on the sabbath day I shall have to preach three times. You see, the Lord finds me work, and, as I love it, I have plenty of it. He gives me favour in the sight of the people. The places for preaching are too small for them: they flock like doves to their windows." He was here visited by a female, an old acquaintance, who once, with her husband, walked in the light of God's countenance, but had also, with him, retraced her steps to the world. Through his preaching and conversation they were again roused from the torpor of spirit which had seized them; and to render their return to the church of God more secure, he entered the name of the female into his memorandum-book, in order that he might be able to give the superintendent of the circuit proper directions, to find out such stray sheep. The woman, said he, "sprang from a good stock. Her grandmother, Ruth Naylor, was a good mother, a good wife, and a good Christian. My creed is, that God will save to the third and fourth generation. This has been the case in my family, and in many a family: yes, and he will bless to a thousand generations."

While going from place to place, several

other friendships were revived. At Swinefleet he entered among the friends of Mr. Knight; at another place he met with a ship-captain, a religious character, in whose vessel he had preached a sermon during his last visit to London; and at a third place, out of the Snaith circuit, he had several interviews with his friend Mr. Thompson, of Armin. Amid many pleasing remembrances, however, there was one connected with the early history of Martha, which was the occasion of much painful feeling. "Yesterday," he observes on writing home to her, "I preached at Garthorp, in Marsland, near the place where you lived when you were with J. H. The house you lived in is now pulled down, and a new one built. The chapel which I preached in is built over against it. The congregation was large; and I took tea with the blacksmith. He knew you well; but he is now going off: he has been in a dying state for the last twelve years. I assure you, I thought of your journey out of Lincolnshire; I could scarcely ever get you out of my head;—to think of your usage with that ungodly man! But he has gone to his reward. I thought of your journey, when you could not keep your shoes on your feet; but the roads are *stoned* and very good now. I wish you were here, to see your old friends. I have heard you say, that the blacksmith's wife was very good to you, when you were ill. I saw the flag that parts the counties. But I will tell you more, if I am spared to get home." In addition to this, he had been informed of some misunderstanding among some of the friends at Micklefield, which had warped their better feelings toward each other. On this, he remarks, "I hope you have got peace proclaimed, and all jarring buried. I will *say* the funeral service over it,—'Earth to earth, dust to dust, ashes to ashes.' The sooner it is buried the better. Love cannot dwell where there is prejudice and party spirit. Give my love to all my neighbours and friends: tell them I am happy, and in a good state of health."

Armin, which was one of Samuel's favourite places, in consequence of Mr. Thompson granting him perfect liberty to follow the bias of his own mind, often became the scene of strong religious excitement, and through that excitement, of permanent benefit to those who were its subjects. Separate from domestic worship, morning and evening, Samuel had his prayer meetings with the servants and neighbours. It was agreed one night, in the course of one of his visits, between the servants and himself, that they should have a prayer meeting early the next morning. Samuel was up, as usual, by four o'clock. On descending from his chamber to the kitchen, he found the windows closed, and no appearance of wakefulness among the inmates of the house. He returned to his chamber, and having prayed and sung alone—his morning hymn having in all probability reached the ears of the sleepers—he was soon joined by the group. But as they had not given him the meeting at the hour and place appointed, he insisted on their stopping with him in his room. This was not very well relished by some of the servants, who knew that Mrs. C., on a visit from London, slept in an adjoining chamber. But it was of no importance to Samuel, who very likely thought that the good lady would be as profitably engaged with them, as lying in bed, at an hour when the birds were beginning to wake into song, and heaven was alive to their melody. Samuel commenced the devotional exercise in good earnest; they prayed—they sung—they met in band; and Mrs. C.—for sleep was in vain where there was only a partition between the rooms—was compelled to keep watch with the party, and, to render the noise at all supportable, had to join in the devotions of the morning as she lay on her couch.

The evening was generally occupied in the same way. On one occasion, when Mr. Thompson and Mr. P., one of the preachers, went to Howden, to evening preaching, Samuel was left behind. On their return, they heard an unusual noise in the house; and on opening the door, they found the servants and neighbours encircling him like a living wall of fire—every one breathing forth the spirit of devotion—Samuel's own lips touched with live coals from the altar—in all the glory of a revival. Mr. P. was for dismissing them, but Mr. Thompson, who knew both Samuel's weaknesses and his excellences, interposed his authority, and requested him not to interfere, without at the same time appearing to give the meeting his own decided sanction. One man was so powerfully affected, that several persons were obliged to hold him; and an old man, eighty years of age, was confirmed in his religious experience and principles, which Samuel—not having had a previous knowledge of him—mistook for conversion. The missionary meeting succeeded this; and Samuel, being called upon to move or second a resolution, took occasion to give a detailed account of the principal circumstances of the meeting the night before. Having, however, omitted the case of the old man, and being reminded of it by Mr. Thompson, he suddenly turned around upon him, and in a loud and sharp tone, with a good deal of fire in his eye, which showed that a portion of his own spirit was infused into it, and as though he thought it "well to be angry" for the Lord, replied, "Heh! and you were none so well pleased with it either"—exciting the smile of the auditory. He supported what he deemed opposition, or indifference, in a revival, with but an ill grace occasionally. Mr. P., who could not endure the noise in the prayer meeting, was obliged to take up his cross in another way. He had Samuel for his bed-fellow one night; and long before "tired nature" had recruited herself with "balmy sleep," he had to struggle between slumber and song, at an early hour in the morning, till his mate, whose instrument was always in tune, had carolled a hymn composed of about ten verses, as he lay by his side.

His eccentricities in a prayer meeting were not always to be endured with gravity. While at Mr. Bell's, of Temple Hurst, a man was praying very devoutly for the conversion of his wife. Samuel knew that there were other prerequisites besides prayer; and supposing him to be a little defective in some of the milder qualities of the mind at home, stopped him, and turning around, as he elevated himself, said, "Set a trap for her, man, and take care to bait it with faith and love"—settling instantly down to his devotions as before, adding to the person, whose voice had been interrupted for the moment, "There, you may go on again."

Any improper feeling, as manifested on the platform, toward Mr. Thompson, was quickly swallowed up in the finer flow of divine love, which pervaded his whole soul, and was let out on the most insignificant portions of the unintelligent creatures of God. Speaking to Mr. Thompson one day, on the subject of religious experience, he said, "I had a field of wheat once; the crows picked it, and scarcely left a single grain; I felt something rise within me, that said, 'I wish I had you all in a *band;*'" then, looking at his friend, he continued, as if afraid of being suspected of indulging a disposition for cruelty, incompatible with what he deemed a high state of grace—"But, mind ye, I was not sanctified then."

While in this neighbourhood, he solicited

subscriptions for the proposed chapel at Goole—preached to every society in the circuit—assisted in holding four missionary meetings—and was frequently entertained by respectable families, who were not in membership with the Wesleyan body. The latter pressed him to repeat his visits.

Samuel took a particular interest, as will have been perceived, in the welfare of persons of his own trade; and an instance of usefulness may here be recorded, as given by a blacksmith in a religious assembly, when Samuel was remote from the sound of his voice. "I thank God," said he, "for what he has done for my soul. I lived long in open rebellion against him—sinning in the face of light and knowledge—and training up my children for the devil. My father, who was pious, reproved me, but I regarded him not. He entered my house once, while I was playing at cards with my children, and spoke to me on its impropriety. My passion rose—I swore—took hold of him, and turned him to the door. Samuel Hick came the next day to our place to preach; and going around to invite the people, he came and pressed me to attend. He saw I was throng; but to accomplish his purpose, said, 'If you are fast, I will help you;' nor would he leave me till I promised to attend preaching. Accordingly, I went; and the Lord met me. All my sins were placed before me, and pressed me heavily. I cried aloud for mercy; Samuel came and prayed with me; I prayed for myself; and it was not long before the Lord blessed me with Christian liberty. He filled me with peace and joy through believing, and has preserved me in his ways to the present time."

He left Snaith and its neighbourhood about the end of April; and after paying one of his "angel visits" at home, visited the York, Pocklington, and Tadcaster circuits: and three of the places in which he was unusually favoured with the divine blessing were Hessay, Acomb, and Moormonkton, at the latter of which he observed, "They sang like angels." When at Hessay, in the month of November, having been from home some time, he found himself, as usual, nearly drained of cash by his charities, one of the last of which consisted in contributing toward the purchase of a pig for a poor woman, who had lost one by some accident or distemper. "She was sorely distressed," said he, "for she had fed and brought it up, and could not buy another without the help of her friends. She was a good Christian; and I gave her the most of what I had in my pocket." But his purse was soon replenished. His son-in-law, Mr. W., had occasion to be in the country; and on finding that he was in the neighbourhood of York, sought him, and found him in conversation with a friend in the street. Laying his hand on his shoulder, Samuel turned around, and was surprised to find the face of a relation peering in his own. As Mr. W. was just passing through the city by coach to London, he could only propose a few brief questions, one of which was, "How does your pocket stand affected?" to which Samuel replied, "It is very low." Mr. W. knew the generosity of his nature; and dipping deep into his own pocket, gave him a handful of silver. Samuel considered this a providential supply, saying, "When I was nearly done with my money, the Lord sent my son to York, who gave me more. I want for neither meat, money, nor clothes; and my peace flows like a river." At this period he often preached once a day in the course of the week, and two or three times on the sabbath.

He had been employed in the course of this year, too, in soliciting subscriptions for Rider chapel, a village near Cawood, forming part of the Selby circuit. The summer, the autumn, and the beginning of 1829, were spent in different directions; and wherever he was followed, the people bore a lively recollection of his visits. Traces of him were invariably found in the conversations of the friends; his works and his walk left as distinct an impression upon the mind, as the print of the human foot to the eye, after a person has crossed the sand of the seashore.

Samuel was in York in the latter end of March, 1829; and the friends in Easingwold wishing him to pay them a visit, a farmer and his good wife, both of whom had been brought to God some years before, through his instrumentality, when residing in the York circuit, were deputed to give him the meeting in the city, and to convey him to the place. He arrived at Easingwold on the 4th of April, and was entertained chiefly at the house of Mr. William and Miss Mary Dixon. Being well acquainted with Mrs. Roadhouse, he deposited with her two pounds, saying that he was afraid of losing it; adding, with a smile, "I have cheated Matty out of this." Mr. R. had been his banker in the Snaith circuit, but having dealt the separate portions out to him with parsimony, from an impression that he gave indiscriminately, he thus made a change. His liberality, however, was again put under arrest; and when he was prevented from giving the whole away, he went among the more opulent and begged that he might be made their almoner. One instance of unnecessary, though not inconsiderate bounty, occurred while here. He stepped into the house of a barber, and requested to be shaved. Inquiring of the man whether he had any other means of supporting his family, and being answered in the negative, Samuel put a shilling into his hand. This produced a grateful feeling, and the man, in Samuel's estimation, was prepared for any thing that might follow. He talked to him on the subject of religion, and then proposed prayer. The different members of the family were speedily on their knees, and the worshipping group were open for the inspection of the next customer that might turn in for the same operation that had been performed upon the officiating priest. A thousand persons might be found to part with their money in the same way, but a thousand persons of the same piety might be found, who, in the same place, and under the same circumstances, could not have brought themselves to act thus, and might be justified in such conduct without being disposed to enter a sentence of condemnation against Samuel.

Of the affection and attention of the Rev. Messrs. Roadhouse and Garbutt, he spoke in grateful terms; and besides preaching, attended, in connection with them, several missionary meetings. Descanting on a part of his labours, he remarked in his own peculiar way, "I preached last night (April 24th, on the other side of Hambleton Hills; and the Lord, and Mr. Roadhouse, and me, held a missionary meeting;" denoting that the Divine Being was as signally present in the influence of his Spirit on the hearts of the people—and without whose presence all missionary meetings are vain to the persons assembled—as though he had been rendered visible to the eye. "It is a mountainous country," continued he, "but very pleasant. The people came from all quarters—from hill and dale: the chapel was crowded, and we had a good time. I never saw friends more kind." Here, too, as at Snaith, in the bosom of the mountains, he realized the truth of the proverb of the wise man, "As iron sharpeneth iron, so a man sharpeneth the countenance of his friend." Early recollections—such as extended to the days of childhood—were revived. One person, in particular, he noticed; and his joy was full, because of his meeting her on Christian ground. "I have found some of my own country friends here; one of them, a woman, born at Aberford. Her maiden name was Barker; she married Mr. Wilkinson's steward, who is now dead. Her eldest son and daughter have died very happy; and if I live till next week, I shall have to preach her funeral sermon." He then spoke of the joy he experienced: further stating his belief that the Lord had "as surely sent" him "into the circuit, as he sent Jonah to preach to the Ninevites. He waters my soul with the dews of heaven."

Hawnley was another of the places which Samuel visited, where he rendered himself amusingly popular by waiting upon the clergyman of the parish, requesting him to "give them a speech at the missionary meeting." The reverend gentleman declining, Samuel tried him on another point.

Samuel. "Will you please then, sir, to give us a pound for the missions?"

Clergyman. "That is too much, and I have no silver upon me; but if you will give me silver for a note, I will give you half a crown."

Sam. "Nay, give the note, sir; it is a noble cause."

Samuel's companion, having a little more delicacy of feeling about him than himself, and perceiving that the pound was more than it was prudent to urge, offered, in order to relieve the clergyman from his importunity, to give him twenty shillings in silver. Samuel immediately, in an altered tone, said,

"Give the gentleman five shillings."

Cler. "That will not do."

Sam. "Ten then, sir."

Cler. "I will give you half a crown."

Sam. "Not less than five shillings, if you please, sir."

The full change was given, and an apology was offered for Samuel, for whom it was fortunate an apologist was at hand. Samuel, on the other hand, dropped upon his knees in the room to improve the occasion, and prayed devoutly and fervently for the divine blessing upon the clergyman. Whether as a rebuke, by way of intimating that instruction was necessary, or as a token of respect—which at least was singular—the reverend gentleman sent one of his written sermons in the evening, accompanied with his regards, to Samuel's companion.

Without placing the least dependance upon works, he toiled as though heaven were alone to be won by them. "If I had ten thousand bodies and souls," said he, "they should all be spent in the service of God." At Carlton, Sheriff Hutton, and several other places, the word of exhortation was made a blessing to the people. His usefulness and popularity appeared to advance with his age. Persons who had heard of him were prompted by curiosity to attend his public addresses; and those who had benefited by them followed him from place to place: so that with the curious, the profited, and the stated hearers, the chapels were generally crowded. In addition to evening preaching, travelling, and visiting the sick, he attended three missionary meetings in one week—moving about in the 70th year of his age with the apparent vigour of youth, and with the fire of a new convert. At one of those meetings he met with the Rev. G. Marsden, from Bolton, who pressed him to take another journey into Lancashire, which he resolved to perform in the course of the year, should he be favoured with health and opportunity. He exulted, too, in the prospect of meeting with his friend Mr. Dawson, at a missionary meeting in the month of May. That month arrived; but the 14th was a day to be remembered by Samuel and his friends. He was on his way from Easingwold to Hemsley Black Moor, to attend a missionary meeting. When about three miles from Hemsley, his horse took fright at a chaise, upon which some white bags were suspended, enclosing some fighting cocks, wheeled around, and he fell off. "Though no bones," says Mr. Dawson, "were either broken or dislocated, yet the shock was felt through his whole frame. He nevertheless attended the meeting; but soon found it necessary to leave, when he was taken to the house of a friend." The scene which followed would form a subject as suitable for the pencil of Wilkie as for the pen of a divine. Bleeding being deemed necessary, a medical gentleman was sent for; but in consequence of absence, his place was supplied by one of his pupils. On his appearance, Samuel threw off his coat, and turned up his shirt sleeve, as if about to enter on the business of the smithy. Had the arm been composed of wood, or belonged to some other person, he could not have manifested greater self-possession, promptitude, and apparent want of feeling. Stretching it out—his hand meanwhile grasping the handle of a long brush, and pointing to the vein, "There, my lad," said he, "strike there;" having the phleme and the quadruped present in his mind, rather than the lancet and the human being. The youth, under the impression of fear, pricked the vein, but no blood appeared. "Try again," said Samuel. The experiment was again fruitlessly made. He instantly turned up the sleeve of the other arm, as if going to another job, or as if he intended to give additional strength to one at which he had just failed, and determinately pointing to the spot, said, "Try here, lad; strike here, and see if thou canst get any thing." This experiment, with the exception of a few drops, was as ineffectual as those that preceded. The youth was overcome with fear, and withdrew. Fortunately for Samuel, the surgeon himself came, about an hour afterward, and bled him copiously, after which he was placed in a bed. While bleeding, he said, "Glory be to God! if I die I'll get the sooner to heaven." In the course of the same evening, while Mr. Dawson was preaching, the vein was opened by some accident, when Mrs. Bentley, who was at chapel, and at whose house he lodged, was sent for, and through her kind attentions, aid was procured, and the arm again bandaged. Samuel thought his work was done, and said to the friends around him, in a tone of holy triumph, "I am *bown* home;—glory be to God! I am *bown* home." He expressed a wish to see Mr. Dawson again, who had called upon him before, and who no sooner closed the service in the evening, than he made all possible speed to his lodging. On entering the room, Samuel accosted him, with a full flow of spirit and of tears, "I am *bown* home, *barn!* Glory be to God, I am very happy! I should have bled to death, *barn*, but I happened to awaken." He next proceeded, "I want my will made, and you must make it." Mr. D., not deeming him so near his exit as he imagined, and adapting his language and imagery to Samuel's thinkings and knowledge of words, answered, "Well, Sammy, if it is to be so, you are a *brown sheller;*" referring by that, as Samuel well knew, to the *ripe* fruit—*brown*, and ready to *drop* from the tree, and which, when taken into the hand, falls out of the *husk*. He was acquainted with Samuel's character, and beheld him as *ripe* and *ready* for a blessed immortality. "Yes," replied Samuel, "I am *bown* to glory." The will was drawn up according to the best directions he was able to give; but as Martha was both cashier and accountant, he knew very little of his own affairs, and of course found it necessary afterward to have it altered.

He met with his accident on the Thursday, and on the Saturday was so far restored as to be able to return to Easingwold in a gig. The friends at Easingwold, knowing that the beginning of the week was the period fixed for his return to Micklefield, proposed that he should preach to them on the Sunday—accompanying the proposal with a hope that it would not seriously injure him, while employing every argument to accomplish their wishes, at the risk of his health and life.* He received the proposi-

* This, to say the least, was inconsiderate, being only the day after he had been shaken a good deal by his removal from Helmsley; and were it not for others than the friends at Easingwold—to whom the following remarks are not intended to apply beyond the point of inconsideration just noticed—farther observations would have been withheld. What between *conscience* on the part of the preachers, and *thoughtlessness* on the part of the people—a *willingness* to expend the utmost of their strength in the cause of God in the one, and *anxiety* for them to be useful, founded on the value of immortal souls, in the other, the men very often become martyrs in the work. The people are especially culpable in urging a *willing* servant of God to work, in cases of great debility; and instances have been known, when, instead of preventing men from running the most imminent danger of relapse, or something worse, those very men have been tortured in every possible way by reasons why the pulpit should be supplied;—the tormentors themselves sitting like philosophers all the time, as if coolly making experiments upon human nature, to see the utmost point to which it would go, then returning with the languishing sufferer, administering their *hopes*, like cordials, that—after they have wrung from him the last mite of physical strength, he will be no worse, but improved—by thus throwing the fever into his system, with a night's *sound repose*. Such conduct, if practised in civil life, would be viewed in no other light than as the result of mere *brutal feeling*. The only difference between an ungodly man *overworking* his servants, like a set of West Indian slaves, and persons who are criminal in the case in

tion with his wonted cheerfulness—preached on the sabbath evening—assisted in conducting a prayer meeting on the Monday evening—and proceeded to York in a gig on the Tuesday morning. Reduced as he was in his bodily strength, such was the unconquerable nature of the spirit he possessed, aided by the prospects of a better world, that he appeared more like a person who had just risen from slight indisposition, rather than as having walked a few paces back into life again from the verge of the grave.

He complained of great internal pain at first; and although it pleased the Lord to raise him again from his couch, and permit him to engage in his usual labour of love, he was more sus-

hand—and to no other the subject can be applied—is, that the former are *driven*, and the latter are *dogged* to it, through indiscreet zeal—incorrect notions of duty—sympathy for the multitude, with a kind of callous feeling toward the individual. Persons should be exceedingly careful not even to lay *temptations* in the way of *zealous*, but afflicted men, to take too early the exercise of the pulpit. A man of God has that within him which will not allow him to remain inactive longer than it is necessary. In such cases, the *people* should stand between the *couch* and the pulpit, and employ the *check* rather than the *incentive*. It is a hard case, when a man is under the necessity of killing himself to prove that he is poorly: and the worst is, that there is neither any *conscience* made of the matter, on the part of these *overworkers*, nor any tribunal at which to try them for their conduct. They go free, though the man of God may lose his life. He is afraid of their uncandid *reflections*, if he do not work; though without reasonable and serious reflection themselves; and to crown the whole, as it is done under the guise, so it is laid to the charge, of Christianity. A man may, perchance, survive it; but no thanks to the task-masters for the pain imparted, any more than for the life next to miraculously preserved.

ceptible of cold, while his friends perceived an evident decay both of memory and of corporeal strength.

Having preached in his own neighbourhood a short time, he left home for Lancashire in the early part of July. His route appears to have been the following. He remained two days at Swillington Bridge, in consequence of the rain, and spoke of the kindness of Mr. Gilgras. From thence he proceeded to Wakefield, where he preached, and at which place he had often experienced the kindness of S. Stocks, Esq., and other friends. Barnsley was his next place, prior to reaching which, he spent two days with Mr. Myers, who quaintly told him he was not to think of "making a road over his house." When he arrived at Barnsley, the friends prevailed upon him to remain until their missionary meeting. While in that neighbourhood, he preached at Burton and Cudworth. This was no new ground of labour to him; and at the latter place, particularly, he was rendered extremely serviceable to Mr. G., who afterward became a useful local preacher, but was in a state of mind verging toward despair, when met by Samuel. They slept in the same room, and every groan fetched up from the soul of the one was the signal for prayer to the other; nor was it an ejaculation with Samuel, uttered in a state of repose upon the pillow, which cost him nothing; for he rose again and again, and wrestled with God, like Jacob, both in the dark and at daybreak. He gave himself no rest, till rest was found by him who sought it. He had here an excellent coadjutor in the general work, in William Smith—a man of a very differently constructed mind, but in no respect his inferior for simplicity, zeal, and disinterestedness.

He remained some time also at the house of John Thorneley, Esq., Dodworth Green, near Barnsley, and was the minister of mercy to a number of poor families in the village of Dodworth. Here, as in other places, in seasons of distress, his funds, though often replenished by Mr. T. and others, were as often drained of the last mite. Cases of distress multiplying upon him, as is usual with those who take the trouble to seek after them, and having received supplies from his own friends, he inquired, as he had done at Burnley on a former occasion, whether there were not some opulent characters in the neighbourhood, who might be willing to contribute of their abundance toward the relief of the poor. He was told of one gentleman, by his friend, William Rhodes, but received only such hopes of success as unbelief could afford. Faith, in Samuel, could perceive no obstacles; he proceeded, therefore, to Mr. C.'s residence, and found him; and knowing less of circumlocution than the legal gentleman himself, entered directly upon the case. Mr. C., either to get rid of him, or being touched in a way which was as rare to himself as it was astonishing to others, took from his pocket a handful of silver, and gave it—feeling like a person, on Samuel's departure, who, in an unguarded moment, had suffered himself to be imposed upon, and wondering at his folly for having been so far overseen on the occasion. But the truth is, there was so much of God, of justice, of humanity, and of mercy, in all Samuel's applications, that they carried with them the authority of a command, and became unaccountably irresistible to the persons to whom they were made.

While he was at Dodworth Green, his respected friend, Edward Brooke, Esq., of Hoyland Swaine, sent his servant and gig for him. On seeing the conveyance, the tear started into his eye, and turning to Mrs. Thorneley,* he falteringly observed, "He will kill me." The zeal of Mr. B. was too much for Samuel's years; and such an expression, from such a man—one who counted not his life dear to him in the cause of God—must have been wrung from him in the agonizing reflection of past suffering. Of this, however, Mr. B. was not aware; and with his wonted kindness furnished him with a new suit of clothes. After labouring here a few weeks, he proceeded to Bolton, where he was on the 10th of August; and had

* This excellent lady, who knew how to estimate Samuel's piety and labours, has since been called to her eternal reward. The writer does not proceed beyond his personal knowledge when he states, that Mrs. T. was modest—retired—intelligent—liberal to the poor—hospitable, without parade—a perfect model of domestic order and happiness, without bustle—a great sufferer, but with the invincible patience and fortitude of a martyr—crowning the whole with the most exalted Christian spirit and demeanour.

it not been for this Lancashire tour, he would have proceeded into Derbyshire, for which Mr. Thorneley had made every preparation, in order that he might be rendered beneficial to the men employed in working his coal mines.

Not content with preaching in the chapels, he took his stand in the streets, and proclaimed the Saviour of sinners to the multitude. Taylor and Carlile had just been there, and had engaged the attention of a few of "the baser sort," who had become venders of their blasphemy. One of these attacked Samuel while he was addressing the people in the street; and Samuel, possessing greater confidence in the truth of God than ability to defend it, imprudently committed himself, by telling the man, that if he would suffer him to proceed without interruption to the close of the service, he would go into any private house with him, or with any number of the same persuasion, if there were a hundred of them, and he would take them one by one and conquer them. But the man was desirous of public conquest; and in the lowest slang of the two infidel missionaries, so famous for stooping and raking up from the very depths of the common sewers of infidelity all the filth of which a depraved heart is capable of conceiving, told Samuel that the Saviour he preached was a thief—that he could prove from the Bible itself he stole an ass from one person, and corn out of the field of another. Samuel immediately rebutted the charge, by insisting, that, as the Creator of all things, the earth, the corn, and the cattle upon a thousand hills, were his; that he only laid claim to his own property. This was as good a reply as the low, ignorant attack merited. The man was prevented from making farther disturbance, and Samuel was dissuaded from giving him the meeting. It was a heavy affliction, however, to his mind. He returned repeatedly to the subject, and felt all his sensibilities in operation for the honour of his Saviour. "I have heard of my dear Lord," said he to some of the friends, in his conversation afterward, "being called a wine-bibber, a gluttonous man, and a friend to publicans and sinners; but I never heard him called a thief and a robber before, though crucified between two." Then he would sob and weep over the charge, as though he wished to sympathize with his Divine Master, while lying, as he supposed, under this odium.*

* Messrs. *Taylor* and *Carlile* were itinerating the kingdom at this time, and in the true spirit of *infidel philanthropy*, after having charged the ministers of Christianity with making a *gain of godliness*, issued their tickets and their circulars to try what they themselves could accumulate in the way of *business*. The originals, which are in the writer's possession, are curiosities. The *ticket* specifies, that, "The Rev. Robert Taylor, B. A., will deliver an Oration this evening, July 6th, at half past seven, at the Manor Court Room, Brown-st., Manchester. *Admission to the Boxes*, 3*s*. —*to the Area of the Room*, 2*s*." So much for the modest *market-price* of infidel commodities to moneyed characters: and as there were no *free seats*, their system of *benevolence* does not, of course, reach the case of the *poor*. If Christian ministers were to admit their auditors into their places of public instruction at 2*s*. and 3*s*. per head, some of them would make an excellent concern of their "*orations*."

Prior to the tickets being offered for sale, the different

While at Bolton, he received a letter from Grassington, near Skipton, stating that a niece of his was very ill—not likely to recover—and wished to see him. He no sooner was inform-

ministers of religion were furnished with the circular referred to, of which the following is a copy:—

"The Rev. Robert Taylor. A. B., of Carey-street, Lincoln's Inn, and Mr. Richard Carlile, of Fleet-street, London, present their compliments, as infidel missionaries, to ——, and most respectfully and earnestly invite discussion on the merits of the Christian religion. which they argumentatively challenge, in confidence of their competency to prove that such a person as Jesus Christ, alleged to have been of Nazareth, never existed; and that the Christian religion had no such origin as has been pretended; neither is it in any way beneficial to mankind: but that it is nothing more than an emanation from the ancient pagan religion. The researches of the Rev. Robert Taylor on this subject are imbodied in his newly published work, 'The Diegesis,' in which may be found the routine of their argument. They also impugn the honesty of a continued preaching, while discussion is challenged on the whole merits of the Christian religion."

It is difficult to command sufficient muscle for gravity, in the perusal of such a document.

First: Robert Taylor comes forward as the avowed enemy of Christianity; and yet, without even a vestige of that Christianity, continues to cling with the tenacity of life to its *honours*, by still retaining the title of *Reverend*, which is one of the distinguishing honours of its ministers, and which he himself would never have thought of assuming, had it not been for his original connection with the church that conferred it, as is evident from its being withheld from his compeer, Richard Carlile, who is honoured with the less dignified title of *Master;*—thus contemning that by which he is still anxious to be exalted;—furnishing another exemplification of the fable of the proud jackdaw, which, not being satisfied with the plumage with which *nature* had favoured it, decorated itself with a few peacock's feathers;—slipping off with a pair of stilts—as confident of his own littleness, and mounting them on every convenient occasion.

Secondly: His title of A. B., still connected with his *once* Christian profession, is one to which no one will dispute his right—showing his progress in learning—having reached the

ed of this, than he took the coach for Skipton. The day was exceedingly wet; and he being on the outside, his clothes were drenched with rain. He arrived a few days before his niece

first two letters of the English alphabet;—halting without being able to arrive at D. This may be deemed sheer puerility. It is; nor is any thing else intended: but then the writer is led to it from a perusal of the "CIRCULAR," which speaks of the astonishing "*researches*" of the *Reverend* gentleman. And to what do they amount? To the amazing vastness of—NOTHING. For,

Thirdly: He undertakes "*to prove*," and that too "*argumentatively*," that "such a person as Jesus Christ never existed;"—that is, in plain language, to *prove* a *negative*. This is beating the *air* with a vengeance; and to say the least, he will certainly have *something* to do, in prosecuting the *task* of *proving* NOTHING.

To take the gentleman, however, on his own ground of *nothingness*, we ask—and ask seriously—if Christianity has not been "*any way* beneficial to mankind," in what solitary instance has infidelity been of service to the human species? Robert Taylor may be told of *one* "way"—and *one* will be as good as a thousand for the writer's purpose—in which Christianity, in its effects upon the human heart, has benefited man by man; and in *that* "way" infidelity has *something* not only to do, but to *learn;*—it is in the way of MERCY. This is one grand objection which every feeling heart must have to infidelity—not in its *professions*, for in these it is opulent, but in its cold-blooded *realities*. As infidel missionaries can *prove negatives*, they cannot with any grace object to their *assertion:* and there is *one* thing which may be averred—*that infidelity never gave birth to a single benevolent institution since God made the world, or man fell from his steadfastness*. No: they are *Christians* alone who plume the wings of genuine CHARITY. Among *infidels*, with all their boasted benevolence, the sacred form of charity appears sickly and inactive—the pulse at her heart beats languidly—no expression flashes from her eye—and her pale lip attests that no seraph has ever touched it with a live coal from off the altar. When, in pursuance of Mr. Rose's Bill, authentic information was for the first time in any country laid before the public, of the number of paupers, and of the amount of the poor rates, it appeared that upward of 700,000 persons were died, but received his own death-stroke by the journey; for he caught cold, which settled upon his lungs, and from which he never fully recovered. In a letter to his partner, dated September 10th, he remarked, "I have been very ill since I came here. I was taken with a *stoppage* in my breathing about midnight. If I had not got bled, I believe I should not have been writing to you just now; but as soon as the doctor bled me, I found instant relief. I was very happy, and found that God was the God of my salvation." In speaking of his niece,

enrolled in *Benefit Societies*. The advantage of even these societies might be fairly inferred from their antiquity. They are known to have existed in some of the ancient Greek republics; traces of them are found among our Anglo-Saxon ancestors; and what is still more remarkable, institutions have been discovered of a similar purport in some of the South Sea Islands, among a people still barbarous enough to delight in devouring the flesh of their enemies. But are these institutions shoots from the stock of infidelity? Or if they were, do they deserve the epithet BENEVOLENT attached to them? By no means; for no one receives help from *these* but the person, who, by his subscriptions, *first* helps *them*. It has been, therefore, and may still be affirmed —That CHRISTIANITY *alone* is a system of HUMANITY, which *leads* to acts of *kindness* and *benevolence*. This is *one* "way" in which it has been useful to the indigent part of mankind; and in *this* "way" infidelity has been worse than a *blank* in God's creation.

N. B. It would seem that Messrs. Taylor and Carlile had set too high a value on the article of infidelity at first, and like other wares, there has been a great reduction in the price. The latter gentleman was lecturing in Manchester, in the autumn of 1833, when the prices of admission stood at *sixpence* and *threepence*, the highest sum being paid for a seat near the person of the lecturer. This is a sad reduction in the space of about two years; and augurs fair not only for *free*, but *vacant* seats, if not the necessity of having to *hire* persons to hear them.

he said, "We are waiting for a convoy of angels, and are expecting them every day, to carry her soul to the regions of eternal glory, where there is day without night, pleasure without pain, and where eternity shall seem as a day. She has obtained a title and a preparation for her heavenly inheritance. She has oil in her vessel, and has on the wedding garment. The Lord has taken a vast deal of pains with her, but he has proved the conqueror. She can give up all; and when this is the case, we receive all. It takes a great deal of grace to say, 'Thy will be done.' My son-in-law, Wrathall, wishes me to stop with her till she finishes her course. Mr. Knight's family being ill, he is obliged to return to London."

It was during one of his Lancashire journeys that he was on the outside of one of the stage coaches, as on the occasion of his going to Grassington, in one of the heaviest falls of rain to which he had ever been exposed: "And ah, *barn*," said he to a friend, as though a Lancashire shower had something peculiar in it—"ah, *barn*, when it rains there, it *does* rain! the hills look white with it, as it dashes down the sides." His heart, as on other occasions, was in the right place. A young woman sat next him, who was much annoyed, being but ill prepared to resist the downward force of the torrent. He looked at her; and while pitying her, he felt happy in his soul, audibly blessing the Lord for all his mercies. Whenever his female companion complained, he as quickly hitched in a pious sentiment, exclaiming on one occasion, "Bless the Lord! it is not a shower of fire and brimstone from heaven." This sentence took effect; it was like a nail fastened in a sure place; she became thoughtful: and he had the happiness to learn, that, in consequence of his behaviour and conversation, she became a steady convert to Christianity.

He preached twice during the sabbath, while here, at Grassington and Hebden. Having written to his daughter Ann in London, and home to Martha, but receiving no answer, he was rather anxious. "Whether," said he to the latter, "you do not think it worth your while to write, or whether you are too busy, I cannot tell: but I am sure, if I had sent word that you had a legacy of a hundred pounds left you, I should have had a few lines before now, to know where and when you were to receive it." Yet he strove to excuse her because of the harvest. "Many a time," continued he, "I have set my face over the brown mountains toward Micklefield. I have seen you in mind in the harvest field, cutting down the corn. If I had wings like a dove I would fly to you, and look at you. We have had a great deal of rain here, almost every day, except last week. When I saw the clouds burst against the mountains, I thought it would stop the rain from reaching you. If you have had as much rain as us, you have had a very wet harvest. But I hope you have got the most of it in, and are shouting 'Harvest home.'"

Samuel soon added, "Ten minutes past five our niece departed this life. She died in the Lord: and blessed are the dead that die in the Lord. May you and I be found ready when the message comes!" Mr. W., who appears to have remained at Grassington till the solemn event took place--having been more sudden than expected—observed in the same letter, "Father will be at home, if all is well, about Monday."

On his return home, "he was only able," says Mr. Dawson, "to preach a few times, and attend two missionary meetings, one at East Keswick, in the Tadcaster, and another at Garforth, in the Leeds East circuit. He now began to sink fast, though not confined to bed till a short time before he died." About a month before he quitted this transitory state, he said to his friends, "I am going home;" and then informed them of some arrangements he had made for the improvement of his death. In these he had only the good of his fellow-creatures in view; and through the whole of them the same distinctiveness of character, the same simplicity, the same benevolence, the same peculiarities which marked his previous life, were conspicuous,—some of them, to those who knew him not, bearing the stamp of ostentation, yet perfectly remote from it,—an increasingly sweet, meek, hallowed feeling pervaded every word, look, and act, alike expressive of the mellowing influences of the Holy Ghost upon his soul, thus checking the lighter feelings of the visitant, who might be tempted to obtrude—the visitant himself feeling that the being before whom he stood had the consecrating hand of God upon him—that death was hovering over the ground which supported him—and that through that same Being he was brought to the immediate confines of an eternal world, ready to open and receive him in any moment of time.

With the exception of a desire to have his will altered, he appeared to have no other wish of importance to gratify; and even in this he was preserved in "perfect peace." Mr. Dawson visited him on the Wednesday before his death, and attended to some of his last requests relative to his will, and other affairs. Martha occupied her accustomed chair, when he entered the house, fast approaching to her 80th year, with her glasses on, and a voice less feminine than that of most of the softer sex. She received him as the friend of her husband, who was in an upper chamber; and although he was so ill the night before that it was uncertain whether he would see the returning day, he no sooner heard the voice of Mr. D., than his spirit revived within him, like that of old Jacob; and gathering up his feet, he in effect said, "I will go and see him before I die." He was quickly on the ground floor, and took his chair in the corner by the side of Martha. He told Mr. D. that he wished to have his will altered. This was soon done, as his effects were not large, owing to his charities, his gifts to his children, and the property of which he had been deprived. He further observed, that he wished to be buried at Aberford—that his friend Simpson was to bake a sack of meal into bread—and that two cheeses were to be purchased. Mr. D., who was scarcely prepared for the reception of the last two items, wished to know the reason of such preparation, when Samuel replied, "There *will* be a thousand people at my funeral. As soon as I am gone, you must advertise it in the Leeds papers, and my friends will all come." Mr. D. very properly but affectionately remonstrated with him, suggesting to him the probable cost, the propriety of persons not specially invited providing for themselves, and the serious effect it would have upon the little he had to leave. "That's *raight*," responded Martha, who heard what was said; "persuade him off it." Samuel, who still retained his ancient spirit, exclaimed, with the tear starting in his eye, "Expense, *barn!* I never was a miser while I lived, and I should not like to die one." Being again pressed to dismiss the subject from his mind, he said, "When the multitudes came to our Lord, he could not think of them fainting by the way." He reminded Mr. Dawson of the text (Isaiah xlviii, 18) which he had previously told him to select, from which to improve the occasion of his death. On Mr. D. leaving the house, Martha, being too infirm to accompany him, sent her voice across the room, and said, in allusion to the funeral sermon, just as he stood in the doorway, "See that *de'nt* set him *te heigh.*" This was in true character. She knew Mr. D.'s high opinion of Samuel; and although she dearly loved her husband, yet her stern sense of justice, and her jealousy for the honour of God, led her to give what she deemed a timely caution. On a friend visiting him, and employing in prayer the common expression, "Make his bed in affliction;"—"Yes," responded Samuel, with promptitude and energy, "and *shak* it *weel*, Lord!"

His thoughts were now solely directed to his "departure," and he gave directions to one of the persons that attended him to take the dimensions of a closet on the ground floor, in order to ascertain whether it was sufficiently large to admit the full length of his body after his decease. This being done, he said, "As soon as I die, you must take the body down and lay it out; for you will not be able to get the coffin either down stairs, or out at the window."

Two young men, members of the Pontefract Wesleyan society, watched with him during the last night of his life; and from one of these—Mr. James Foster—some interesting particulars have been communicated. "While I was in London," said he to them, "Dr. C. encouraged me to preach full sanctification, and I *will* do so. It *shall* be done: faith laughs at impossibilities, and cries—It shall be *done*. Sing, joys, sing." In compliance with this request, they sung the well known *doxology*, composed by Bishop Kenn,

"Praise God from whom all blessings flow;"

a hymn which will never cease to be heard in heaven by warbling millions of redeemed intelligences from earth—its strains no sooner dropping by one individual, or one part of the militant church, than resumed by another—the continuous song flowing on, till the last saint of God shall wing his way from time to eternity. On one of the young men asking him whether he had any wish to be restored so far as to be able to preach again, he replied, "No;" then added, "If it would glorify God, and do good to souls, I should be willing."

In the course of the night, he repeatedly exclaimed, "Glory, glory, glory!" then in an ecstasy broke out—"I shall see him for myself, and not for another. The Lord has wrought a miracle for me. He can—I know he can—I cannot dispute it. Christ in me the hope of glory. I am like the miser; the more I have, the more I want." His ear, like his heart, seemed only tuned for heavenly sounds. "Sing the hymn," said he,

"Who are these array'd in white,
  Brighter than the noon-day sun,
Foremost of the sons of light;
  Nearest the eternal throne?"

during the whole of which, he continued to wave his hand in triumph. Then again, with untiring perseverance in the exercise of praise,

"My Jesus to know, and feel his blood flow,
'Tis life everlasting, 'tis heaven below."

The hymn being finished, he said, "Blessed Jesus! this cheers my spirits." It was said to him, "You will soon be among the dead, Samuel." "No doubt about that," he replied; "but I am ready to be offered up—glory be to the Lamb! Some of the friends in London told me, that I did not know how to pray; but I know better than that—glory—glory—glory! Mercy of mercies! Lord, save me!" He was again asked, "What must we say to your friends, who inquire after you?" "Tell them, joy, that I have all packed up—that I am still in the old ship, with my anchor cast within the veil—and that my sails are up, filled with a heavenly breeze. In a short time, I shall be launched into the heavenly ocean." A mariner, and even some landsmen, might be able to discover a confusion of metaphor here; but the Christian can look through all this, and can perceive a soul in readiness for a state of endless felicity.

A heavenly smile played upon his countenance, and the joy he experienced gave a vivacity to his eye which scarcely comported with the general debility of his system. Prayer occupied some of the short intervals between hymns; and such was the influence of God upon every exercise, that it seemed as though other tones were heard than those from mortal lips, and the room itself was "the gate of heaven." One of the persons who attended him observed, "I have spent whole nights in reading and prayer: but the night spent by the bedside of Samuel Hick exceeded them all."

In the afternoon of the day on which he died, some of his friends came from Sherburn to see him. Unable audibly to pray with them himself, he requested them to pray, and with great feebleness gave out the first verse of one of his favourite hymns,

> "I'll praise my Maker while I've breath;
> And when my voice is lost in death,
> Praise shall employ my nobler powers."

To a neighbour, he observed, with unusual solemnity, "I have as much religion as will take me to heaven;" then pausing a few seconds; "but I have none for Matty;" adding, with another pause, "and none for the children." This is the key which unlocks the secret of his real feelings, and shows that there was no thought of funeral parade in what he had previously observed—nothing beyond a wish that his remains might admonish the living on the subject of mortality. He found that he had nothing of which to boast—no more religion than was barely necessary—and wished to impress upon those around the importance of personal piety. Some of his last words were, "Peace, joy, and love." As evening drew on, his speech began to falter; yet every sentence uttered by those around appeared to be understood; and when that hymn was sung,

> "Ye virgin souls, arise," &c.,

he entered into the *spirit* of it; especially when the friends came to,

> "The everlasting doors
> Shall soon the saints receive,
> Above yon angel-powers
> In glorious joy to live;
> Far from a world of grief and sin,
> With God eternally shut in;—"

at the enunciation of the first line of which verse he lifted his dying hand, and waved it around till it fell by his side; still feebly raising and turning around his forefinger, as the arm was stretched on the bed, betokening his triumph over the "last enemy," and showing to those who were with him that he was—to use language previously employed by him—going "full sail toward the harbour," and had an entrance ministered to him "abundantly into the everlasting kingdom of our Lord and Saviour Jesus Christ." Just at the moment that the vital spark, which had been some time twinkling in its socket, was emitting its last ray, he opened his eyes, and feebly articulated, "I am going; get the sheets ready," and died. This was about eleven o'clock, on Monday night, November 9th, 1829, in the 71st year of his age.*

On the day of interment, which was the succeeding sabbath, such was the sympathy excited in the neighbourhood, that the people for

* The age here specified is that which was on the *breast-plate* of the *coffin*. His brother, it may be proper to notice, is of opinion that he was two years older than there stated. The writer, not having had an opportunity to consult the register, is unable to decide between the dates.

some miles around, uninvited, attended the funeral. "Some hundreds," says Mr. Dawson, "went to Micklefield, which is about two miles from Aberford. The funeral procession swelled as it proceeded; and when all met at Aberford, it was computed, on a moderate calculation, that not less than a thousand persons were assembled together." This rendered Samuel's "thousand" almost prophetic, and in the dark ages would have won for him the character of a seer. Without any pretension to such gifts, the fact itself of such an extraordinary concourse of people, in a comparatively thinly populated district, affords an eminent instance of public opinion in favour of integrity, usefulness, and unassuming worth. Mr. D. adds, "Had not the day been rather wet, and the roads very dirty in consequence of it, it is probable many more would have been there. The church was crowded, and scores could not obtain admission. The worthy vicar would not permit his curate to read the service, but went through it himself, as a mark of the respect he bore to the deceased, and was much pleased with the excellence of the singing. It was truly affecting to see the crowd press to the grave, to take their last look of the coffin that enclosed his mortal remains. They gazed awhile;—they turned aside, and wept, exclaiming, 'If ever there was a good man, Sammy Hick was one.'" Mr. D. might have added, that the infirm and aged, who were unable to follow the corpse, appeared in the doorstead of their houses, wiping away the tears as the procession passed; and that, pleased as the clergyman was with the singing, the tear was seen glistening in his eye in the course of the service.

His death was improved the sabbath following, by Mr. Dawson, who took the text, which, as noticed, Samuel had selected. The chapel was incapable of containing one half of the people that assembled; and though there had been a considerable fall of snow in the course of the forenoon, the preacher and congregation were under the necessity of worshipping in the open air. Such was the anxious solicitude of the people to pay respect to his memory, that no less than nine additional funeral sermons were preached, in different parts of the Tadcaster circuit, besides others in those of Selby and Pontefract; and some of the simple-hearted were heard to say, "I love heaven the better, because of Sammy Hick being there."

CONCLUSION OF THE MEMOIR.

1. In Samuel Hick we are presented with an additional exemplification of the numerous facts which go to support an argument pursued in a small, but interesting tract, entitled, "GREAT EFFECTS from LITTLE CAUSES." It is there shown, that every man, woman and child can do something—can do *much;* that we cannot *stir*, without touching some string that will vibrate after our heads are laid in the dust; that one word of pious counsel, uttered in the

hearing of a child, may produce an effect upon children's children whose influence may be felt on the other side of the globe, and may extend to eternity; and that it is not improbable that eternity will disclose to us, how the astonishing events of this age sprung at first from the closet of some obscure saint, like Simeon and Hannah of old, "praying to God alway, and waiting for the consolation of Israel." What has resulted from the labours of Samuel Hick, emphatically one of "the *weak things* of the world," is beyond the power of any one, except an Infinite Intelligence, to calculate. He set many a human being in motion for heaven, and accelerated the march of others.

2. The admirable economy of Methodism is unfolded, in accommodating itself to the bestowments of God to his creatures, whether he confers upon the individual the lesser or the more exalted intellectual endowments—and the designs of that God in holding every talent in requisition for the general good of mankind. No disparagement is intended to other Christian communities, by stating that the Established Church, the Calvinists, the Baptists, the Society of Friends, could not, agreeably to their economy, have found employment for such a man as was Samuel Hick. They would have been at a loss to know what to do with him; and would have been ashamed of him as a *preacher*, however they might have borne with him as a *Christian*. But Methodism, while she lays her hand upon the pounds, has never dis-

dained to stoop to the pence; and it is in the *pence*—the pence, in more senses than the metaphorical one intended—that she finds her strength. "Gather up the fragments that remain, that nothing be lost," will apply in a thousand cases besides the one which called forth the remark from the Son of God.

POSTSCRIPT.

In the month of January, 1832, just as some of the last sheets of the third edition of the memoir of her departed husband were passing through the press, Martha was summoned into the presence of her Lord. With all the prudence and care which characterized her proceedings, a proper occasion, as will have been perceived, was all that was necessary to draw out the truly noble and independent spirit which she possessed, and of the credit of which she had been deprived from the heedless exuberance of her husband's givings. The profits of the first edition of this volume were sacredly set apart for her benefit; and when Mr. Dawson presented her with the first-fruits, he was accosted by her with—"I cannot think of taking any thing, till I know that Mr. —— shall suffer no loss by it;" and it was not till she was satisfied on this point, that she could be induced to accept the offering. Her faculties were greatly impaired before she died; but she left the world, if not with Samuel's triumph, in Christian peace.

NOTE.*

The order of God, and the confusion of man, viewed in connection with religious assemblies.

On the visit of the apostles to Ephesus, "the whole city was filled with confusion. Some therefore cried one thing, and some another: for the assembly was confused; and the more part knew not wherefore they were come together."† Similar effects have followed in every age, and in almost every city, town, and village, since that period, on any *extraordinary work* of God, in the awakening and conversion of sinners. The stillness and serenity of the midnight hour seemed to enwrap the slumbering citizens, till Paul, "finding certain disciples" who had only been baptized "unto John's baptism," and who, like many moderns, whatever they may have "*heard*," have not known "whether there be any Holy Ghost," "laid his hands upon them," and preached in their hearing the faith of Christ.‡ No sooner could it be affirmed, that "the Holy Ghost came on them"—that "they spake with tongues and prophesied"—and that Paul "went into the synagogue, and spake boldly—disputing and persuading the things concerning the kingdom of God"—than "divers were hardened, and

* See page 163. † Acts xix, 29, 32. ‡ Acts xix, 2, 6

believed not, but spake evil of that way before the multitude."* Among the worst of these were "certain of the vagabond Jews," whose representatives in the present day are to be found in the lower ranks of society, among the vicious and uninstructed.† When the Lord, however, began to make bare his arm in judgment as well as in mercy, "fear fell on them all, and the name of the Lord Jesus was magnified."‡ But among those who were alarmed, there were only a certain number that "believed"—"confessed"—"showed their deeds"—and "burned" their "books," by which they had "used curious arts."§ Up to this period, the opposition was a good deal confined to the vulgar, as Christianity laid the axe to the root of their *vices*. But when "mightily grew the word of God and prevailed," affecting the established religion of the place, to which the *secular* interests of many of the worshippers were linked, it was then that the higher orders of society considered themselves justified in supporting the virulence of persecution. "Demetrius, a silversmith," who "made silver shrines for Diana"—a business that "brought no small gain unto the craftsmen," led the way. Noble and ignoble being now engaged—the one in support of their *vices*, and the other of their *gains*, "the whole city was filled with confusion." It is a remarkable fact, however, that the *confusion* belonged not to the *disciples* and *brethren*, but to

* Acts xix, 6, 9. † Ver. 13. ‡ Ver. 16, 17. § Ver. 18, 19.

the *mob*;—to the latter also was the *conflict of opinion* to be charged, some crying "one thing, and some another;"—and that to them, finally, was the most profound *ignorance* to be attributed, since "the more part knew not wherefore they were come together."*

"NOISY MEETINGS," so called, in modern times, are religious assemblies which have been generally distinguished for *sudden awakenings* and *conversions*. Some writers of respectability, under an impression possibly that such meetings are discreditable to Christianity, have laboured to remove the *noise*—as an *effect*, by referring the *cause*, *sudden conversion*, to apostolic times, and by representing such change as the result of miracle, in order to confine it to the first age of the Christian Church; arguing from the cessation of the one, the absurdity of the other. Among those who are desirous of referring every thing "*quick* and *powerful*" to primitive days, Dr. Mant takes a distinguished stand. His language is, "Where the conversion was sudden or instantaneous, it was the consequence of miraculous evidence to the truth. When the preaching of Peter on the day of pentecost added to the church three thousand souls, they were men who had been *amazed* and *confounded* by the effusion of the Holy Ghost, and the supernatural gift of tongues." Had the learned prelate paid proper attention to the subject, he would not have selected this portion of Scripture history for the establish-

* Acts xix, 29, 32.

ment of his non-experience theory; for it appears,

1. That the *apostles* and *brethren*, who were *all members* of the *Christian Church*, about one hundred and twenty in number, were assembled in an *upper room* in Jerusalem.*

2. That the apostles and disciples were the *only* persons that *saw* the cloven tongues of fire—were *filled* with the Holy Ghost—and *spake* in different languages.†

3. That on a *report* of this being "noised abroad, the multitude came together."‡ These, it ought to be observed, had neither *seen* any thing that had occurred, nor even *then* received the Holy Ghost.§ Having only *heard* of the descent of the Spirit, their evidence of course—allowing a trifle for lapse of time—was similar to what is furnished to every man in the present day, who is confirmed in the truth by a *perusal* of the fact in the sacred pages.

4. That when they heard the apostles speak in different tongues, they, in common with all who read the account with seriousness and attention, "were *amazed* and *marvelled*."‖

5. That instead of being equally *convinced*, much more *converted*, they were all "in *doubt*;" and some not only hung in a state of suspense, but "others *mocking*, said, These men are full of new wine."¶ In this state, *amazed*, *marvelling*, *doubting*, *and mocking*, each part sustained by different persons probably, as in a drama,

* Acts i, 12, 15. † Acts ii, 1, 4. ‡ Ver. 5, 6.
§ Ver. 38. ‖ Ver. 7, 12. ¶ Ver. 12, 13.

the *miracle* left them; *unconvinced* and *unconverted.* To attempt, therefore, to get rid of modern instantaneous conversions, by attributing those in the apostolic age to *miracle*, not only evinces a defect in Biblical knowledge, a disposition to confine the Spirit's influence to peculiar modes and seasons, but an awful incapacity—from a want of experience—to treat on a subject so immediately connected with personal salvation and the sacred office.

Turning from the *miracle* and its *effects* of *amazement*, *&c.*, we find Peter publicly addressing the "multitude" convened on the occasion.* The general topics on which he enlarged were the predictions of the Old Testament in reference to the Messiah—the signs of his coming—the blessings of his kingdom—his character—his miracles—his crucifixion—his resurrection—his ascension—and the gift of the Holy Ghost.† What, then, are the facts of the case? They are these—and the appeal is made to the sacred records:—

1. That the probability is in favour of Peter having addressed the multitude in his own tongue, the language spoken by the Jews at the time; thus, he accosted them, "Ye men of Judea, and all ye that dwell at Jerusalem," including both natives and strangers, to whom by their residence the language was familiar.‡ In his more private conversations, and in his addresses to select parties, belonging to different

* Acts ii, 14. † Ver. 14–36. ‡ Ver. 14.

nations, he, together with his brethren, employed their own separate tongues.*

2. That it was through the *preaching* of CHRIST *crucified*, and *not* through the *miraculous gift* of *tongues*, that the multitudes were awakened: hence it is affirmed, "*Now*, when they *heard* these things"—*heard that God had made that same Jesus, whom they had crucified, both Lord and Christ*, "they were pricked in their hearts, and said unto Peter and to the rest of the apostles, Men and brethren, what shall we do?"†

3. That it was not till *after* the delivery of the general discourse, that *signs* of *genuine conversion* succeeded—Peter being obliged to urge the subject home to the bosoms of his auditors, with "Repent, and be baptized, every one of you, in the name of Jesus Christ, for the remission of sins, and ye shall receive the gift of the Holy Ghost;"‡ the whole, up to this moment, being deemed impenitent, unbaptized, unpardoned, and without the saving influence of the Spirit of God. It was only *subsequent* to this period that the inspired penman could observe, "Then they that gladly received his word were baptized; and that same day there were added unto them about three thousand souls."§

From the whole of this statement, it is evident, that it was not the *medium*—not the *tongue*—not any number of *tongues*—not even the *miracle* imparting the gift of those tongues,

* Ver. 8–11. † Ver. 36, 37. ‡ Acts ii, 38. § Ver. 41.

that produced the change, but the *subject matter* of the Christian ministry: the one—viz., the gift of tongues, as well it might, filled the *mind* with *amazement;* the other—the words of God, effected the *conversion* of the *heart;* and it is still *that* "*word*," accompanied by the energy of the Holy Ghost, which the Divine Being has employed down to the present time, as the grand and leading instrument in the conversion of sinners. If, agreeably to the original commission, the gospel was to be preached to every creature, and throughout every era of time;—if the same end was to be accomplished by it, which could only follow by the same accompanying influence; it is rational to suppose, since the same *necessity* exists, that it will prove as much "the power of God to salvation" in the present, and in Great Britain, as in the first century at Jerusalem. With the same instrument, operating on similar subjects, we are not only authorized to expect the same grand internal change, but also minor, external, and often incidental effects, to exhibit themselves.

By paying a little attention to the subject, the difference between an *ancient* and a *modern revival* will be found not so great—and therefore not so alarming—as some persons are led to imagine. The following are a few of the points of agreement:—

AN ANCIENT REVIVAL IN JERUSALEM.	A MODERN REVIVAL AMONG THE WESLEYANS.
1. Prior to the religious commotion in the holy city,	1. The preaching of the gospel invariably *precedes* a

"the word," as has already been observed, was preached by the apostles, Acts ii, 14.

revival of the work of God among the Methodists.

2. The people were "pricked in their heart," verse 37.

2. *Conviction of the aggravating nature of moral evil* is experienced, and a desire, according to rule, to flee from the wrath to come, is expected in all who unite themselves to the society.

3. There was a great *inquiry* among the persons seriously *affected*; anxiously asking, "Men and brethren, what shall we do?" Acts ii, 37.

3. *Inquirers*, denominated *sincere seekers of salvation*, multiply on those occasions; their *earnestness* and *language* varying, according to the degree of *feeling excited*.

4. The serious inquirers "continued in prayers," verse 42.

4. Though *prayer meetings* are regularly established throughout the connection, they are much more numerous under a quickening influence of the Spirit of God than at other times. *Then*, more than at other seasons, they pray "without ceasing;" so much so, indeed, as frequently to annoy their prayerless neighbours.

5. To prayer, they added the "breaking of bread," Acts ii, 42, 46.

5. As no mention is made of *wine* in this case, and the *private members* were engaged in "breaking bread from *house to house*," it is warrantable to conclude, that an allusion is made to the Αγαπαι, *lovefeasts*, to which young converts are extremely partial, and which

constitute a part of the *prudential* means of grace among the Wesleyans.

6. They gladly "received" the "word" preached, verse 41.

6. Ministers are looked upon as angels of God—and their message is the joy of the soul; and the man who is most useful in a revival is most beloved.

7. A love to the sanctuary of the Most High followed; for they continued "daily with one accord in the temple," Acts ii, 46.

7. Places of worship are crowded—old chapels are enlarged—and new ones are built. The language of the people is, "How amiable are thy tabernacles, O Lord of hosts!" In a moment's absence, they are ready to exclaim, "My soul longeth, yea, even fainteth, for the courts of the Lord."

8. The religion of the temple entered their dwellings, in attestation of which, "they ate their meat with gladness and singleness of heart" —— "praising God," Acts ii, 46, 47.

8. At tables, where "grace before meat" was never heard, and in houses where a family altar was never erected, the voice of prayer is poured forth, and the voice of praise makes melody to "them that are without."

9. "They continued steadfastly in the apostles' doctrine and fellowship," verse 42.

9. Uniting themselves in church fellowship to the body, the young converts conduct themselves agreeably to the gospel, and to the rules and regulations imposed upon them by a conference of Christian ministers.

10. The most expansive benevolence was manifested,

10. There is, perhaps, not a Christian community in

as a fruit of the Christianity possessed: they "sold their possessions and goods"—"parted them to all, as every man had need"—broke "bread from house to house"—"and had all things common," Acts ii, 44, 45, 46.

the world which supports a more extensive system of charity than the Wesleyans. Such are their givings, that they have been advanced as an objection against the preachers, as though they were too liberally supported; and these have increased and decreased with the spiritual life of the body.

In what, then, consists the principal difference? In Jerusalem, the converts "had favour with all the people;" in modern times, an objection is taken against *revivals*, because of the occasional *noise*, which forms an accompaniment.

There are persons that merit an apologist, and may be excused for the part they take in attempting to quell an apparent tumult, when persons professing unusual sanctity, and who have been disciplined in the midst of such assemblies, have taken offence at them. They have sometimes raised as great a clamour for *order*, as the clamour has actually amounted to which they have attempted to silence. ORDER, DECORUM, CONFUSION, &c., very often mean just as much as we are disposed to make of them. Imagine a magnificent edifice, in the course of erection, rivalling, in its splendour, the noble minster at York. Persons totally unacquainted with the plans and designs of the architect, on seeing a hundred men employed in different places, crossing and recrossing each other's path, hewing wood, drawing water, mixing, chiseling, hammering, moulding, with a hundred other *et ceteras*, would be ready to label the whole as one immense mass of *confusion*. But the architect himself, confident in the harmonious movement of his own plans, and who can connect the whole from beginning to end, sees that *every man* is in his *proper place*, and that the *building* is *regularly rising*—proceeding with *order*—going on toward *completion*. This, though not a perfect, is a sufficient illustration of a PRAYER MEETING. A hundred persons are associated together, with a hundred wants, in a hundred different states, with a hundred objects in view, and with as many different modes of accomplishing their purposes. Here is one dumb, and as a beast before his Maker, capable only of expressing himself by a *sigh*. A second, more deeply wrought upon, gives utterance to his sorrow by a heavy *sob*. A third breaks silence with a *groan*. A fourth, drinking still deeper of the wormwood and gall, actually *roars* out for the disquietude of his soul. A fifth is *wrestling* with God in *mighty prayer* for the blessing of *pardon*, while a dozen more *penitents* are *smiting* on their *breasts*, and each responds to the prayer publicly offered, "God be merciful to me a sinner"—a score of voices lifted up at the same time, and striking in, like the people of old, with a hearty "*Amen.*" Two or three persons, in the midst of this, having obtained *peace* with God, being very differently affected, are ready to commence a *song of praise*, and nothing but the word "*Glory*" dwells upon their lips. Though the prayer *publicly* presented to God is *one*, yet the *states* of the people *differ*. It cannot perhaps reach *every case*, because every case is *not known* to the person who is the mouth of the audience; and persons will be *affected* in proportion as it reaches themselves—thus passing from one to another: and till every case is reached, agony itself will compel the penitent to throw in his sententious and ejaculatory interruptions, in order to hasten the blessing. If the people were in *one state*, had all arrived at the same stage of *religious knowledge*, had the same *strength* of *intellect*, and the same *views*, they might then be brought to keep tolerable time with each other, like a number of clocks or watches. Until this is the case, the character of a meeting, composed of persons taking the kingdom of heaven by holy violence, will vary: and to a person entering into a place at the period just described, the whole might appear a scene of *confusion*, and he might, by way of hushing it into stillness, *bawl* out more lustily than any of them for *order* and for a *constable*. But such a person should recollect, that MAN's *confusion* is very often GOD's *order*. The Divine Being, who sees not as man—man, who is unable to look beyond the veil of humanity—beholds the *same* SPIRIT at work, though *various* in his *operations*—the *same* grand WORK going on, though in *different persons*—the work of *prayer*, *praise*, *conviction*, *repentance*, *pardon*, *holiness*, *love*, *joy*, *peace*, all proceeding in *regu-*

lar order, not *confusedly mixed* up in *one* human *soul* at the *same moment* of time, but *distinct*, in *different persons*. A few varied *gestures* or *movements* to the *eye* of the *beholder*, or a few *jarring sounds* to the *ear* of the *hearer*, may *confound* the individual himself who thus looks and listens, but cannot change the distinct character of the work. A thousand congregations met at the *same moment*, under the immediate eye of God, engaged in *prayer* and *praise*, though in different places, are not more distinct, or less to be charged with disorder, than the separate characters in a prayer meeting, each of whom has his distinct work of grace upon his heart, and his distinct sentiments, "uttered or unexpressed," on his tongue. There is nothing irrational in different *men* in different *states* being differently *affected*, and manifesting those *internal* effects by *external* signs. Confusion in the *mass* to man is order to God in the *individual*. They have only to be *separated* to appear so to their fellows. A partition of burned clay, three inches thick, will settle the difference even with man, between *confusion* and *order*; on each side of a half dozen of which partitions separate groups may be differently engaged, one in sighing, another in groaning, a third in singing, a fourth in murmuring accents, like the noise of many waters, following the minister in the Litany, or in any part of the Church service. Let men only be saved systematically, with the charm of brick and mortar between them, and the work at once becomes genuine! But the moment the *groaners* blend with the *sighers*, the work loses its character, as though the ear of the Saviour could not distinguish sounds, the eye of the Saviour could not discover the shades of difference in the work, or the different workings of the heart! A worthy gentleman who wished to systematize matters, and have every thing done decently and in order, feeling, as a member of the establishment, for the honour of religion, discovered his concern for, and insight into, divine things, in rather a singular manner. There was a revival of religion among the Wesleyans in Manchester, in the summer of 1816, and the grand place of resort for the devout was Oldham-street chapel. As there was an occasional mingling of voices in the chapel, and these had risen so high as to bring the assemblies under the imputation of "noisy meetings," the gentleman referred to, knowing that Dr. Law, then bishop of Chester, was about to visit Manchester, took the alarm, and went to an influential member of society, to see whether the work, or in other words, the meetings, could not be suspended awhile, till the dignitary had left the town, that the credit of the town might not be injured in his estimation. The manufacture of the town will at once account for the gentleman's notions; going on the supposition that the work of God might be managed like the machinery in a cotton mill, put in motion when we please—worked slow or fast—or laid to rest between meals! The work might be suspended *here*, if it could be effected *hereafter*; but this can only be shown on popish principles, and on the principles of the bishop himself, who hesitated not to pray for one of the royal family after her demise, and which prayer is yet in print, in the funeral sermon delivered on the occasion. Certainly, groans in the living are as justifiable as prayers for the dead, and earnestness in religion as praiseworthy as indifference.

THE SUBSTANCE OF AN ADDRESS.

"Rejoice evermore. Pray without ceasing. In every thing give thanks: for this is the will of God in Christ Jesus concerning you. Quench not the Spirit. Despise not prophesyings. Prove all things: hold fast that which is good. Abstain from all appearance of evil. And the very God of peace sanctify you wholly: and I pray God your whole spirit, and soul, and body, be preserved blameless unto the coming of our Lord Jesus Christ," 1 Thess. v, 16–23.

I HAVE to tell you, that you have only an old blacksmith in the pulpit to-night, and that you may look for very plain truths. When I first began to preach, I was sadly afraid lest I should not be able to recollect my text, for I could neither read nor write. But now, blessed be the Lord, I can do both. The Lord is a wonderful teacher; and when he undertakes any work, he can soon make a job of it. I cannot preach a learned sermon; but I can give you the word of God just as I have it before me.

"REJOICE EVERMORE." The text says, "*evermore*." What! rejoice in tribulation, in famine and nakedness—when there is no money in the pocket, and no meat in the cupboard? was there ever a man, think you, that could do so? O yes, my friends, I can find you a man that did. What says Habakkuk? "*Although the fig tree shall not blossom, neither shall fruit be in the vines; the labour of the olive shall fail, and the fields shall yield no meat; the flock shall be cut off from the fold, and there shall be no herd in the stalls: yet I will rejoice in the Lord, I will joy in the God of my salvation."* Do you think I cannot find you another in the word of God? O yes, I can. What says Job, after all his losses and sufferings? "*Naked came I out of my mother's womb, and naked shall I return thither: the Lord gave, and the Lord hath taken away:*" and what then? Why, "*Blessed be the name of the Lord!*" Who would have expected this? Not the infidel, I am sure. He would rather have thought that Job ought to have said, "And cursed be the name of the Lord!" And do you think, friends, that we are going to be beat by these Old Testament saints—those that lived in the dark ages? No, no. St. Paul speaks about being "*joyful in tribulation.*" In the text, he says, "*Rejoice evermore:*"—"*and again I say, Rejoice.*" You may do as you like, friends; but for my part, I am determined to enjoy my privilege—to "*rejoice evermore,*" as here commanded.

"PRAY WITHOUT CEASING." That is, live in the *spirit* of prayer; and pray with your *voice* as often as you have opportunity. You may pray when you are at your *work*, as well as when you are upon your *knees*. Many a time have I prayed while shoeing a horse; and I know that God has both heard and answered me. Were it not for this *inward* prayer, how could we "*pray without ceasing?*" St. Paul did not mean, that we were to leave our business, or our families, and be always upon our knees. No, no. I have my business to mind, and my family to provide for: and, glory be to God! while we "*provide things honest in the sight of all men*," we may "*work out*" our "*salvation*" by praying secretly to him. But this is not all. We should have *set times* for prayer, both *public* and *private*; we should pray with our *families*, and also in the *house of God*. It would be a sad thing, if, in the day of judgment, any of our children were to rise up and say, "I never heard my parents pray; I may have heard them curse and swear, and tell lies, but not pray." Other children may say, "We have heard our parents pray—for they said the Lord's prayer; the very first word of which was a lie in their mouths. They knew that God was not their '*Father*;' they neither loved nor served him, but were *of their father the devil.*" O, my friends, this *outside*, this *formal* religion will not do; we must get it into our hearts. Then our prayers will be acceptable to God, and useful to ourselves.

"In every thing give thanks." What! for a bad debt, or a broken leg? for parish pay? for a dinner of herbs? for a thatched cottage? Ay, praise God for *all things*. He knows what is best for us. We have more than we deserve; and we should neither take a bite of bread, nor a drink of water, without giving thanks for them. If we were more thankful for our mercies, God would give us more: but we are by nature so very ungrateful—either murmuring against providence, or expecting so much more than common food and raiment, that we need a positive command before we will give thanks for what God gives to us out of his free bounty. You must give *thanks*, then; "*for this is the will of God in Christ Jesus concerning you.*" Now, the *will* of God should be the *law* to MAN; and you hear that it "is the will of God in Christ Jesus" that Christian men should "rejoice evermore, pray without ceasing, and in every thing give thanks." Another part of the text is,

"QUENCH NOT THE SPIRIT." You that have the Spirit of God, see that you do not quench it. Grace is a very tender plant, and may easily be destroyed. You need not go to bed drunk to quench the Spirit. It may be quenched by *neglecting* prayer, by giving your minds to foolish and trifling objects, by attending to earthly things, by refusing to do good, by not praying with your families. The master with whom I was an apprentice never used family prayer: I have often thought of it since: and it was no wonder that we grew up so very wicked. When I got converted, it was as natural for me to pray with my family as it was to live. I should be like a fish out of water without prayer. But we may also grieve or quench the Spirit, by refusing to *do* our duty, and by speaking rashly with our mouths. I remember quenching the Spirit of God in this way once. A man came into my shop, and asked me to do a job for him. Being afraid he would never pay, I felt vexed that he should ask me, and hastily told him that I would not do it. But I soon felt that I had done wrong, and would have given almost any thing to have had my words back again. Besides, I thought the refusal might lose the man a half day's work. But I was off my guard; the devil gained his point; and pride hindered me from confessing my sin. Well, what was to be done? Satan had gotten me down; but I was not to lie there, and give all up. No. I said to my wife, "I have lost my evidence of the favour of God; I will go to Mr. Bramwell—he is a man of prayer, and will help me to obtain it again." He did so, and I found it—glory be to God!

"DESPISE NOT PROPHESYINGS." Do not turn your backs upon the word of God; for "*faith cometh by hearing, and hearing by the word of God.*" I told you that you have only an old blacksmith for your preacher. But you must not think, that, because of that, you have no need to repent and turn to God. What I say is true; and if I speak according to the will of God, you have as much right to attend to what I say, as though the greatest preacher in the world were in the pulpit. You may not think me a very *wise* preacher, but I am a very *safe* one for *you;* for if I preach at all, it must be the gospel of Jesus Christ. I know nothing else; and if I were to lose my religion, I should not offer to preach another sermon. But I must get on, or I shall preach too long—and long sermons do no good. In the first age of Christianity, some were for Paul, some for Apollos, and some for Cephas. Some said one thing, and some said another: but we are to "*try the spirits whether they are of God.*" And St. Paul says,

"PROVE ALL THINGS." Do not be content with any religion that comes to hand, but examine it, and see if it be right according to Scripture. Some folk boast about not changing their religion, and that—however they may live—reckon they will not have to seek their religion at last. Alas, for them! They are called Christians on no better ground than Turks are called Mohammedans—merely because their fathers and their grandfathers were called so. When I first became religious, I thought I would join the *best* people and be right, if possible. I knew what the Church was; so that I did not need to try it. I went to a Catholic chapel, as the Catholics say they are the *oldest* Christians in the world, and make great pretensions to be the true Church. But I did not understand their Latin prayers and monkish ceremonies, and found I could get no good to my soul there. I then went to a Quaker meeting; but there was never a word spoken; and I wanted to know how I might love and serve God. After that, I went to the Baptists, and the Calvinists; but the Methodists suited me best. Still I am not slavishly bound to any party; and if I could find a *gainer*, a better, or a cheaper way of getting to heaven, I would willingly go that way. "*Hold fast that which is good.*" Having found religion, don't be so ready to part with it. Hold it fast. The world, the flesh, and the devil, will strive to get it from you; but be determined sooner to part with your life than make shipwreck of faith and a good conscience.

"ABSTAIN FROM ALL APPEARANCE OF EVIL." This is a capital direction. How many people get wrong through self-conceit and proud confidence! "O," say they, "there is no harm in such a thing, and such a thing; it is not clearly forbidden in Scripture." They are not sure whether it is right or wrong; so they will even make the venture, although the Scripture says, "*He that doubteth is damned*"—that is, condemned in his conscience. If there be an "*appearance of evil*," do not venture. When I go anywhere on business, I always strive to get out of the way of wicked men. I am like a fish out of water here again: I cannot live out of my element; I am always afraid of being corrupted by them. "Can a man take fire into his bosom, and his clothes not be burned?" Now, I am coming to the very best part of the subject: I am sure I can say something about sanctification, for I love it best.

"AND THE VERY GOD OF PEACE SANCTIFY YOU WHOLLY THROUGHOUT SPIRIT, SOUL, AND BODY." It seems to me that man is made up of three parts—a spirit, which is immortal—a soul, which he has as an animal—and a body which is the dwelling-place of the soul and spirit. The body will soon die; and of each it may soon be said, "Earth to earth, ashes to ashes, dust to dust." But when that part of us which is taken from the earth shall join again its "kindred dust," it will then have passed into another state, and will either be "numbered with the blest," or "with the damned cast out." Should it have been made holy during the time it was united to the body, it will go to a place of happiness. If unsanctified, it will be driven to a place of misery. Some men have thought that the terms "*spirit and soul*," in the text, refer to the powers and dispositions of the mind; but whichever way it is, and whether you divide man into three parts, or thirty parts, St. Paul means to include them all in this entire sanctification. We are first to be sanctified, and then to be "*preserved blameless unto the coming of our Lord Jesus Christ.*" The justification of a sinner is a great work, which none but God can perform; but to sanctify that sinner wholly is almost more than the mind can understand. There are many who stagger at the doctrine of entire sanctification, and cannot think that it refers to any state of grace upon earth. But St. Paul prays that the Thessalonians may be thus sanctified, and often speaks of it in his other epistles. He declares that "*this is the will of God, even your sanctification.*" I had doubts about this doctrine once; but I was convinced of the truth of it one day, while going through a wood. I saw two trees which had been felled. One of them had been cut away to make a ship, or a coffin, or something else: but the *stump* was left in the ground, and young trees were again growing out of the old one. Ah, thought I, this is like a man who is justified. The *stump* of his evil nature remains, and fresh evils spring up and trouble him. Well, sirs, I came to the other tree. It was laid upon the ground, but the roots were *stubbed* up, so that it could not grow again. I said to myself, This tree is like a man in a sanctified state; the strings are cut that tied him to the world; and the earth is no longer about his roots; "*the world is crucified*" to him, and he "*unto the world.*" I got a fair view of the doctrine of sanctification that day; and it was the Lord himself that made use of these two trees to teach me what I desired to know. I sometimes compare religion to the best coin of the realm. First, there is repentance: this may be compared to a seven-shilling piece; though there is but little of it, still it is good. Then comes pardon: this is like half a guinea. Next comes sanctification: this is like a guinea. Now, who would be content with seven shillings, or even with half a guinea, when he might just as well have a whole guinea, by applying for it?

What a blessed world this will be, when the Christian Church zealously contends for the doctrine of Christian holiness! Nearly the whole of our natural disorders are owing to our sins. If people were more religious, there would not be so much need of doctors; and when the millennium comes, they may get a fresh trade; for as there will then be no more sin in the world, so there will be no more pain or sickness. This state of holiness is not without its trials. As you got into it by faith, you may get out of it by unbelief. You must not think that the battle is ended, or the work is done, when you have stepped into this liberty of the gospel. No: you are to be

"PRESERVED BLAMELESS." When persecution or tribulation arises, whether from the devil or man, do not part with your sanctification. It will abide a storm. Do not slip into a state which is more dangerous, though not so much exposed; and if you should lose your hold, strive to get it again. It sometimes happens, in a great battle, that a particular house or barn is taken and retaken many times in a day. I have lost this sanctification at different times, but I always got it again. I have suffered a good deal for sanctification. The devil once got hold of me thus:—A cunning man came into my shop one day, and asked me what good I got by going to love-feasts, and other meetings, and whether it was not possible to live to God without so much trouble, and so much praying? What he said set me a reasoning. I thought I could, and began to try; but I soon *lost* my evidence of sanctification, and as soon *felt* my loss. I was like old Pilgrim, who had lost his roll, and went back to find it.

There are people who believe that sin will

never be destroyed, but by death; and thus they make death a mightier conqueror than Jesus Christ. The founders of our Church had other views, for they taught us to pray, that the "thoughts of our hearts may be cleansed by the inspiration of the Holy Spirit." If the thoughts are cleansed, we are sure that the words will be holy and the life good; for it is out of the heart, as the fountain, that all evils flow. The language is nothing but the bell, and the hands the index, to show what is within. If there was no clock-work in the inside, we should never know the hour of the day. The promise of the Saviour is, that the gospel shall be preached as a witness among all nations, and that then the end shall come. The end of what?—the end of the world? No, no; the wickedness of the wicked shall come to an end, and the earth shall be filled with the glory of God. This doctrine I will preach to the end of my life. If the king were to make a decree, that if any man dared to preach the doctrine of sanctification he should have his head cut off, I would willingly go and lay my head upon the block, and would shout with my last breath, "*May the very God of peace sanctify you wholly throughout body, and soul, and spirit, and preserve you blameless unto the coming of our Lord Jesus Christ.*" O, friends, get this sanctification of the heart—pray to God for it earnestly—believe that it is your privilege to enjoy it—and claim the blessing by faith in Jesus Christ.

The papists talk of a purgatory after death; but I have been in one in this life;—

> "'Tis worse than death my God to love,
> And not my God alone."

I never mean to be in this purgatory again. While I live in the enjoyment of this religion, I will invite others to partake of it. Yes, I will preach this sanctification

> ————————"While I've breath,
> And when my voice is lost in death,
> Praise shall employ my nobler powers."

Sin has led many a man to destruction, but I never heard that holiness ever injured any one. I had a man that lived with me; he was a very good workman, but determined to live in sin. He would never come in to family prayer, and it grieved me sadly that any man should live in my house who was such an enemy to godliness. He was such a spendthrift, and reprobate, that he had hardly any clothes to his back, and was always in debt at the alehouses and shoemaker's. Well, I thought, "This must come to an end;" and I determined to part with him. While reasoning one day upon it, I thought again, "How many years has God had patience with thee, Sammy? Why, five and twenty years!" Then, I said to myself, "I must have a bit more patience with this poor fellow, and try some other means to bring about his conversion." Well, sirs, I set a trap for him, and baited it with faith and prayer. I got him persuaded to go to a lovefeast. The people wondered to see him there. He went out of curiosity, to hear what the friends had to say, and, it may be, to make sport of them. But God found him out, and brought him into great distress of soul. This ended in his conversion. God made *a bran new man* of him; and he now finds that godliness has the promise of this life. He looks a hundred pound better than he did. He soon began to pay off his old debts, and now lives without making fresh ones. Did sin ever do a man any good like this? No. It promises much, but it never performs what it promises. The truth is, it has nothing to give; for "*the wages of sin is death.*" Every sinner will shrink from the payment of those wages which he has earned by a life of sin.

It is religion that makes good husbands, good wives, good children, good masters, and good servants. It is the best thing a man can have in this world, and it is what will fit him for heaven. May God save you! I hope I shall meet you all in heaven. I feel such love to you that I could take you all in my arms, and carry you into Abraham's bosom. O, that every person in this congregation may turn from his evil ways, and become a new creature! May "the very God of peace sanctify you wholly, and preserve you blameless in body, soul, and spirit!" Amen!

CONTENTS

TO

THE VILLAGE BLACKSMITH.

CHAPTER V.

CHAPTER VI.

CHAPTER VII.

CHAPTER XI.

CHAPTER XII.

CPSIA information can be obtained
at www.ICGtesting.com
Printed in the USA
BVHW041430150819
555988BV00011B/566/P

9 781318 664597